▌PRAISE FOR STEALING OUR DEMOCRACY

"*Stealing Our Democracy* is every bit as compelling as Kafka's *The Trial.* The governor's book reveals how the Department of Justice, used as a political weapon, is threatening America's democracy. Siegelman's story is astonishing, compelling, and infuriating." — THOM HARTMANN, America's #1 progressive talk show host and *New York Times* bestselling author

"Don Siegelman was the most successful Democratic politician in post-Wallace Alabama. His new book tells an amazing odyssey involving two federal prosecutions and a conviction forced by a corrupt judge. Following explosive disclosures of political manipulation by Republican whistleblowers, the constant that links many strands of the governor's political assassination is Karl Rove." — SCOTT HORTON, contributing editor, *Harper's Magazine*

"Don Siegelman's story is nothing less than an American tragedy. *Stealing Our Democracy* should remind us all of what can happen when federal prosecutors' powers are used to target not conduct but people, when the criminal sanction becomes a substitute for the ballot box, and when ambiguities in the law are exploited to damage a reputation and destroy a life. Siegelman's description of the Kafkaesque nightmare that enveloped him and his family should cause both heartbreak and outrage. Understanding the abuses he experienced may well be the first step to ending them and to healing our broken politics." — JOHN J. FARMER JR., former New Jersey attorney general, former dean of Rutgers Law School, currently law professor and director of the Eagleton Institute of Politics, Rutgers

"If you doubt that politics are the mortal enemy of justice, read *Stealing Our Democracy.* Terrible things happen when prosecutors forget that they are duty-bound to prosecute cases based solely on evidence and the law. Former Alabama Governor Don Siegelman's book is a sobering reminder of the vast powers the federal government has wrongfully used as a sledgehammer to achieve a conviction at any cost." — DAVID C. IGLESIAS (R), former U.S. Attorney, District of New Mexico

I STEALING OUR DEMOCRACY

STEALING OUR DEMOCRACY

How the Political Assassination
of a Governor Threatens Our Nation

DON SIEGELMAN

FOREWORD BY JOHN J. FARMER JR.

NewSouth Books
Montgomery

NewSouth Books
105 S. Court Street
Montgomery, AL 36104

Publisher's Cataloging-in-Publication Data
Names: Siegelman, Don, author. Title: Stealing our democracy: how the political
assassination of a governor threatens our nation / Don Siegelman.
Description: Montgomery : NewSouth Books, 2020.
Identifiers: LCCN 2020933134 (print) | ISBN 9781588384294 (hardcover) |
ISBN 9781588384300 (ebook)
Subjects: Siegelman, Don, 1946– . | Governors—Alabama—Biography. |
Prisoners—United States—Biography. | False Imprisonment—United States. I. Title.

Printed in the United States of America by Sheridan Books.

To the proposition that America's thirst for democracy will win out in the end. To all who remain hopeful while facing overwhelming odds. To all working for a positive change and spending themselves in a worthy cause—the Greta Thunbergs, the Malala Yousafzais, the Bryan Stevensons of the world. To all seeking freedom, working for justice, and democracy. Especially to my family and to other families who have been victims of crime or have been or will be wrongfully convicted and sentenced, some to prison, others to death.

Don is engaged in two important fights: One, for his own freedom and, the other, to save our democracy. As Americans, we have a responsibility to protect our democracy from those who would take advantage of it and abuse their power.

— Former Vice President Al Gore,
in a 2008 letter to supporters

Don Siegelman, Alabama's first progressive governor, was elected with a majority of black and white voters. He advanced the cause of justice for African Americans and women, appointing more African Americans as judges than had been elected or appointed in Alabama's history. This drove Republicans crazy. The coup de grace was that Governor Siegelman was going to give free college education and free early learning to all Alabama children.

— Congressman John Lewis

Pressing for the Education Lottery, October 1999.

CONTENTS

FOREWORD

By John J. Farmer Jr.

I became aware of the prosecution of Don Siegelman when I, and over one hundred other former state attorneys general of both parties (I am an independent), signed an amicus brief challenging the application to Don of the federal bribery statute. As a former federal prosecutor, state attorney general of New Jersey, and criminal defense attorney, I was well aware of the potential breadth of the "theft of honest services" statute, and had worried about its potential for partisan abuse.

Don's case confirmed my worst fears.

Don was sentenced to over seven years in federal prison for conduct that is engaged in every day by politicians of both parties and has been throughout our history. His appeal was denied by a Supreme Court that acknowledged, in a subsequent case, that "theft of honest services," could mean anything the prosecutor decides. All 113 state Attorneys General joined Don in his request for clemency. It was denied by President Obama who, like all presidents, appointed people as ambassadors whose sole qualification was that they had raised millions of dollars to support the president's campaign. No one has suggested that our presidents be prosecuted or impeached for this practice.

What did Governor Siegelman do?

He supported the establishment of a state lottery to fund and help to improve education in Alabama. The Governor accepted a $250,000 contribution to the campaign committee supporting the lottery raised by Richard Scrushy, a prominent businessman. Governor Siegelman reappointed Scrushy to an unpaid health care advisory board to which he had been appointed by three prior Governors of both parties.

Neither Governor Siegelman nor any of his family nor his election campaign benefited one penny from the contribution. Scrushy, for his part, who had supported Don's opponent in the governor's race, was without question qualified to sit on the board to which he was reappointed.

In short, the case against Don Siegelman was inexplicable as a matter of impartial justice or accepted political practice; it makes sense only in the realm of partisan retribution, only as an attempt to nullify the Alabama voters' choice of Don as their Governor.

Stealing Our Democracy tells the story of the politics that destroyed Don's career and nearly ruined his life. Its impassioned pages bring home the outrage, the heartache, the grief, and the ultimate resilience of this remarkable man and his family.

Don's story is also a cautionary tale for our time. Several years ago, I was asked by the State Department to travel to Armenia, to assist a legislative commission that was investigating the violence—including twelve homicides—that had accompanied recent elections. The partisan stakes in that country were daunting; the parties viewed their adversaries as illegitimate. As a consequence, we had to meet the opposition party clandestinely, outside the capital, because its leaders had gone into hiding for fear of arrest and prosecution.

We haven't quite reached that point in the United States. Yet.

Stealing Our Democracy serves as a stark warning. Loss of liberty should not be the consequence of winning or losing an election. Yet it is hard to escape the conclusion, that Governor Siegelman's true "crime" was winning a statewide election as a liberal Democrat in Alabama.

Beyond its heartbreaking personal story, therefore, Don's book should serve a broader purpose as an antidote to the "lock her up" mentality (the chant evoked at rallies for Donald Trump in 2016) that has entered and begun to pervade our politics. In retrospect, Don's prosecution may well be identified as the first major case in which the "lock her up" approach succeeded.

My hope is that Don's book will be as politically transformative for the reading public as it was personally cathartic for Don. As readers live through in vivid detail the outrage and injustice visited upon Don and his family, perhaps they will begin to rethink their attitudes toward those with whom they politically disagree.

What Don and his family endured will never be "worth it"; if, however, through Don's story, we can begin to restore a sense of mutual respect and shared legitimacy to our two-party system, his and his family's suffering will not have been in vain.

John J. Farmer Jr. is University Professor of Law and former dean, Rutgers School of Law, and director of the Eagleton Institute of Politic at Rutgers University.

President Clinton greets Dana and Joseph as he exits Air Force One,
October 24, 1996. (Courtesy Clinton Presidential Library)

▌PROLOGUE

By Joseph Siegelman

On September 11, 2012, my mom, sister, and I delivered my father to federal prison. Dad was the former Governor of Alabama. He was running for reelection in 2002 when, in a stunning turn of events, he was indicted for bribery. We were prepared for the somber occasion; a month earlier he had been handed his prison sentence of six and a half years. Only we hadn't expected this day to arrive at all.

An unprecedented, bipartisan coalition of more than one hundred former state attorneys general came to my father's defense, as did eminent law professors and scholars from across the country. We felt sure the U.S. Supreme Court wouldn't disregard such prominent support. But it did.

As I'm watching my father walk away from us and toward the prison, I can't help but think, how did we get to this point? A lingering question remained: how did he get convicted? I'd seen my dad devote most of his life to public service. I knew my father wouldn't have intentionally done something that warranted the court-mandated punishment. He was accused of bribery—appointing an Alabama Fortune 500 CEO, Richard Scrushy, to an unpaid position on a state board (to which he had been appointed by three previous governors) in exchange for a campaign contribution to a state referendum to benefit public education. But how did the jury become convinced that this campaign contribution was a bribe?

I saw my father enter the prison. He was now no longer visible. The air in the car seemed to thicken as our heads collectively sank into our chests.

I wanted to be at peace and understand how the jury became convinced that my dad committed a crime. I couldn't accept this unjust punishment. I knew I would visit him in prison as much as possible, and welcome him home upon his return. I love my father and would continue to love him, but I needed closure on how this had happened. One hundred and thirteen former state attorneys general and many U.S. Constitutional law professors said that what my dad did wasn't a crime. Were all these attorneys general and legal scholars who studied his case wrong?

There was one person who could tell me: Nick Bailey, the government's key witness against my father. Nick had long been an aide for my dad and had landed in his own legal trouble. Then Nick became the government's key witness against my father. I knew and liked Nick when he worked for my father but hadn't talked to him in years and I was uncomfortable talking to him now, but if anyone could tell me why my father was convicted, it was Nick. Having just watched my father disappear behind the prison gate, I knew I had to see if Nick would meet with me.

On October 21, 2012, Nick and I met at a local restaurant in Birmingham, Alabama. I arrived nervous, not knowing what to expect. Would he say, "I hate to be the person to tell you, but your father did some things he shouldn't have"? Or would he confirm what CBS's *60 Minutes* had exposed, that something untoward occurred in my father's prosecution and that his only crime was being a member of the wrong political party? Either way, I had to ask.

We sat out on the cafe patio, away from others, and proceeded into the conversation that ultimately led to years of intense effort by my sister, me, and so many others to "Free Don." After some informal discussion, I explained that I needed someone to tell me why my father deserved to be in prison. Nick cut me off, "But he doesn't deserve to be there, at all."

Certain of his comments are seared into memory. I asked him directly about the crux of the entire case against my father: "Do you personally think there was an agreement between my dad and Scrushy?" "No," Nick promptly replied. I was stunned by how quickly and easily he responded. There was no wavering or uncertainty about it. He insisted not just that he didn't think a bribe occurred but said "it's impossible to bribe your dad."

One might question the reliability of Nick's remarks to me that day, but they are consistent with everything I have learned since. Although Nick at one point in our conversation called his own testimony at trial "bullshit," I presume referring to the inferences drawn from it. Tragically, he ultimately refused to come forward, clarify, or change any of his testimony for fear of retribution from the prosecutors.

Prosecutors have immense power, as do trial judges. The prosecutors in my father's case were led by a U.S. attorney, Leura Canary, whose husband ran the campaign of my father's gubernatorial opponent. She was hell-bent on convicting him, and my father's trial judge, Mark Fuller, who had four years earlier been investigated at my father's direction, eagerly played along. (Later this judge was removed from the bench for bludgeoning his wife and lying about it under oath.) In my father's trial, the verdict hinged on the inferences Nick provided in his testimony, even if by Nick's own account, those inferences were incorrect. Since appellate courts rarely disturb a jury's verdict, my father's case was largely upheld.

We learned later that the Department of Justice had a secret report on my father's case, so I filed a Freedom of Information Act lawsuit seeking its disclosure. The court handling the case found "evidence of bad faith in the investigation and prosecution of Governor Siegelman" but turned over only limited, heavily redacted portions of the report. Much of this evidence of the government's bad faith is contained in the Legal Notes at the end of the book.

This book provides a vivid account of the bad faith that's known, exposes a vulnerability in our democratic system, and answers the question I had when we delivered my father to prison that day: How did we get to this point?

With Joseph in Birmingham, after my release.

Dana helping me tally election results, 1986.

Fishing with Joseph, 1998.

Family outing at the State Attorneys General Conference, Wyoming, 1990.

Lori celebrated with children at the First Lady's children's art festival 2001 (and she and I danced).

❙ ACKNOWLEDGMENTS

To former U.S. Vice President Al Gore and Congressman John Lewis.

To members of Congress who stood with me: The late John Conyers, former chairman of the U.S. House Judiciary Committee; Committee members Jerry Nadler, Steve Cohen, Hank Johnson, and Linda Sanchez; Congresswoman Terri Sewell; U.S. Senator Tammy Baldwin; former Congressman Robert Wexler; and Democratic Whip, Congressman Steny Hoyer.

A special thanks to all 113 former state attorneys general, including my dear friends and colleagues Bob Abrams of New York, Bob Stephan of Kansas, Grant Woods of Arizona, and Jeff Modisett of California, and Lynne Ross, former director of the National Association of Attorneys General.

To former Rutgers Law School Dean John Farmer Jr. and former U.S. Attorney David C. Iglecias, New Mexico.

To constitutional law professors Jesse Chopper, Daniel A. Farber, Erwin Chermerinsky, Alan Brownstein, Lawrence Alexander, Robert O'Neil, L.A. Powe, Martin Redish, Bennett Gershman, and the Constitution Project, Washington D.C.

Deep gratitude to my family, Lori, Dana, and Joseph and my brother, Les; also to journalist Susan Edwards and author Carolyn Haines, who consulted with me on the manuscript; and to dear friend Diane Alvis, who devoted untold hours poring over, proofing, and making correctional edits: to Barbara Tarburton, my "prison AA"; to Sharron Williams, who edited photographs; and others who helped and encouraged, including Anita and Claibourne Darden, Joe Giattina, Joe Perkins, Keith Givens and the Cochran Firm, Dr. Parker Griffith, Maze Marshall, the late Reverend Fred Shuttlesworth, Charles Steele and the SCLC, the New South Coalition, the Reverends Tommy Lewis and Gregory Clarke, Brent Blackaby, Bren Riley and members of organized labor, Nichols Collado, Clint Brown, Mimi Kennedy, Maria Florio, Pam Miles, Chip Hill, John Aaron, Leigh Ann Bishop, Tracey Hale, Danny Sheridan, Richard Dorman, Bobby Timmons, Cynthia

Mosteller, Carol Collingsworth, Paige Horace, Josh Coleman, Pete Bullard, Peter Neuman, John Griffin Jr., Elliott Peters, Saul and Peggy Shorr, Tack Mims, John Crowder, Norman Estes, Tom Goodwin, Peter Mirijanian, Terry Leirman, Gary and Judy White, Dr. Phillip Bobo, Amy Methvin, Mark Bollinger, Seiko Shihan Y. Oyama, Ambassador Jim Jones, and my dear friend Ambassador Chuck Manatt.

To my primary lawyers: Joseph Siegelman, Peter Sissman, Greg Craig, Clifford Sloan, Vince Kilburn, David McDonald, Susan James, Redding Pitt, Bobby Segall, Joe Espy, David Cromwell Johnson, Robert Blakey, Hiram Eastland, Sam Heldman, Jack Drake, Doug Jones, and Glennon Threatt.

To Republican whistleblowers Dana Jill Simpson, Tamarah Grimes, and Thomas Gallion.

To the free press, especially including Alabama journalists who have been fair, and national media: Robert Barnes, Adam S. Cohen, Scott Horton, Dan Abrams, Chris Hayes, Rachel Maddow, George F. Will, Jeffrey Toobin, Adam Zagorin, Thom Hartmann, Amy Goodman, Greg Palast, Robert F. Kennedy Jr, Mark Crispin Miller, Craig Unger, Andrew Kreig, Steve Wimberly, Paul Alexander, Larisa Alexandrovna, and Brad Friedman.

I STEALING OUR DEMOCRACY

CHAPTER I

JUDGMENT DAY

In the late afternoon of July 28, 2007, I stood in the marble hallway on the top floor of the new federal courthouse in Montgomery, Alabama. I was waiting to be sentenced for a "crime" that was invented by Republicans who wanted to destroy me.

My real crime was that I, a Democrat, had been elected in succession Alabama's secretary of state, attorney general, lieutenant governor, and governor.

Even as trumped-up charges were being concocted against me, I was running for a second term as governor. I expected an easy win and then planned to challenge President George W. Bush. Republican leaders, starting with Bush White House political strategist Karl Rove and his political associates had other plans for me. They had set out to defeat my grip on Alabama politics. Now, in 2007, they were winning.

I faced sentencing by the same Republican Judge Mark Fuller who had just presided over my trial and who had a longtime grudge against me. Judge Fuller had been an Alabama district attorney. Right after he was handpicked by Rove and appointed by Bush as a federal judge, I appointed his replacement as district attorney. The new DA found Fuller had illegally raised his deputy's retirement by some $300,000. It went to court. Fuller lost, the pay raise was reversed and Fuller was embarrassed by the negative publicity. Now, it was payback time.[1]

I had been charged with racketeering, but the jury had acquitted me of those charges. I was now being sentenced for "bribery" on a campaign contribution and an obstruction of justice charge, for a motorcycle I had bought with my own money.

I believed in the law. I had believed our system of justice would work for me. I was mistaken. I now saw how our system of justice can be corrupted.

I was awaiting sentencing for an innocent act—raising money for a state referendum to benefit public education. Karl Rove's client, Bill Pryor, who was Alabama's attorney general, and the U.S. attorney, Leura Canary, who was the wife of Karl Rove's associate, Billy Canary, and Mark Fuller, a hostile judge, had convinced jurors that what I had done was a crime. Judge Fuller's corruption would later be exposed, and he would be forced to resign in disgrace, but for now he remained all-powerful.

The trial was started in May of 2006 and dragged on until the Friday before the Fourth of July. When the jury was unable to reach a verdict that day, the judge told them, "Look, I've been appointed for life. I can keep you here until next July if I want to. Bring me a verdict or a partial verdict."

Finally, the jurors gave him what he wanted. While acquitting me on most of the drummed-up charges, they nevertheless convicted me on two felony counts that could carry a long prison term.

As my brother Les and I entered the courtroom to hear the judge pronounce my fate, Les noticed how many federal marshals were gathering.

"They're going to take you out of here," Les said.

"No, that won't happen," I protested. Normally, someone sentenced is given time to get their financial affairs in order before entering prison.

"Trust me, they'll take you away as soon as you're sentenced. They don't want you talking to the press. Give me your car keys and wallet."

Suddenly I feared Les was right and grimly handed him my wallet and car keys. "Give 'em to Lori," I said, speaking of my wife, who had been so courageous throughout this ordeal. Lori was in the courtroom today. Our children, Dana and Joseph, were on a trip to Israel. We believed that, in the event of a prison sentence, the experience would be too terrible to inflict upon them.

Meanwhile, I clung to hope. When a previous Republican governor, Guy Hunt, used $200,000 of his inaugural fund for personal matters, he was forced from office and sentenced to community service. I had been convicted of supposedly trading an appointment to a non-paying state board in exchange for a contribution to a state referendum to benefit public education. I never received a penny. Why should I go to prison?

But Rove-related prosecutors and a vengeful judge had called this bribery, and had won convictions against both me and businessman Richard Scrushy. Scrushy, who made the campaign contribution to the lottery referendum, had become a multimillionaire by founding a chain of healthcare rehabilitation centers.

As we re-entered the courtroom, I spoke to friends and tried to appear confident. It was late. Going on 9 p.m. When I saw my codefendant I whispered, "Richard, they are going to take us out of here after we're sentenced."

"Tonight?"

"Look around," I said. "There are marshals everywhere."

The judge entered the courtroom. Mark Everett Fuller was in his forties, clean cut, with closely cropped reddish-blond hair. He took his seat and soon professed to be outraged that I had refused to admit guilt. That I would not do, even if my refusal might worsen my sentence. I was an innocent man.

I felt weak, helpless, and nauseous as I stood to hear my sentence:

"Eighty months for Defendant Scrushy and eighty-eight months for Defendant Siegelman," he said. "Marshals, take them away."

People gasped in disbelief. My lawyers tried to argue that I should be free on bond while I appealed but the judge gaveled them down. I looked around for my wife, brother, and friends but all I could see were marshals. They hustled us out the aisle and to a side door.

"Face the wall," they said. "Put your hands over your heads." My new life had begun.

They patted us down and told us to remove our coats, ties, shoestrings, and belts. Handcuffed, with chains around our waists and legs shackled, we were taken into a dimly lit basement room. Somehow my lawyers made their way there.

"Governor, how are you?" they asked.

"I'm fine," I told them. "Don't worry about me."

"We'll get you out of here," vowed Vince Kilborn, my lead trial lawyer.

I knew my lawyers would fight for my freedom. I also thought they had perhaps made mistakes in defending me but this was not the time to talk about that.

Richard and I were taken from the basement and placed in the back seat of an old Chevrolet sedan. It was hot and humid, even as a summer rain fell. The car radio blared country music as we drove away from our families, friends, and the lives we had known, toward unknown and uncertain lives in prison.

The handcuffs and shackles were chrome-covered steel and locked so tightly, they were painful. I tried to move them up and down my ankles to ease the pain. Emotionally exhausted, I slept fitfully for part of the 160-mile trip to Atlanta. As we arrived at 12:45 a.m., an ominous nineteenth-century fortress loomed ahead. A federal prison.

One of the marshals opened the car door and I stepped out into the light rain. The marshal walked alongside me, gripping my arm as we entered the huge, old wooden doors to the dungeon-like prison. The oldest maximum security prison in the nation. Ordered by Congress in 1899. I was to learn that this was the prison where Al "Scarface" Capone, "Bugsy" Siegel (no relation), and other mafia thugs had been sent. I felt uncertainty and disbelief, but not fear.

I was greeted by framed photographs of President George W. Bush and Attorney General Alberto Gonzalez. I mused, silently, where was Karl Rove's picture. He was the one who brought me here. He was the powerful White House aide they called "Bush's brain." I imagined he'd received the good news by now. His plan had worked to perfection. Alabama would continue to have a Republican governor with the state's most popular Democrat locked inside a federal prison. George W. Bush wouldn't be challenged by me.

I never doubted Rove's role in my downfall. President Bush would soon ask Rove to leave the White House. Congress would investigate his role in my prosecution and his central role in appointment of partisan U.S. attorneys to bring charges against Democrats. *Time* magazine commented, "In this new Republican landscape, Siegelman emerged as one of the few Democratic stars . . ."

Rove's close political ally Billy Canary was a national Republican political operative who had worked with Rove on the Bush-Quayle campaign in 1992. Billy was married to my prosecutor, Leura Canary. Vetted by Rove, she had become the Bush-appointed U.S. attorney in Alabama. Billy Canary was being paid to defeat me while his wife was conjuring up charges against me. He was running my Republican opponent's campaign while she was seeking to destroy me. The Department of Justice had written that there was "no actual conflict." WTF? When Leura Canary's conflict of interest became too blatant to defend, she in theory disqualified herself as my prosecutor, but she secretly continued to oversee my case.

CHAPTER 2

LOCKED AWAY

Now, inside the prison, our shackles and handcuffs were removed. We were fingerprinted and told to take everything off.

"Turn around, spread your legs and cheeks," ordered a guard. We were given faded orange clothing and taken on a long walk through the old prison's grim corridors. It was now the middle of the night. Finally, after being led though old underground brick-lined corridors secured with iron doors, we stopped before a small cell, the last in a series. "This is it," one guard said. "We're out of room. You two will stay here."

He opened the iron door and we entered. As it closed behind us, the guard told us to back up to the door, stick our hands, cuffed behind us, through a thin slot opening in the door. Then our cuffs were removed. In this surreal situation we unexpectedly found something to smile at: a bit of graffiti that an earlier prisoner had scribbled boldly on the wall:

THE GOVERNMENT DOES THE WORK OF THE DEVIL

That night, as I lay on the top bunk, I tried to put aside my bewilderment, the questions of how we could be convicted of something that didn't happen, my anger at Rove and his Alabama cohorts, and my disbelief over our system of justice that had completely failed me. I focused on the love and support of my family, many close Alabama friends and countless people around the country who were rallying around my cause. They were people I'd never met and those who had elected me to public office. All who still believed in me. I thought of my mother and father. I was glad they had lived to see me elected governor but not to see this disaster. I knew seeing me here would have hurt them far more than it could ever hurt me.

An appeal would free me. I knew I could survive. I would exercise regularly; my years of karate training would help me stay strong. Push-ups could keep me healthy and fighting for my freedom could keep me sane. Inevitably, my thoughts took me back over my life, to recall its joys.

I knew my lawyers, family, and supporters would be working nonstop to free me. Within the week, I received a rhyming message from D. E. Alvis that captured what happened and made me smile:

This boy grew up in Bama. He loved the southern state, of mind, of heart, its future bright, its schools that could be great. But when he was the Governor, despite his dreams and plans, they stole his re-election; he'd overplayed his hand.

Then Rove and friends, Jeff Sessions too, sought out a friendly judge, with much to gain, his "Honor" gave the jury one more nudge. His dreams were sins, the verdict read, hung jury, twice denied; the Governor, chained and shackled, had no chance to say good-bye.

Railroaded. Lies were written, ask two jurors, not the News. Ask Abramoff, Pryor, and in casinos are some clues. The Governor gone, no lawyer, pen, or paper. In solitary confinement, truth jailed, the lies were safer.

Political prisoner. His dreams on hold, conditions grim, he said, "I'm fine, don't worry about me, we're fighting now to keep America free. Democracy first, keep that in mind. Don't worry about me, I'll be fine."

CHAPTER 3

EARLY YEARS, VALUES LEARNED

I was born in Mobile in 1946 and grew up in a small, two-bedroom home my parents bought with my dad's World War II severance pay and money they'd saved by their frugal lifestyle. My brother, Les, was three years older. We were close as children and that never changed.

My parents were kind, thoughtful people. Each contributed to the values I would live by.

My dad and my mom were my first and best teachers. Dad taught me to value education, the reward of hard work, and to treat everyone with respect. My mom taught me to be kind and caring to others.

I attended Woodcock Elementary School, a short walk through the field behind our house and a couple of city blocks away. One afternoon I returned home and was surprised to find my father there. He worked downtown, managing a music store, and usually arrived around six.

"Daddy, you're home," I called out. He asked me to join him in our kitchen and soon asked me questions I had not expected.

Integration was coming to Alabama. The Supreme Court had in 1954 called for public school desegregation in *Brown v. Board of Education*. In February 1956, a young African American, Autherine Lucy, had been admitted to the University of Alabama by a court order, only to be forced to withdraw by white mobs.

I knew nothing of all this and there had been no black students in my school. But race was a burning issue throughout Alabama and it was the reason my dad was home early that day.

"Your mother told me you used a bad word this morning," he said and told me what he meant. Now we sometimes call it the N-word, but in Alabama in those days it was often just "nigger."

"Where did you learn that word?" he asked.

"I heard guys at school say it."

"Donnie, go bring me the dictionary," he told me.

I went to our small second bedroom where a bookcase held our Bible, a dictionary, issues of *Reader's Digest*, a few novels and a set of encyclopedias Mom had bought with S&H Green Stamps. We also had a separate glass bookcase that contained a late-nineteenth-century edition of *Encyclopaedia Britannica* which we all loved. Our *Webster's Dictionary* was probably acquired by Mom with Green Stamps. She often would give me the job of licking the back of the stamps and putting them in the "books." I took the dictionary to my dad and he told me to look up the word I'd used.

I finally admitted I couldn't find the word.

"Let me tell you why you can't. That word isn't in the dictionary. It's a slang word. An insult to other people. We don't use that word. Now look up *Negro*."

I did and he told me to read the definition.

"That's the correct word and the only word you should ever use, no matter what other people say. I want you to address every Negro man by saying Sir, and Negro women as Ma'am."

I would not use that word again, even though I would hear it more and more in school and in other public places as well.

My dad asked if I would like to help his piano delivery man that Saturday. Of course I would! I spent Saturday helping a young African American who revered my father. My dad had not only told me what was right but made me see for myself why we didn't insult people because of the color of their skin.

My dad, Leslie Bouchet Siegelman Sr., was born in 1914. His father, Ralph, born in Cairo, Illinois, was a railroad man. His mother was of French heritage. My grandfather brought his family to Mobile when he became involved in the Railway Clerks Union. I'm sure being a union man contributed to my dad's political beliefs. My dad held President Franklin Roosevelt in great esteem, and his admiration extended to Harry Truman, Adlai Stevenson, and John F. Kennedy.

In the 1950s he supported our colorful governor, Big Jim Folsom, a Democrat, and liberal by Alabama standards, who did what he could to advance civil rights. My dad supported Folsom when George Wallace challenged him for governor in 1962. Wallace by that time had branded himself as a segregationist. After losing a race for governor in 1958 to an open segregationist, John Patterson, Wallace had vowed never to be "out-segged" again. His success as a fiery racist and emergence as a national figure became a tragic turning point for Alabama and the nation.

In 1960, when I was fourteen, dad and I watched the Kennedy-Nixon debates on television. He was 100 percent for Kennedy. Only three years later we watched news of the Kennedy assassination together as well. I had heard the awful news earlier at school that day. Some students cried. Some cheered.

That day was the first time I saw my father cry.

My mother, Catherine Andrea Schottgen, had an equal influence on us. Her father, the son of a German immigrant who was a blacksmith, worked for the water department in Mobile. Mom dropped out of school at sixteen to care for her sick younger sister. She became a beautician and was working downtown near my dad's music store when they met and fell in love.

My mother was our religious rock. She took Les and me by the hand to Sunday school whether we wanted to go or not. Sometimes in church I would hold her hand and feel the roughness of her fingertips and see the cuts from exposure to chemicals she used as a beautician.

Mom taught me the value of helping others. One day when I was about ten she asked me to help an elderly lady across the street. My mother must have known that it would make me feel good to help others. She was teaching me that it was gratifying to help people, that religion wasn't confined to church,

Above, with our parents, 1948. Below, Les and me, 1952.

and that good works should be central to our lives.

Those lessons would shape my life in politics.

Mom was an outgoing woman who loved to sing and dance around our living room and play our borrowed piano. When Les and I were teenagers, she persuaded dad to convert our screened-in porch to a beauty shop with two chairs for her and a friend. She loved working at home near her sons —and she doubled her income.

But there were troubles ahead.

After the war, Dad had been an accountant for a Chrysler-Plymouth dealership and later joined the Jesse French Music Company to manage its store in Mobile. He had worked there for more than three decades when, in his mid-fifties, he suffered three heart attacks, one of them severe. He came home from the hospital, determined to return to work, and he did, but he suffered a flare-up and had to take time off to recover.

On Christmas Eve of 1968, his boss, Jesse French, came to Mobile to "check on" my father. Dad gave him a drink and they sat before the gas fire in our living room. He told my dad, "We can't use you anymore, Les. You've had three heart attacks. You need rest."

Dad protested that he would soon be back to work, but Mr. French would not yield. He took out a small box and asked Dad to open it. The box contained a watch inscribed "For Les Siegelman for your 33 years of service."

Dad was crushed. He had built that store up from nothing and made it a success. Aside from his family, that job had been his identity, his purpose in life, and suddenly it was gone. After that, I would always believe working people deserved health benefits and job security.

Dad's agony was painful to see. He was often in tears, beyond consoling. He would sit for hours at the kitchen table. When I was home, we would talk about President Nixon and the war in Vietnam. I would try to ease his depression. He slowly came around. Mom was struggling to pay the bills from her income as a beautician. Dad, who had always been good with tools, began painting houses and putting up wallpaper. He took pride in his work and agonized over every detail, which meant fewer jobs and less money, but he was himself again. He was helping to provide for his family.

When Alzheimer's disease struck Mom, Les and I lived hours away in

Birmingham. We tried to help, visiting every opportunity, but Dad would say, "Your mother is my angel and I'll take care of her."

Our neighborhood was by then fully integrated. Some of our neighbors moved out, but Dad would only say, "Our new neighbors are good people." One day we had a call from the young black man who lived across the street. The mailman had knocked on our front door and received no answer, so he had asked the neighbor for help. They opened the door and found Dad unconscious on the floor. They called 911 and then called us.

At the hospital the doctor said Dad had suffered a minor stroke. He needed rest and he reluctantly agreed that Les and I could find a nurse to help with both him and Mom. We converted my mother's former beauty shop into a small apartment and found a full-time nurse to live there. God bless that wonderful woman. She was with them until the end.

CHAPTER 4

PUBLIC SCHOOL EDUCATION

My first political race, confronting religious prejudice and bullies, my first speech, compassion for the physically challenged, and my first appearance in court all came early on.

I attended Mobile public schools, where I made good grades and was a good, but not great, athlete. I made my political debut in the second grade when I was elected class representative. I think we held one meeting and I have no idea what we were supposed to be doing.

I started at Woodcock Elementary but our school zone had changed to effectuate integration, so I was transferred to a different school for the fourth grade. My first day at my new school, a fellow came up to me outside the school. "Hi, I'm David Raider," he said. We talked and when he went into school he added, "I'm Jewish." That fact meant nothing to me.

In my new homeroom, we recited the Pledge of Allegiance and someone read a Bible verse. Then the teacher asked us to introduce ourselves and tell what our religion was. Almost everyone was Southern Baptist. One girl said she was Jewish, and everyone turned to look. When I said I was Catholic, the girl in front of me turned and said, "You don't look Catholic." That baffled me. What did a Catholic look like?

The next morning, after Dad dropped me off at school, I looked for my new friend David. I found him surrounded by some bigger guys. One of them hit him in the face. I ran up, swung my fist, and bloodied the attacker's mouth. They all retreated.

"Thanks, man," David said. "They're fifth-graders and wanted to pick a fight."

My brother had warned me that there might be bullies at the new school and my father had told me, "Son, if you're right, stand your ground."

The next year I returned to Woodcock. In the sixth grade I was elected captain of the safety patrol, taken on a tour of the Mobile police department, and a photo of me with Sergeant Don Keebler ran in the *Mobile Press-Register*.

The next year I advanced to Barton Junior High, just as my brother left there for Murphy High. Les urged me to seek class office, so I ran for class treasurer. Dad printed up my name and message on index cards I could hand out. My opponent, Roberta Murphy, was one of the prettiest girls in school. She put her picture on her cards and beat me like a drum.

Roberta and I became friends. She and her friends lived in big houses near the Dog River. They were called the River Rats. They all took Latin, so with encouragement from my dad, I took it too. In my three years at Barton I mostly focused on Latin, literature, girls, and football. I wasn't a bad tight end. I caught a few passes thrown by our star quarterback, Bill Kaiser, a great all-around athlete.

When I entered Murphy High, I found new challenges. Mobile was a social town. Rich families put on Mardi Gras balls that competed with anything in New Orleans. Guys wore tuxes and girls became Southern belles in their ball gowns. There were open bars and great bands that played for dancing. I was glad to be welcomed into that world by my "River Rat" girl friends.

Our high school had fraternities. Boys were "rushed" according to their social standing. I joined Sigma Phi Omega, or SPO, my brother's fraternity. Most of the guys were from working families. I felt at home with them.

I had hoped to play high school football, but the coach didn't want players who joined fraternities. He said I had to choose. I didn't like his ultimatum, so I chose the fraternity but played on SPO's intramural team. It was just as tough as the school team but with less equipment, fewer rules, no referees, and more concussions. My first year, I was elected class representative.

In my junior year, I ran for class president. All the candidates were to speak before a school assembly. I drafted a speech, only to have my friend Danny Sheridan read it and warn, "This will put everybody to sleep. If you want to win you have to stand out. I'll write a speech for you."

Our school had just been integrated and tensions were high. Police and teachers were stationed around the school to watch for trouble. There were white bullies who picked fights in the hallways between classes. Everyone was on edge.

My speech had ignored all that. Danny's version did not. It began: "My fellow inmates, guards, and wardens." I went on to urge the students to put a big X by Don Siegelman's name for junior class president. To dramatize, Danny insisted I stand on tiptoes and make an exaggerated X with my right arm. Reaching as high as I could, and then bent down low, nearly touching the floor with my right fingers, I completed my big, dramatic X.

The audience howled with laughter and I won without a runoff. Then the principal called me to his office. "What were your intentions with that speech?" he demanded.

"Sir, I wanted to say something the students would remember."

"Well, you certainly did," he conceded. "Go back to class."

Sigma Phi Omega, like most high school and college fraternities in those days, was segregated. No Jews, and certainly no . . . blacks. We were hazed, shined shoes, and had our butts beaten with razor straps. It was all part of the game. But we were also required to maintain good grades and take part in community service.

We volunteered for the Red Cross and raised money for the March of Dimes. My work with the Mobile Boys Club opened my eyes to the struggles facing kids from poor families. I was constantly reminded how blessed I was.

In October of 1963 I organized a group of volunteers to escort children with physical disabilities to the Greater Gulf States Fair. The children were driven to the front entrance of the fairgrounds, which was muddy because of rain. I met my new friend, a girl of twelve with serious physical issues. Her wheelchair was useless in the mud, so I picked her up and carried her inside. Holding her in my arms we walked to her very first carnival ride ever. She couldn't speak clearly, and her arms and legs were crippled, yet she smiled as we rode the "Spider." With the safety bar pulled down tightly, the machine began spinning us around as each arm of the Spider rose and fell abruptly. I could see the joy in her eyes. She didn't want to stop. We rode that ride over and over. She touched my heart and helped shape my life. I had never felt so content in helping someone else smile.

When it came time to select new members for SPO, I put up my friends Bill Kaiser and Danny Sheridan. Danny was Jewish. For years Danny and I had met after school to shoot hoops. He had written my speech that had gotten me elected and a trip to the principal's office. No high school fraternity had ever admitted a Jewish member. Some guys objected because Danny was a Jew, but I promised that Danny would be a popular member of SPO, and he was.

The night that Danny and our high school quarterback, Bill Kaiser, were initiated, a fraternity party was planned. I proceeded to do something extremely stupid.

I was driving myself and my friend Bill to the party in my brother's 1960 Austin-Healey Sprite convertible. I took a pint of my dad's vodka and had hidden it in the trunk. Then I decided that it might not be enough and drove to a liquor store in a part of downtown where I was unlikely to see anyone I knew.

Since I was far too young to buy alcohol legally, I hoped to find an adult to do it for me. In the store's parking lot, I saw a Negro man, perhaps sixty years old, getting out of his car. I asked him if he would buy me a pint of vodka.

"You boys look awfully young," he said uncertainly. "Can you handle this?"

I assured him we could. He was dubious but we were white boys in a sports car so he took my money, went inside and returned with a bottle in a paper bag. "You boys be careful," he said.

Just then a man stepped out of a nearby car.

"What have you got there, son?" he asked. He spoke with authority as he told us to get out of the car and the Negro man to stay where he was. The undercover policeman told me to lock my car and come with him. The man who had helped us was handcuffed and put into a police car. I'll never forget the pained look on his face.

At the police station we were fingerprinted, then put in a cell with a couple of drunk men. The iron door slammed shut. We had no idea what was next and were fearful about our futures. Bill was worried about what this might do to his football career. Then, to our immense relief, a chance to make a phone call. My parents were at my uncle's house. My mother answered the phone.

"May I speak to Dad?" I said.

"Are you in trouble?" she asked. Mothers know.

"Where are you?" Dad asked. "Are you in jail?"

"Yes, sir."

"I'll be right there."

He and my uncle arrived soon with Bill's mother and we were released.

The next day's paper carried an account of our embarrassing escapade. At school we had to face the principal and the coach. "I got Bill involved," I told them. "It was all my idea." After having Bill run some laps, the coach was glad to blame the fraternity and forgive his star quarterback.

In court the arresting officer told the judge what he'd seen. "You boys are on probation for six months," the judge told us. "If you stay out of trouble this won't go on your records."

The Negro man was called up. "What you did was bootlegging," the judge said.

I raised my hand.

The judge asked if I wanted to speak.

"Yes sir, judge," I told him. "This man didn't want to buy the liquor. He refused at first but I talked him into it."

"Thank you, son," the judge said. He conferred with the police officer and then told the man, "I'm dismissing the charges against you."

The man, almost in tears, said, "Thank you, sir."

As we left the courthouse, he thanked me too. All I could do was tell him I was sorry. I could tell my mom and dad were proud that I had spoken up for the Negro man.

I survived the incident. I was ashamed to have done something so stupid. As I looked ahead to college I hoped to do better.

CHAPTER 5

COLLEGE, A POLITICAL EDUCATION

As a college activist, from 1965 through 1968, I was busy supporting student rights, confronting George Wallace, opposing the Vietnam War, dumping LBJ, and bringing Robert Kennedy to campus.

When it came time to ponder my future, I thought it might be a good idea to be a dentist. They couldn't be fired like my dad. They were their own boss. I learned that Brown University in Rhode Island had an excellent school of dentistry so I thought I should go there, until my parents broke the news that they couldn't afford Brown.

Les was about to graduate from the University of Alabama in Tuscaloosa and Dad said they could financially handle that. I decided not to pledge a fraternity right away. I needed to make good grades.

I made all A's and B's except for a C in, of all things, political science. I was asked to join Delta Kappa Epsilon, the same fraternity George Herbert Walker Bush had joined at Yale and Teddy Roosevelt before him. George W. Bush, I would learn, was a DEKE at the very same time I was. This was the first of the overlaps I would have with the younger Bush through the years. George W. Bush had joined the Air National Guard and did a stint in Montgomery, Alabama. Earlier, I had been in the Air National Guard in Birmingham. Like his dad, George W. became president of DKE at Yale.

At Alabama, I continued with my political activities. I was appointed the DKE Inter-Fraternity Council representative. In my junior year, I was elected SGA senator, representing the College of Arts and Sciences, and chairman of an academic reform committee. We presented student power and student rights resolutions that shook the campus. We advocated for students to evaluate teachers, students to organize public housing projects for better living conditions, and to establish a New College to teach courses in current world affairs, including the war in Vietnam.

But another urgent issue faced the university and all of Alabama. George Wallace, whose only real issue appeared to be racism, had first been elected governor in 1962. In June of 1963, he made his infamous "stand in the schoolhouse door" speech, as a political show for his voters, in defiance of a federal court order admitting two black students to enter the university. The Kennedy administration, backed by federal troops, saw that the students were admitted. Wallace vowed "Segregation forever!" and began his long career of what was known as "race baiting"—stirring up fear among white voters.

In 1966, barred by Alabama's constitution from running to succeed himself, Wallace ran his wife, Lurleen, in his place against a progressive state senator, Gene McClain from Huntsville, whom my political friends and I supported. But the voters overwhelmingly elected Wallace's wife, and she became Alabama's first female governor. While the common perception was she would be George's puppet, she later asserted herself in her own right, pushing for increased funding for the mentally ill.

Through Lurleen, George Wallace continued his battle against integration. She proposed legislation allowing her to take over all systems of higher education, including the University of Alabama. The university's president, Dr. Frank Rose, strongly opposed such an outrage, as did our Student Government Association. In retaliation, segregationists in the state legislature demanded an investigation of "communist activity on the University of Alabama campus" by the U.S. House Un-American Activities Committee. Nothing came of that.

In the spring of 1967 I ran for SGA president. I met Bruce Payne, a student from Yale who was teaching at Stillman, the historically black college in west Tuscaloosa. Friends wanted me to talk to Bruce about the National Student Association, NSA, which brought together colleges on political issues. Two friends and I drove to an old frame house. Bruce greeted us and spoke of the asset NSA could be to me as SGA president.

After winning my election, I attended an NSA conference at the University

I ran for and won the University of Alabama SGA presidency in 1967.

of Maryland that summer. I heard eloquent statements of support for civil rights and opposition to the war in Vietnam. Most importantly, I met Al Lowenstein, who delivered powerful and persuasive reasons why President Johnson had to be "Dumped." Al would become important in my life and was instrumental in ending the political career of President Lyndon Baines Johnson.

Weeks later Al called and asked if I'd drive him into Mississippi. Al was determined to elect delegates committed to nominating a "peace candidate" at the upcoming 1968 Democratic National Convention in Chicago. We met with black civil rights leaders like Aaron Henry and Charles Evers, as well as white civil rights activists.

As SGA president, 1967–68, my senior year, I stirred up students and the administration, pushing for new campus initiatives. One project helped tenants of public housing push for better living conditions. In another, college volunteers provided after-school tutoring to high school students. And we joined in a lawsuit to support a student editor's right to publish an editorial critical of George Wallace.

I urged the founding of the Alabama Association of Student Body Presidents so that leaders from all colleges could work together. I met with the student-body presidents from Stillman College, Tuskegee Institute, Alabama State, Alabama A&M, all historically black colleges (HBCUs), and worked with Auburn University's SGA president to sponsor a resolution for our school bands to stop playing "Dixie," a tribute to the Old South, at our football games. Behind the scenes, Dr. Frank Rose, president of the University of Alabama, made it happen, the end of "Dixie," at least the song, on our campus.

CHAPTER 6

WORKING FOR PEACE

I was proud of my work on campus; but for all of us who cared about America, there was one great national issue that cried out for our attention. The Vietnam War kept expanding and more American soldiers were getting slaughtered and innocent civilians were being killed in our ravage bombing. Lyndon Johnson refused to seek peace, lest he be politically damaged for "losing" Vietnam—which was never ours to lose.

AL LOWENSTEIN AND ROBERT KENNEDY

Meanwhile, my new friend Allard K. Lowenstein was speaking against the war all across America. Al first tried to get Senator Robert Kennedy to enter the fray against President Lyndon Johnson. When Senator Kennedy first refused, Al went to Eugene McCarthy.

Al then supported Senator McCarthy who agreed to enter the 1968 primaries and challenge Johnson for the Democratic nomination. Many still hoped that Senator Robert Kennedy might do the same—with a better chance of success.

In that spring of 1968 Senator Edward Kennedy was scheduled to speak on our campus. Then just two weeks before the speech, Senator Kennedy called and told me he had to cancel his appearance. My heart sank. I protested that everyone was so anxious to hear from him. He laughed and said, "Well, if it's okay I have a substitute for you. My brother Bobby."

It was beyond belief that on March 21, 1968, just five days after announcing his candidacy for the Democratic nomination for president, Bobby Kennedy would be on our campus! Just five years earlier, RFK and his brother, President John Kennedy, had forced the integration of our University. Robert Kennedy had confronted Governor George Wallace, the national symbol for racial bigotry and, in response, in April 1963, Wallace had raised the Confederate Battle Flag over Alabama's state capitol. Five months later, September 15, 1963, the Ku Klux Klan set off a dynamite bomb at the 16th Street Baptist Church in Birmingham, killing four African American children attending Sunday School.

I was at the airport to meet Bobby Kennedy's plane. I was thrilled. I had no doubt that Kennedy would win the nomination and become our next president. Then, finally, the war would end, and sanity would return to America.

Robert Kennedy delivered a charismatic speech as thousands cheered. He spoke not only about ending the war but about the civil rights struggle.

Greeting Bobby Kennedy at the Tuscaloosa airport, 1968.

He was emerging as the kind of inspiring leader we had not seen since his brother.

"Al Lowenstein asked me to say hello," I told Kennedy.

"How do you know Al?" he asked, surprised that a Southern student-body president would know the celebrated anti-war activist. I explained that I had met Al at the NSA convention and traveled with him to Mississippi in search of anti-war delegates to the upcoming Democratic convention.

I mentioned that Al was talking of running for Congress.

"He's been a strong voice against the war," Kennedy said. "I wish this nation had more men like Al."

"We're lucky to have one," I said.

On our way off campus, astronaut John Glenn rode in the front passenger seat, with Robert Kennedy sandwiched between me and my friend and future lawyer, Redding Pitt, in the backseat of a sedan. RFK instructed us to roll down the windows. He rolled up his sleeves and reached out both sides of the car, over Redding and me, to touch the outstretched hands of admirers who lined the way. Ten days later, President Johnson told the American people he would not seek nor accept his party's nomination.

My Conscientious Objection to the War

As my graduation neared in May 1968, my future was far from clear. I was thinking of law school but what I really wanted to do was attend the Democratic National Convention and work in Bob Kennedy's presidential campaign. But I faced a more urgent decision. I was nearing draft age. I had friends who were applying for conscientious objector status or thinking of going to Canada to avoid the service in Vietnam. One friend insisted, "Don, you have a future in Alabama politics but if you become a C.O. or go to Canada, you'll kill it."

He offered an alternative. His father was a general in the Alabama Air National Guard. "Maybe he can find a slot for you." I talked to the general and he said he could use me.

I struggled with my decision but seized that opportunity. I would have to leave for basic training right away and miss the Democratic convention that I believed would nominate Kennedy. On the evening of June 5th, the day of the California primary, the day I hoped Bobby Kennedy would seal the nomination, I and others flew from Alabama to Lackland Air Force Base outside San Antonio, Texas. We lined up on the runway, awaiting orders.

Then a sergeant bellowed out devastating news:

"That no good, communist son of a bitch, Robert Kennedy was shot and killed last night!"

I couldn't believe what I was hearing. Bobby Kennedy dead! The man I had been with just three months before, America's hope for peace, the man I thought would bring sanity to the nation, was suddenly and senselessly as dead as John Kennedy and Dr. King. Was there no end to the madness?

I completed my basic training and decided to postpone law school. I thought I might lose my mind if I didn't stay involved in trying to end the war. I called Al Lowenstein to volunteer for his Congressional race in Long Island. He agreed to pay for my travel and find me a place to stay.

I arrived on Long Island the first of September and was immediately asked to go door to door canvassing. I told people I was there because Al wanted to end the war. Many others had come to support him, including economist John Kenneth Galbraith, the conservative writer William F. Buckley Jr., and two young men my age, Bill Clinton, a future president, and Greg Craig, future White House Counsel for President Obama. President Johnson's vice president, Hubert Humphrey, won the Democratic nomination with the support of "party bosses" but lost Democratic support because he was too close to LBJ's war policy.

I learned a lot in the next two months. How to attract and use volunteers, how to raise money, frame issues, win over undecided voters, and deal with the media. In the end, while Hubert Humphrey lost to Richard Nixon, Al won big in his Congressional race. At least we would have a strong anti-war voice in Congress.

That Christmas of 1968, I drove my 1959 Mercedes 190 (my first car, bought used for $600) and arrived at a party at the home of a gorgeous, bright, and fun young woman, Victoria Barney. I soon embarked on my first serious romance. However, I was scheduled to fly out the next day with two college friends to work with refugees in Biafra, which had been engaged in a civil war with Nigeria. When we arrived in London, the Red Cross plane to Africa had been delayed by three weeks. I couldn't wait that long because I had to be back for my monthly Alabama National Guard meeting. I did have time to take trains to Paris and Rome and fall in love with Europe.

Back home after my two-week excursion, I took a temporary job that enabled me to spend time with my mom and dad. At night I would sit and talk with them at our kitchen table, and I wrote extensively to Victoria, who was in school at the University of Colorado in Boulder. Victoria and I would remain bound in heart and spirit through law school and my postgraduate work at Oxford. Then political work consumed the time needed to maintain our relationship. It was a sad but important lesson for me. Early in June 1969, Al Lowenstein called and asked me to join him on another trip to Mississippi, to attend the inauguration of Charles Evers as mayor of Fayette, Mississippi. He was the brother of the slain civil rights leader Medgar Evers.

When Al asked about my future plans, I said I would attend law school, but I needed time away from Alabama. He asked where I might go. "Probably the University of Virginia," I said. "They've offered me a grant."

He saw that I wasn't excited about UVA and asked where else I'd been accepted.

"Georgetown and Alabama," I said.

"Then why don't you come to Georgetown and work in my Congressional office?" Minutes later we stopped in a Dairy Queen for Al to buy a chocolate milkshake and I called Georgetown Law School and accepted their offer. It was a decision that changed my life.

I was excited to be joining Al in Washington. Nixon's "secret plan to end the war" remained a secret. Al was his most fierce and determined critic. I felt I was headed into the eye of the storm.

Because I was in law school I mostly worked in the afternoons and nights, often driving Al from one speech or meeting to another for days on end. I was proud to be helping Al, and helping in my own way to end the war. But by the time he ran for reelection in 1970, Al was on Nixon's "enemies list" and the Republicans had redrawn his district to give it a vast Republican majority. Al lost the election. It was the first time I saw clearly how politicians can change the rules to win the game.

College campuses were engaged in massive anti-war protests. Police violently responded to the student protests at the University of Alabama, Tennessee, four Kent State students were killed by the Ohio National Guard, and eleven days later, two more students were killed and a dozen injured when Mississippi police opened fire on anti-war demonstrators at Jackson State College. I was in front of the U.S. Capitol watching Captain John Kerry when medals were tossed over a chain link fence, later I was trapped in George Washington University with protesters and Allen Ginsberg to avoid being tear gassed. Congressman Lowenstein asked Greg Craig, another staffer, and me to organize Congressional hearings on the campuses—hearings on police and national guard violence. I was with Al when he made his report forcefully to the U.S. Deputy Attorney General for Civil Rights, demanding the Justice Department to take action.

When Al was leaving office, I called the DOJ and found a new job at the Justice Department as a law clerk working on the excessive use of force by the national guard and police.

While I awaited my security clearance, Senator Jim Allen of Alabama arranged for me to be hired by the Capitol police. After a few days of training I and other recruits met the police captain. He wasted no words: "Men, the most important thing to remember is that cop killers don't live to tell about it. If a fellow officer is shot, you shoot back to kill. Then you have a throw-down knife or weapon so there's no doubt you shot in self-defense." I couldn't believe it. In the basement of the Capitol, an officer of the law was telling us how to get away with murder.

In 1971 Al was elected national president of the liberal Americans for Democratic Action and I was elected to its board along with renowned economist John Kenneth Galbraith and Barney Frank. Barney was later elected to Congress from Massachusetts. When I was about to graduate from Georgetown Law, our dean, who was also my International Law professor, Ambassador Adrian Fisher, recommended me for postgraduate work in international law at Oxford University in the UK. In 1963, Ambassador Fisher had been instrumental in negotiating President Kennedy's Limited Nuclear Test Ban Treaty.

That summer I worked on delegate selection and voter registration projects for the National Youth Caucus in Washington State, Mississippi, and Florida. After the Democratic convention in 1972, I signed on with the DNC to run the McGovern campaign in Alabama. I worked closely with Bob Vance, the chairman of the Alabama Democratic Party, who became my friend and mentor. McGovern lost in a landslide, but I learned a great deal about Alabama politics.

All over America, young politicians were wondering how to impact our country and state and indeed the world. One such young man was Joe Biden. I had heard of Joe during the McGovern campaign of 1972. Leaders in the peace movement were determined to reshape the country. Some like Sam Brown, one of the triumvirates running the Moratorium to End the War in Vietnam, and gonzo journalist Hunter Thompson would run for local office. Joe took a big step to run and win a U.S. Senate seat. He caught my eye and helped give me the self-assuredness to make my first statewide race in 1978.

After that school year at Oxford in 1973, I considered New York or Washington, D.C., but was drawn back to Alabama, where I thought I could do the most good.

I signed on to work with Bob Vance's four-man law firm and to coordinate Bob's campaign for reelection as Democratic Party Chair. Bob was being challenged by a man supported by Governor Wallace. Governor Wallace wanted to take control of the state party and use it as a vehicle to run for president again.

CHAPTER 7

BACK TO BAMA

From 1973 to 1978, I was back in Alabama and continued my undaunted fight for things I thought important: Number one was stopping George Wallace from taking over the Alabama Democratic Party. Most importantly, I would meet Lori Paige Allen who would become my wife and the mother of my children. I also learned how to be a lawyer, working side by side with Bob Vance and would enter my first race for public office.

Robert S. "Bob" Vance Sr., was chairman of the State Democratic Executive Committee and loyal to the national Democratic Party's presidential nominee. This put Bob in direct conflict with Governor Wallace and his Dixiecrats who were trying to take over our state party for Wallace to use as his base for another presidential run. Wallace had been crippled by a would-be assassin's bullet in 1972. I rallied support for Bob's reelection as Democratic Party chair among people whose loyalty was to the national party, not to segregation. So, with Governor

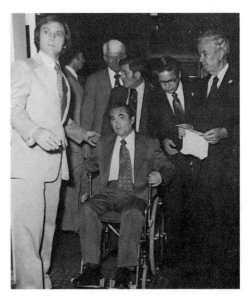

Above: as executive director of the Alabama Democratic Party, with George Wallace and Senator John Sparkman. Below: in 1976, I campaigned for Jimmy Carter and introduced him at an event in Birmingham at Samford University.

Wallace on the floor for the vote, smoking a cigar, he looked shocked as we pulled off an upset and reelected Bob over Wallace's handpicked challenger.

We did beat back the Dixiecrats, but for me something else was happening as well. With Bob's support I was making plans to run for Secretary of State. I traveled endlessly around Alabama. I met with all sixty-seven county Democratic chairmen and scheduled regional meetings at which we trained thousands of people in the basics of political action.

Bob was a friend, both a legal and political mentor, and inspiration. He gave me the chance to learn Alabama politics, and to work with African American political leaders who had split from the Alabama Democratic Party because of Wallace and to bring them and moderate supporters of Wallace back into the party. We kept the Alabama Democratic Party loyal to the DNC.

In December 1977, after Bob was nominated by President Jimmy Carter to be a federal judge, I set out to win my first statewide political office.

MEETING LORI

In the midst of my campaigning, something else important was happening in my life. One day I was outside the building that housed my law office when a beautiful young woman walked by wearing blue jeans and a plaid cotton shirt. She had long dark curly hair and a backpack. Intrigued, I followed her into our building and onto the same elevator.

"Floors, please," the operator said.

"Four," she said.

"Five," I said, although my office was on the third floor.

As the door was opening for her to exit, I said, "I'm Don Siegelman. Would you mind giving me your name and phone number?"

She smiled but said, "Sorry, I don't give out that information."

She exited and we went up. "Good try, sir," the operator said.

I had him take me back to the fourth floor. I waited until she returned to the elevator. Flustered, I said something inane but true:

"You have such pretty eyes."

Lori eventually agreed to my calling her and gave me her number. We met the next Wednesday evening after her classes. When I rang her doorbell.

Lori greeted me along with her puppy Kelly, a golden retriever.

We took Kelly for a walk and Lori told me she'd left her car at school because it wouldn't start. I'd driven plenty of old cars and had jumper cables in my car. We drove to her 1964 yellow Mustang convertible. I used my jumper cables and her car started easily, as did our relationship.

Several dates followed. Lori was bright, funny, articulate, and a wonderful diversion from politics. She was a student at the University of Alabama in Birmingham and a dancer. In time, we drove to Dauphin Island and stayed in my parents' small cottage overlooking the Gulf of Mexico. It was a romantic place. Walks on the beach, her Golden, Kelly, fetching driftwood sticks. It all felt right.

Meanwhile, my campaign continued. I drove the wheels off my dad's old station wagon. I was building on my travels for Bob Vance and the state party.

My campaign received a boost when I got to know our former governor, Jim Folsom, often called Big Jim or Kissing Jim. He was a colorful character and had been a good governor. One evening, I saw him in the Gulas restaurant in Birmingham, and went over to his table to tell him I would appreciate his support. He stood up—Big Jim was around six-foot-seven—and startled me by announcing he was descended from Vikings. Then he asked, "Son, are you Jewish?"

"No sir, I'm Catholic."

"Well, you'd better convert to Baptist before you run for office in this state."

In my speeches I often won laughs by quoting Jim's remarks to me. Such as when I'd said, "Governor, will you help me?" And his reply, "With a name like Siegelman you'll need all the help you can get."

The Governor asked about my education. I told him I'd studied international law at Oxford University in England. Big Jim replied, "Son, you'd better say it was Oxford, Mississippi. Folks will like that a lot better."

Alabama's Secretary of State oversaw elections, and I wanted to make it easier for people to register and vote. "I want to make our elections more fair and honest," I would say. "Some counties have more voters than they have people. When elections are close, sometimes the dead have been known to rise from the grave and vote."

I hoped to start my campaign with front-page coverage in the *Birmingham News*, the state's largest paper, so I went to their senior political reporter, Al Fox. He agreed to interview me, but the story didn't turn out as I'd hoped.

"Why do you want this job?" Al demanded. "Secretary of State has always been a job for women." That was true. But I thought I had a right to run, despite that tradition, to pursue my concern about elections.

Al's story, buried on a back page, began "One candidate has the right name for the job." He explained that part of the Secretary of State's job was to certify documents with the Great Seal of Alabama and that Siegelman

Lori made her public debut as my partner at the 1979 inaugural ball.

in German meant "the keeper of the seal." Thus, he conceded that at least I had the right name for the job.

My name became an issue of sorts. Rumors persisted about my being Jewish, no doubt encouraged by my opponents. It was true that Lori was Jewish and that I'd had a Jewish grandfather. But I was Catholic. I responded with a radio spot that said, "Siegelman, Diegelman, Tiegleman—No matter how you say it, Don Siegelman still is the most qualified candidate for Secretary of State."

I led the ticket, winning more votes than Fob James, who was elected Governor.

CHAPTER 8

SHAKING THINGS UP AS SECRETARY OF STATE

My inauguration took place on a cold day in Montgomery early in 1979. My mother and father were on the podium and nearby were my brother Les and my future bride, Lori. Dad administered the oath and Lori made a glamorous debut as my very significant other at the inaugural ball.

IMPACTING RACISM

As a candidate for secretary of state, I knew it would be wise to meet the office's current employees at the Capitol and ask for their support. I was greeted warmly. Before leaving, I asked if there was anyone I had missed. "Well, there's one more," I was told. The way she emphasized the word "one" I knew this employee must be black. "His name is Mark Gilmore. He runs errands and delivers the mail."

"Where is he?" I asked.

"Downstairs in the basement," I was told. "Do you want to see him?"

Again, with emphasis on "him" I knew I had assumed correctly and that Mark would be an African American.

"I want to meet everyone." That was basic, something I had learned from former U.S. Senator Jim Allen: you shake every hand.

I made my way to a room that had once housed a furnace and found a hefty African American about thirty-five years old. He presided over a warehouse filled with copies of the state code and bound volumes of the legislature's sessions. Mark proved to know a lot about Alabama politics.

I hadn't expected to encounter such political sophistication. Soon after taking office I made Mark my assistant Secretary of State for administrative affairs. "But he's just a laborer," someone protested. "He delivers the mail."

I saw potential in Mark. One day he told me he was thinking of running for the Montgomery City Council and asked for my support. I knew it would be hard. The mayor was a Republican and would oppose him. But Mark had told me of his mother's role in the Montgomery Bus Boycott. Mark said he had been beaten by police for walking through a public park closed to blacks. He deserved my support. I made calls and helped him raise money. He ran hard and won. After that it was a pleasure to see City Councilman Gilmore walk proudly into my office.

My fraternity brother Charlie Graddick had been elected Alabama's Attorney General. Charlie was a fiery "law and order" Democrat. He vowed to "slam the jailhouse door" on criminals and, for those on death row, "to fry 'em till their eyes pop out and green smoke comes out of their ears." He put forth a draconian package of criminal laws, promising more prison for more people, which passed over the strong objections of black legislators.

Our new governor, Fob James, had been elected as a Democrat in 1978, although in the 1990s he would return as a Republican. He had been an All-American football star at Auburn University and become a wealthy businessman. He was happy to sign Attorney General Graddick's tough crime bill, but he didn't understand that it had to be signed within a certain amount of time. Various people chose not to enlighten him. When he called a press conference for the bill-signing, it was too late. The deadline had passed, and the bill had fallen victim to a "pocket veto," a major embarrassment for both him and Alabama's new Attorney General.

Les and I visited my friend, former Congressman Al Lowenstein in New York in early 1980. Al was proud of my political career. He liked to joke, "You'd have been elected sooner if you hadn't met me." In 1977, Al was appointed by President Jimmy Carter as the U.S. Representative to the

United Nations Commission on Human Rights, where he served with the rank of ambassador until he resigned in 1978. Al again ran for Congress from Manhattan, without success.

TRAGEDY STRIKES MY MENTOR

In March of 1980, Al, from whom I'd learned so much, was murdered in his office by a deranged gunman. My dear friend was fifty-one and left behind his wife and two children. I attended his funeral in St. Patrick's Cathedral, in New York, where Ted Kennedy and William F. Buckley Jr. delivered eulogies. Al was a patriot who changed many lives, including my own. It was then I used my power as Secretary of State to demand computerized background checks before purchasing a firearm.

MY LIFE WITH LORI

On October 12, 1980, Lori and I were married in the backyard of our home in Montgomery, with just our parents, siblings, our dogs, and a Jewish rabbi and Episcopal priest, who presided. I made a bouquet for Lori to carry and gave her flowers for her hair. Since Lori was Jewish, she intended

Lori and I wed in a backyard ceremony in Montgomery in 1980.

to raise our children in her faith. I was Catholic. I figured at some point our children would decide for themselves what they believed.

Later, my dear friend and Catholic priest, Father Bill James, dropped by our home and married us again just to make sure we were covered. We lived in a small house that I bought from the mother of Montgomery's mayor for $37,000. Lori and I enjoyed working with my dad to fix up the house.

CHAPTER 9

A LIFE-CHANGING TRAGEDY

After my reelection as Secretary of State in 1982, I began exploring a race for the U.S. Senate.

My reelection was mostly uneventful. My opponent in the Democratic primary was weak and my general election opponent was the vice chairman of the state Republican Party.

As promised in my campaign, I made it easier to register, extended the hours to vote, and easier for those physically challenged. Barbara Crozier, who had been Miss Wheelchair Alabama, became my chief of staff. Barbara was a quadriplegic due to polio. She had a beautiful spirit and she enhanced my understanding of the lives of those who lived with physical or mental challenges.

We worked to make the Capitol more accessible to people in wheelchairs. After the assassination attempt on him in 1972, George Wallace was confined to a wheelchair. In 1982, Wallace was once again elected governor. Barbara and I went to the Governor and asked for his help in making the Capitol accessible to people in wheelchairs. He ignored our request. He was well taken care of and perhaps didn't realize that others in wheelchairs needed help, too. Barbara later filed a lawsuit and won concessions. The Capitol became accessible to those physically challenged.

I had another serious confrontation with Wallace when a new law required budgets to be adopted before other legislation could be passed. Governor Wallace wanted it placed on the ballot at a time that was not permitted. I refused to do so. He tried to overrule me with an executive order. I filed a lawsuit. "Secretary of State Sues Gov. Wallace." The court ruled with me.

For Alabama's young Secretary of State to defy the legendary Governor Wallace was big news. I assumed it helped me with some people and hurt me with others. Wallace was by then in his fourth term and had declared he had been wrong to vow "Segregation forever!" He sought black votes, even as he maintained strong support among Alabama's older white voters.

Our occasional dealings were cordial enough, but I could never forget his long history of racism. I could not forgive his embrace of white supremacy, when he had the Confederate flag fly over Alabama's Capitol or the attack by state troopers on African Americans as they attempted to cross the Edmund Pettus Bridge in Selma. The church bombings and the deaths of many civil rights workers could be blamed on Wallace's extremism. Still, when I made a last visit to his bedside, at his home with his son, George Wallace Jr., he was a pathetic figure, in pain and needing constant care. It was impossible not to recognize his suffering.

In 1984, I turned my attention to challenging Alabama's newly elected Republican U. S. Senator in the next election.

As a second-term Secretary of State, I knew I could beat the Republican incumbent, Jeremiah Denton. He had been born in Mobile, was educated at the Naval Academy, and became a Navy pilot in the early days of the Vietnam War. His plane was shot down in 1964 and he began nine years of confinement and torture in Hanoi. Denton was viewed by many as a genuine hero and won election to the Senate in 1980. He was the first Republican elected statewide in Alabama since Reconstruction. His record was that of a Tea Party original: his first priority, he said, was to preserve the family. Yet rumors followed that he pursued young women in his office. He pushed for $30 million to promote chastity proclaiming: "No nation can survive long unless it encourages its youth to withhold indulgence in their sexual appetites until marriage."

Besides chastity, his priority was the Soviet threat. In an interview with *Time*, he warned that unless more was done, "We will have less national security than we had when George Washington's troops were walking around barefoot at Valley Forge." This was when President Reagan had convinced

Consulting with James Carville.

Russia to tear down the Berlin Wall, and future Nobel Peace Prize winner Mikhail Gorbachev was president of the U.S.S.R. and led efforts to democratize Russia. Denton made other odd remarks and there was talk of excessive drinking.

I thought I could easily defeat Denton in 1986. I hired political consultant James Carville who later was hailed for his brilliant political work for Bill Clinton.

On the eve of my birthday, we joined my old friend Danny Sheridan on the Mobile Bay Causeway for dinner. The next morning, Lori and I left early with our dogs for a fishing trip to Dauphin Island in the Gulf of Mexico, a short drive from my mom and dad's home in Mobile.

We stopped for coffee and breakfast at McDonald's, then drove on until the Dog River Bridge was just ahead. I saw an oncoming car swerve at the top of the bridge. It was an older model car, driven erratically. It started swerving from lane to lane, as I told Lori:

"That guy is drunk."

I slowed. The erratic driver stayed in his lane for a second, then swerved all the way off the road to our right. His car was spinning up gravel on the shoulder of the road. I moved to the center of the road and cried out to Lori:

"Hold on!"

Just as we were about to pass the erratic driver, with him on our right and oncoming cars to our left, he jerked his car to the center and hit us head on.

A tremendous crash. Our car spinning. Tires screeching. Shattered glass. The dogs yelping wildly.

In an instant, my life changed forever.

We finally came to a stop. Lori was slumped over her seat, bleeding, terribly injured. I forced my door open and rushed to open Lori's door. Cars stopped. People were running toward us.

I kept assuring Lori, "You're going to be okay . . . you're going to be okay," as I pleaded with people to call an ambulance.

The drunk driver's car had crashed into our front passenger's side, smashed through our windshield, and broken metal of our car had inflicted deep cuts on Lori's head, face and right arm. I saw blood coming out of her ear, and her forehead was split open through her right eye, which was oozing from its socket. Shards of glass were embedded in her face and arm. I gently put my hand over the deep wound on her forehead.

As God would have it, a doctor and nurse, who just happened to be in the line of cars behind us, hurried to Lori's side. After a quick examination, he told me they had to perform an emergency tracheotomy to save Lori's life. I gave permission instantly. He then punched a hole in Lori's throat so she wouldn't choke on her own blood which started gurgling from the opening. She was getting oxygen. All I could do was repeat, "You're going to be okay."

Lori's Kelly was dead. My golden retriever, Brutus, had run into the marshes.

A fire truck arrived, and men began to assist Lori. The other car was on fire with its drunk driver stretched out beside it. An Alabama state trooper appeared.

"An ambulance is coming. The driver is dead drunk. No license or insurance we can see. He has a long criminal record. You're going to Knollwood Hospital. It's the closest."

A bystander handed me his business card saying, "Sir, I have your dog. I'll keep him as long as needed."

"He's Brutus," I said as I put the card in my pocket and thanked him.

The ambulance arrived and Lori was eased in. I followed her inside.

The drive to the hospital seemed to take forever. Finally, in the ER, doctors surrounded her. One said, "Don, I'm Van Carter. I was in school with you at Alabama. I've called our neurosurgeon, Dr. Roger Mudd. He's the best. I would trust him with my family."

I heard a commotion nearby. It was the drunk driver. I implored the state trooper and doctor, "Please get him out of here!"

I was told he was not seriously injured. "We understand," was the answer. He was taken away.

Lori's skull was broken in multiple places. Her jaw was broken, her cheek bone smashed, and her right eye socket crushed. She had lost half her teeth and couldn't use her right hand or arm. Nor could she speak.

Dr. Mudd and Dr. Jim Green, an oral surgeon, stabilized Lori. Dr. Mudd then privately admonished, "You need to get her to the University of Alabama's Medical Center as quickly as you can." I called a friend, an advocate for victims of drunk drivers, who arranged for Lori to be airlifted to Birmingham. UAB sent its plane and we were there in two hours.

Days later, when she was finally able she wrote me a note:

"I am so blessed. So lucky."

Lori had nearly been killed by a career criminal driving drunk. Her life was saved only by the doctor and nurse who miraculously showed up at the scene and preformed an emergency tracheotomy. I will always be grateful for their presence, without which I would have lost my entire family.

On Sunday, one day after the accident, I spoke to District Attorney Chris Galanos about possible criminal charges against Wallace Merritt Manning, the drunk driver. Galanos only planned to charge him with drunk driving. I wanted a felony charge of assault with a deadly weapon. I learned that he had recently been released from prison. His record included nineteen misdemeanors and three felonies: drunk driving convictions, drug charges, reckless driving, and one escape charge.

I told Galanos I would come to the courthouse the next morning to swear out a warrant. When I arrived, Manning was gone. His girlfriend had posted the $500 bond on a drunk driving charge. I learned more about the man who almost killed Lori when I stopped for gas in a small service station between Montgomery and Birmingham. The station operator recognized me and said, "I'm the brother of the man who almost killed your wife. Give him to me and I'll take care of him."

Astonished, I asked what he meant.

"He killed our mother. He was drunk and he tied our mother's horse to the back of his truck and dragged the poor animal to death. He came back and slammed her dog against a cement wall. Then he killed our mother. You get him to me, and I'll save the taxpayers a lot of money."

Somehow, thanks to her courage and brilliant medical care, Lori was out of the hospital in eight weeks, though confined to her parents' home.

Three months later, when Lori felt well enough, we planned a camping trip, a vacation from all the doctors, her thirteen eye operations, and dentists. We went to a wilderness campsite in Alabama's Cheaha State Park, pitched our tent, and built a fire. It was early May and still cool. We made love in our tent. As so often happens, from tragedy a miracle is born. Nine months later, on February 19, 1985, Lori gave birth to our daughter, Dana.

Former President Ford, right, and I spoke on voting rights at the Harvard-Kennedy School of Government while I was secretary of state.

CHAPTER 10

BABY GIRL SETS PRIORITIES

After fundraising trips to California and D.C., and now with a baby daughter at home in Alabama, I began to have doubts about being a U.S. senator. I really didn't want to leave my family. I knew that as a U.S. senator I would be spending weekdays in Washington and campaigning nonstop on weekends.

I spoke to Carville and he agreed that the office of Alabama attorney general could open a door for me to later become governor or U.S. Senator. I believed I could win the AG's race and be home every night with my family. Carville coached me on how to explain my change of plans. "You'll go out and listen to the people. You'll have listening posts. You'll tour the state and when you get back you will have heard from the people that they want you to stay in Alabama."

James Carville was a supreme realist. His very first question was: "How are you and the death penalty?" When I confessed to reservations about the death penalty, he roared at me:

"Let's get this straight. You're a candidate for attorney general of ALABAMA. You are FOR the death penalty!"

After a tough primary, I was elected without a runoff.

As Alabama's attorney general I dealt with myriad issues of life and death, consumer fraud, protecting the state from environmental disasters, of who went to prison, and whether voting rights and civil rights laws were enforced. I removed judges from the bench and impeached sheriffs and mayors, making sure no one was above the law.

I had my political future in mind as well. George Wallace had dominated Alabama politics for twenty years, but by the 1980s, his time was almost over. I had ambitions as did many others around me, including Charlie Graddick, Jim Folsom Jr., Bill Baxley, Fob James, Guy Hunt, and George Wallace Jr.

We all knew each other. Some we liked, some we didn't, and we kept a close eye on our rivals, judging their strengths and weaknesses and how their ambitions might help or hurt our own. The fact that some of us were considered liberals and others were hard-core conservatives underscored how closely divided Alabama was. A race could go either way.

But civil rights were increasingly the central issue in Alabama politics. Republicans, positioning themselves as its opponents, grew increasingly strong, encouraging many white voters to change parties. The shift had begun in 1948 with Senator Strom Thurmond of South Carolina splitting off from the Democratic Party to run as an official segregationist, supporting laws oppressing African Americans and promoting white supremacy. He was the standard bearer of the Dixiecrats. Later he supported Republican Barry Goldwater's 1964 presidential campaign and Governor George Wallace in 1968.

Politicians from city council to mayor to governor, from the House to the Senate, from wherever, were driven to take another step up the political ladder. The end of all our fantasies was the White House where issues that mattered most could be affected with the stroke of a pen, an appointment, or by getting that one last vote in Congress. The odds were long, but someone had to emerge, perhaps a Southerner. In 1976, Jimmy Carter had advanced from governor to president. Bill Clinton would soon do the same in 1992.

Ego, idealism, and ambition were universal. Sometimes leaders emerged who possessed greatness, like John Adams, Thomas Jefferson, George Washington, Abraham Lincoln, Franklin Roosevelt, John and Robert Kennedy, and Dr. Martin Luther King Jr. People not interested in politics might prove their worth in business, in the arts, or sports, but for many politics was the greatest test.

Early in 1987, because of our work for the National Association of Attorneys General, Joe Lieberman and I were invited to the White House to be with President Ronald Reagan when he signed the Omnibus Drug Act. I showed up. Joe had other plans. The White House photographer took pictures of me and President Reagan shaking hands. I asked Reagan aide Billy Canary if I could be sent a copy. He promised to take care of it, only later to report that my photos had been lost.

In other words, no favors for Democrats. Remember that name—Canary. A bird not to be trusted. He will be heard from again.

CHAPTER 11

USING POWER FOR PUBLIC GOOD

I shook up the attorney general's staff. There had been only three black employees when I arrived. I put the highest ranking African American lawyer in charge of all hiring. The AG's office had nearly 28 percent African American employees when I left. Message is simple. If you really want change, put people who want change in charge.

I formed a Victims Task Force that held hearings around the state. A teenage rape victim told how she'd been turned away at a Birmingham hospital. I met with the head of the hospital and we agreed to produce a state protocol on how hospitals should respond to rape victims. We increased funding for domestic violence shelters in Alabama, passed tougher sentences for the cowards who beat their wives or children, and strengthened laws to protect the elderly.

Lori took this picture of Dana, Joseph, and me on a 1989 camping trip.

Robert F. Kennedy Jr., nationally known as an environmental activist, came to me and said, "Big polluters are taking your regulations as options, not requirements." Enforcing the laws vigorously, in my first eight months in office I brought more environmental cases than my predecessor had in eight years. Robert Kennedy Jr. would become a friend and later authored a chapter on my election being stolen and how Karl Rove had been involved in my political demise.

I filed more antitrust suits against corporate cheaters and price manipulators than any AG in history and worked to put Alabama on the side of consumers. To do so reflected my basic political beliefs. To protect individual rights, we must often fight corporate power.

Perhaps my greatest voting rights achievement came when I settled a case mandating new political districts for every local public office on the principle of "one man, one vote," leading to the election of more African American officeholders in Alabama than any other state in America.

One of my two greatest joys in life happened in 1988, September 8th, when Lori gave birth to our son, Joseph. With Dana as his constant companion, I knew Joseph would grow up to be a fine young man. I did my best to be a devoted father to my children as I was to my public service. I took them to school when possible, and with Lori attended PTA meetings, school plays, awards, and sporting events. Lori and I always took them with us to the annual meeting of state attorneys general. In retrospect, I know I could have and should have done more.

Then, I was blindsided by another tragedy.

My Alabama political mentor, Robert S. Vance, then a U.S. Circuit Court Judge, was murdered. Shortly before Christmas of 1989, I was in Birmingham when I received a call from the FBI. "Judge Vance has been assassinated," Louis Freeh said, "By a mail bomb." Mr. Freeh would later serve as FBI director from 1993 to 2001.

I was devastated. Bob Vance, my friend and mentor, the lawyer who had become a universally admired federal judge, had been murdered. Bob had opened a package that arrived in the mail that he took to be a Christmas gift. A pipe bomb killed him instantly. His wife, Helen, standing nearby in their kitchen, was seriously injured.

As co-chair with Bob Dole to fund an Alabama World War II memorial,
I ceremonially drove Dale Earnhardt's #3 car at the Talladega Speedway.

I hastened to the Vance home. As Alabama's attorney general and a family friend, I wanted to be kept informed on the progress of the investigation.

The killer, Walter Leroy Moody, was captured, in part because he had previously been sent to prison for using a homemade bomb. Moody had blamed Bob Vance, wrongly, for his failure to be freed on appeal.

Soon after Bob's death Moody sent another pipe bomb that killed a civil rights lawyer in Atlanta and another bomb to an NAACP office that did not explode. Moody was sentenced to death, and after many appeals, was finally executed, at the age of eighty-three, on April 19, 2018.

Helen Vance had opposed that penalty, even in this heartbreaking case.

CHAPTER 12

A RACE TO THE TOP

As the 1990 race for governor neared I was ready to run. My opponents painted me as a dangerous liberal. I had committed the sin of meeting

with Tom Hayden and Jane Fonda in California. Yet I had many friends and supporters who were moderates and conservatives. As attorney general I had supported tougher drug laws. My support for safe shooting ranges had mollified the National Rifle Association. I regularly attended NASCAR races at the Talladega Speedway, a Mecca for camouflage-wearing, beer-drinking, pickup-truck-driving race fans. The NASCAR fans had children and appreciated my plan to provide free college education. I thought it was time to move up.

Above: Lori congratulated and consoled me on election night in 1990. Below: with Fob James and Jeff Sessions at the 1994 inauguration.

My dad disagreed. "Don, if you run

for reelection as attorney general, you'll win, and then walk in as governor next time. Why rush it?"

"Because I believe I can win and be a better governor than Guy Hunt."

It turned out Dad was right and I was wrong. U.S. Senator Jim Allen had also once told me, "Don, listen to the people and they'll let you know when it's time to seek a promotion." No one had asked me to run. I thought my opponent in the Democratic primary would be one of the usual suspects— "Little Jim" Folsom, Charlie Graddick, or perhaps, Bill Baxley. Instead, it was Paul Hubbert, the lobbyist for the state teachers' union, fondly called the Alabama Education Association. Paul had never held elective office but was well-liked by many of my supporters. Nevertheless, I thought I had more support and a stronger organization. I was wrong. When Paul announced his candidacy, the Alabama Education Association gave him a check for $500,000, which was more than I had raised in several months. On election night, the results were close but I lost. Paul went on to lose to Republican incumbent Guy Hunt.

George Wallace, after losing his first campaign, vowed never to be "out-segged" again. I came away from my 1990 loss determined not be outspent again. To win, you had to have the money to spread your message.

I joined a plaintiff law firm that would later affiliate with the Cochran Firm. In three years I had made far more money than I had in public service. I was hired to represent a motorcycle cop who was hit by a drunk driver, a young girl who lost her leg to a reckless driver, a Hunt Oil Company driver who was burned to death due to the negligence of the company, and I represented a class of plaintiffs against Archer Daniels Midland for price fixing. Perhaps my biggest contribution as a private attorney to the public good was the Alabama taxpayers' class action against Big Tobacco. I really enjoyed practicing law and my family needed the financial benefits I was able to provide but public service was my calling. So, after being actually drafted by friends, I ran for lieutenant governor in 1994. The lieutenant governor also served as president of the Alabama Senate, which carried considerable power in the state legislature. There I could work for progressive ideals. Also, I knew being lieutenant governor could be a path for a run for governor.

I won the Democratic nomination in 1994 against tough opponents including George Wallace Jr. Then, in the general election, I faced the Republicans' strongest candidate, Charlie Graddick. Charlie, who had been my fraternity brother in college, was now, as a former AG, viewed as THE law-and-order Republican. I had a better statewide organization and my record as attorney general had broader public appreciation than his.

I worked harder at fundraising than I had in my failed race for governor. My fellow trial lawyers contributed $700,000 to my campaign. After winning the election, I paid them back in full. I could have saved the money for my next campaign, but I wasn't comfortable feeling obligated.

In the governor's race, Fob James, a jolly born-again Republican, defeated former governor "Big Jim" Folsom's son, known as "Little Jim." At the inauguration I was the lone Democrat standing between Governor James and the state's new attorney general, Jefferson Beauregard Sessions.

KARL ROVE, JEFF SESSIONS, AND BILLY CANARY

Jeff Sessions had no doubt been guided by Karl Rove and Billy Canary. Those two had founded a political consulting network in Alabama after vacating the White House when Bill Clinton defeated President George H. W. Bush in 1992. Canary had married an attractive, dark-haired Alabama lawyer, Leura Garrett. Rove married Darby Tara Hickson, from Mobile, the second of his three wives, and settled in on the Gulf Coast. Alabama was increasingly Republican, and Rove soon applied his talents and shenanigans to expanding the Republican majority.

In 1981 President Reagan had appointed Jeff Sessions as U.S. Attorney for the Southern District of Alabama, where Sessions used the FBI to intimidate Democrats. He charged black leaders with voter fraud to suppress black voter turnout. He sent two civil rights leaders I knew well, Maggie Bozeman and Julia Wilder, to prison on trumped-up charges. He used his FBI agents to discourage political activism among African Americans. For him to become the state's attorney general meant it would be open season on Democrats.

Alabama and Texas were the only two states that gave its lieutenant governor important legislative power. I could oppose the plans of Governor James. I would be president and presiding officer of the Alabama State

Senate, able to appoint all committee chairmen and members and therefore block distasteful legislation. I would use these powers to support education, health care for women, stronger penalties for domestic violence, and other issues important to Alabama's working families.

I pushed for our participation in the Clinton administration's Children's Health Insurance Program. I met with Governor James and the Speaker of the House asking their support for $10 million to make the CHIP's program the first in the nation. They were opposed, but I had the votes in the legislature, and made it happen.

The idea of states suing the tobacco industry for the deadly and painful harm their products caused, and the huge expenses imposed on states, began with Mike Moore, the attorney general of Mississippi, along with trial lawyers Dickie Scruggs of Mississippi and Joe Rice of North Carolina. They asked me to join the effort as lieutenant governor since Sessions as AG was doing nothing.

My trial lawyer colleague Jack Drake and I met with Jeff Sessions, Alabama's new attorney general. We pitched why Alabama should join with other states in the national tobacco lawsuit. Jack explained that the lawsuit could enable states to recover billions of dollars spent on medical costs for those sick and dying of tobacco related diseases.

"Let me make it clear," Sessions said. "The state of Alabama will not sue tobacco companies."

His deputy, Bill Pryor, soon to become Karl Rove's client, added, "It sounds like a way for you and your trial lawyer buddies to make a lot of money. You should know that I've recorded this conversation."

We ignored his inane threat. Alabama law permits lawsuits by taxpayers if the attorney general fails to represent their interests, so I put together a group of plaintiffs. When I filed the lawsuit on behalf of all Alabama taxpayers, Sessions and Bill Pryor bellowed insults and defiance. Their attempt to have my class action dismissed failed. In 1996, after Sessions was elected to the U.S. Senate, Pryor was appointed by Governor James to replace Sessions. Pryor then declared that my lawsuit was frivolous because smoking cigarettes hadn't cost Alabama money since "people who smoke die faster." Other AGs across the country were shocked.

While the tobacco lawsuit took several years to play out, I continued to help organize it nationally. I spoke to Dickie Scruggs. Dickie said they needed my help with North Carolina and California. "If we can bring on California, we can get this case settled," Dickie added. North Carolina was a tobacco-growing state. I knew it'd be a hard sell but I called my friend Attorney General Mike Easley and made my pitch. Then I called Gray Davis. Convincing my fellow Democrat and Lieutenant Governor Gray Davis of California to file a lawsuit on behalf of California taxpayers, brought the national class to the settlement table.

As Alabama's lieutenant governor, I added an amendment to an appropriations bill that ensured any recovery from the Alabama lawsuit against "Big Tobacco" would go to children's health programs. Most members of our legislature knew little about the lawsuit and doubted it would ever bring a dime to Alabama. In time, it would net the state approximately $3 billion over twenty-five years.

CHAPTER 13

CLOSE ENCOUNTERS WITH ROVE AND CANARY

I first became aware of Karl Rove when he and his partner, the powerful Republican political operative Billy Canary, were ejected from the White House after Bill Clinton defeated President George H. W. Bush in 1992. They came to Alabama as political consultants working to elect Republicans. Their immediate cash cow was taking over Alabama's supreme court. Both having married Alabama women, Rove settled on the Gulf Coast at Rosemary Beach and Canary stayed in Montgomery, Alabama's center for political mischief. Rove, who was later to make his fame as "Bush's Brain" and "The Architect" of George W. Bush's ascension to power, was politically linked to Billy Canary. Canary was a Reagan protégé. According to *Time*, RNC chair Rich Bond in 1995 had called Canary "a legend in Republican circles . . . You drop him into a state where something needs fixing and it gets fixed."[2]

The Republican star-makers and I, who *Time* reporter Adam Zagorin later labeled the "Democratic star,"[3] inevitably came into conflict. This conflict heightened as I persisted in beating their strongest candidates, winning five statewide races.

Rove, long on talent and short on scruples, soon made an impact. In 1994, he and Canary used a vile campaign of rumors against Mark Kennedy, an incumbent Democratic Supreme Court Justice, who had established charitable foundations for children. Rumors were spread that he was a pedophile. It was not the last time Rove would be suspected of putting forth nasty rumors about opposing candidates.

Kennedy was narrowly reelected.

That same year, Rove and Canary sabotaged a recount effort in a close race for another seat on the court. Despite my testifying in federal court to stop Rove and Canary from stealing the election, they were successful in discounting valid absentee ballots, which swung the Alabama chief justice's win to a Republican. In retrospect, it was a preview of the tactics Karl Rove used in Florida which gave George W. Bush the presidency in 2000.

Rove guided the Texas governor to the White House. During Bush's two terms as president, Rove arguably had more power than any White House adviser in history. He was political strategist, policy guru, major fundraiser, and leader of his own network of appointees as federal judges and U.S. attorneys. He had effective control over the Republican National Committee, and President Bush gave Rove the credit.

Nicholas Lemann wrote a profile of Rove for *The New Yorker* which discussed Bush's loss of the 2000 New Hampshire presidential primary to Senator John McCain. After that painful setback, the campaign moved on to South Carolina, where "scurrilous material started circulating—dark suggestions that McCain had committed treason while a prisoner of war and had fathered a child by a black prostitute." Bush won the primary, ending the McCain campaign. Rove has been credited as the source of those salacious lies.

CHAPTER 14

BEATING ROVE, CANARY, AND ABRAMOFF

My win of the governor's race in 1998 was an unexpected upset. I won against a Republican incumbent, a major defeat for Karl Rove, Billy Canary, and Jack Abramoff and his client, the Mississippi Choctaw Indian casinos. The gambling money was used to fund their efforts to "stop Siegelman."

After winning the Democratic primary I faced incumbent Governor Fob James, the reborn Republican, who combined peculiar ideas with extreme beliefs. In his first term as governor he had written his own Christian prayer to go into Alabama's constitution. To draw a distinction with me, Fob supported putting the Confederate battle flag in all Alabama welcome centers. Once, to dramatize his opposition to the teaching of evolution in schools, he imitated a chimpanzee during a televised meeting of the state board of education.

I made endless trips around the state to talk with people. Some cafes and restaurants reserved a special table for politicians, called "The Liars Club," with photos on the wall of Jim Folsom and George Wallace. I always stopped there to talk politics with anyone who wanted to exchange ideas.

I was no longer reluctant to ask for money. I agreed with Senator Richard Shelby who said it was just as easy to ask for $10,000 as for $1,000.

I counted on the support of my African American friends, and particularly Michael Figures, even though I knew he dreamed of running for governor himself. My hope was to win in 1998 and for us to run as a team in 2002. After that, I also hoped his time would come.

My dream of Michael being Alabama's first African American governor vanished when Michael's wife Vivian called and told me he had suffered an aneurysm. I rushed to the hospital and stayed by his bed, holding his hand, talking to him with no response. Soon he was gone. At his funeral I delivered a eulogy. Michael was irreplaceable.

My hope for Alabama's working families and for all children was the creation of an Education Lottery that could fund free early learning and free college education. Georgia already had such a program that had brought in billions of dollars. Our program would earn enough money for tuition and books for all students who maintained a B average. Children could go to college or a trade school. The program would also pay for free Pre-K and put first-rate technology in every classroom, to ensure children in rural areas had access to quality education as good as that in the cities.

In 1998, I was described as a "New South" Democrat, progressive on social issues, but with a "law and order" reputation from my years as attorney general. I won the election with 58 percent of the vote against Fob James, the Republican incumbent governor. I was the first gubernatorial candidate in Alabama since 1964 to be elected with a majority of both white and black votes. My victory attracted national attention. If I won reelection in 2002, I thought I could contend for a place, most likely the VP spot, on the Democratic ticket in 2004.

CHAPTER 15

CLINTON, GEORGE W. BUSH, AND AL GORE

After my election, Lori and I went to Washington for the White House Christmas party and a meeting of the National Governors Association. In a private meeting with President Clinton, I felt like I had to tell him that Rahm Emanuel was letting him down by not returning calls. Our discussion became heated when Rahm denied my allegation. The White House party that followed was a delight, a fairyland of Christmas trees, music, dancing, and laughter, as Bill and Hillary greeted friends and colleagues. I admired the political skill that brought Bill Clinton there at such an early age. We were both born in 1946 and had both been AG and governor.

In our hotel lobby, I saw George W. Bush, governor of Texas and the Republican Party's likely presidential nominee in 2000. I went over and I introduced myself. Given my recent victory in Alabama and his in Texas, it was not inconceivable that we might face one another one day. Why not get acquainted?

Bush was happy to talk but as he did my disappointment grew. He was

In 1999, talking politics with Al Gore in his office in Washington.

cavalier, self-indulgent, and arrogant; he struck me as a total lightweight. After we parted I called Al Gore, a likely Democratic candidate in 2000.

"Mr. Vice President," I said, "I just met George Bush. He's both arrogant and ignorant. Al, you have to run. You're the strongest horse in the barn. You have to stop this man from becoming president."

Gore invited me to his office in the Executive Office Building, next to the White House. We talked politics and I again urged him to run—and said I would be glad to endorse him whenever it would help.

I faced a major challenge during the two months between my election and my inauguration. I was still lieutenant governor but my successor had been elected and was waiting to take office. Steve Windom was a Republican State Senator, and an ally of Rove forces headed by Billy Canary. I knew he would try to defeat my lottery proposal in the legislature. I also knew how much power he would have to do that. But I still had those powers and I set out to rewrite the rules of the senate and deny them to Windom, to neuter his ability to destroy my legislative program.

I needed to put the votes together to rewrite the rules of the senate and to get senators loyal to me appointed to the key committees. I had to get the support of Senator Lowell Barron, a man with whom I had clashed in the past. Barron wanted to be President Pro Tem of the Senate. I told him my plan. All I needed was his commitment to help me pass my Education Lottery referendum. I won his support. With the new rules he, as Pro Tem, not the Republican lieutenant governor, would control the Senate.

I also sought assistance from Mack Roberts, who had been George Wallace's assistant highway director and was also my choice for that post. He would continue to dole out funds for paving highways and roads and building bridges in legislative districts. All that money made legislators' salivary glands start flowing. Then I brought in former state senator Dewayne Freeman, my choice for director of Economic and Community Affairs, who would oversee federal funds for many public community projects, projects legislators would want for their districts. Dewayne had just lost the race for lieutenant governor to Windham, had minimal affection for him, and had lots of friends in the State Senate. With Mack and Dewayne on board, soon to wield a great deal of patronage, we met with legislators and won the votes we needed to organize the Alabama Senate and reduce Windham's powers as lieutenant governor, so he couldn't block my Education Lottery legislation.

CHAPTER 16

MY INAUGURATION AND GOP CONSTERNATION

At my inauguration as governor in 1999, I was again the only Democrat standing. I was standing with my two political antagonists, Bill Pryor, the newly elected attorney general, who was Karl Rove's client, and Windham, the newly politically neutered lieutenant governor who was joined at the hip with the Rove forces. Rove could not have been pleased.

It was, for me, a glorious day. In my remarks, I paid tribute to Rosa Parks and Dr. King. The torch had been passed in Alabama politics and I made it clear that African Americans were my friends and allies. We started the morning at St. Jude Catholic Church, one of the staging grounds for the Selma to Montgomery March in 1965. Then we walked on to Dr. Martin Luther King's church, with Dr. King's son, MLK III, and several noted civil

Right: with Lori and Dana at the inauguration in 1999; Below: with Joseph in a wheelchair due to an injury, our family waved to supporters during the inaugural parade.

The **Birmingham News** *said it best: "She never looked better: The crowds at a private rotunda reception and inaugural ball were abuzz over how radiant Lori Siegelman, dangling the new governor on her arm at the Montgomery Civic Center, appeared Monday night."*

rights icons. My master of ceremony was a noted African American lawyer; the prayer and gospel singers were all African Americans. At the beginning of the parade, Lori, Dana, Joseph, and I stood before Dr. King's church and sang the "Negro National Anthem," "Lift Every Voice and Sing."

Jimmy Buffett took the stage and sang, at my request, "Stars Fell on Alabama." Zell Miller, governor of Georgia, whose college scholarship program I planned to copy, swore me in as Alabama's fifty-first governor. After my remarks, still at the inaugural podium, I signed my first executive order, which began over 1,000 new school construction projects to get rid of 3,500 substandard portable classrooms.

Lunch was served in the Governor's Mansion, as thousands of people lined up to shake hands with Lori and me. That evening, Lori was the belle of the Inaugural Ball and fourteen-year-old Dana was glamorous, too. Joseph, eleven, also looked fine, although he was in a wheelchair because of a soccer injury. I couldn't have asked for a better start to the job I had sought for so long and in which I hoped to achieve so much for Alabama.

Less than two months after I took office, Attorney General Bill Pryor and his Assistant AG Matt Hart issued a subpoena for my finance director's computer. Pryor came to see me saying it was a mistake, but I knew an investigation by Karl Rove's client was then underway.

CHAPTER 17

TAKING ON ANOTHER FIGHT

My priority was to win approval of my Education Lottery. The lottery was my way around a legislature that for years had refused to provide money to improve schools. People who bought lottery tickets might not win the jackpot but they would be contributing to education. Given that I had won with 58 percent of the vote, and polls showed an even higher percentage of voters approving the lottery, I was confident that I would be able to give all children the dream of free college.

For too long George Wallace, campaigning for president as a racist, had brought shame on our state. This program could remind Americans that Alabama was breaking new ground in education.

I was soon seeking donations to be used for radio and television ads to sell the amendment and to finance a get-out-the-vote campaign. I made many calls to people who had supported my campaign for governor, particularly the large donors. Then I was asked to meet with one of the richest men in the state, Richard Scrushy. A man who had given my Republican opponent $350,000.

I first asked for a donation from Eric Hanson, a friend from the Mc-Govern campaign days. He had become a lobbyist for HealthSouth, a major healthcare company with headquarters in Alabama. Eric requested a meeting before contributing. Over dinner, Eric said he wanted me to meet his friend and boss, Richard Scrushy, CEO of HealthSouth.

*Campaigning for universal
pre-K and free college for
ALL Alabama children
as part of my Education
Lottery proposal, 1999.*

Scrushy had built HealthSouth into a $2 billion Fortune 500 company. Normally, I would have consented without a second thought, but I knew Scrushy had contributed $350,000 to Fob James. Eric was asking me to meet with someone who had tried to defeat me. I told him I had a problem meeting with someone who tried his best to destroy my career.

Eric persisted. "Don, please do this for me. Richard was the best man in my wedding."

I had met Eric as a teenager; his mother and sister had been volunteers for George McGovern. I had been to their home in Birmingham many

As First Lady, Lori encouraged reading in classrooms all over Alabama. We campaigned with Colin Powell for "America's Promise" to make children and youth a top U.S. priority, 2001.

times. I felt I couldn't ignore that friendship. "OK, Eric, I'll meet with him," I said. "But don't let him forget that he gave Fob $350,000." Goading Eric I asked, "Wouldn't you think it'll take $350,000 for the lottery to start on neutral ground."

Eric sighed with relief. "Thanks, Don. He'll be just as good to you as he was to Fob, you'll see."

Later, I received a call from Gary White, a Republican county commissioner in Birmingham. Gary said, "I understand you're meeting with

Richard Scrushy. I'd like to play a role in introducing the two of you." I told him to work it out with my secretary.

When the day arrived in early July 1999, we gathered in the formal office, the opulent inner sanctum, which was made memorable by Governor Wallace's media interviews. All staff and visitors excused themselves, knowing this was Scrushy's moment to make amends.

We sat face to face at the large ancient mahogany conference table. Richard had been a poor kid from Selma who worked his way through school, became a therapist, and started his own physical therapy company. HealthSouth had mushroomed into a national chain, and he was now one of Alabama's most generous philanthropists.

CHAPTER 18

A BRIBE OR POLITICAL CONTRIBUTION?

"Mr. Scrushy," I said, "I'm glad to finally meet you. Eric has told me a lot about you."

"Call me Richard, please. Eric does a good job as my D.C. lobbyist."

He soon got down to business. "Governor, I screwed up. I supported the wrong candidate. I can't go through four years with the governor mad at me. Is there anything I can do to make things right?"

I appreciated his candor. "Can you support my education lottery referendum?"

"Absolutely. I'll be happy to."

I was also relieved. Our relationship could be important, both in terms of financial support and of my standing with the business community. After Scrushy left, I called my finance consultant, Jim Cunningham.

"Jim, I just had a meeting with Richard Scrushy. He is going to support the lottery."

"What did he commit to giving?" Jim asked.

"I didn't ask for money," I said.

"Damn, Governor, how many times do I have to tell you? Give him an amount. Call him back and ask him for $250,000 and another $250,000 later. And give him a deadline."

I called the next day. "Richard, would you consider giving or raising $250,000 by the end of the month and perhaps help out later if we need you?"

"Governor, that won't be a problem," Scrushy said.

I called Eric Hanson to thank him. "Eric, you were right. Richard is on our team."

"I told you he'd be your friend."

"Is there something I can do to solidify this relationship? A show of appreciation?"

Eric thought a moment, then said, "You can ask him if he wants to be on the Certificate of Need Board. I don't think he does because he just resigned from it, but at least he'll know that you're aware of his interests."

I spoke with my appointments secretary, Raymond Bell, a young lawyer who had been recommended to me by my friend Michael Figures. Raymond confirmed that we had a place available on the Certificate of Need Board, or C.O.N., which certifies the equipment needs and bed space for hospitals and nursing homes. Scrushy had recently resigned from the C.O.N. Board after having served nearly twelve years. I would be the fourth governor to appoint him. I called him. "Richard, I want you to serve in my administration, on the Certificate of Need Board."

Silence.

Finally, "Governor, do I have to? I just resigned from the Board. I've been on there over ten years. It takes up at least two full days each month. Can't I just recommend someone to you?"

"Richard, if you don't serve in my administration, it will send the wrong message. You actively supported my opponent. I'm trying to build a relationship with the business community. It will help me if you'll serve."

"Can you give me a few days?" he asked.

When Richard called back he asked if he could be chairman. The C.O.N. board had already chosen a chairman, but the vice chair spot was open. I offered him that position and he accepted.

Soon, I received a FedEx envelope from HealthSouth in Birmingham. Inside was a $250,000 check. It didn't come from Scrushy but from a company called "IHS" in Maryland. I told the finance staffer to hold the check. "We can't deposit this until we know what these people do." I couldn't take a chance on some misstep. HealthSouth was well-respected, but what was IHS?

I went on raising money for the referendum. The list of people to call seemed endless. I tapped many of my campaign supporters but I wanted to build bridges to the business community. Surely most would support my plan to raise money for education—without raising their taxes!

We were doing well on fundraising. Saul Shorr, my media consultant, had some great television ads up and running, even as I was giving interviews and making speeches about keeping lottery dollars in Alabama. There was opposition from conservative evangelicals but they didn't seem likely to have the money for television time. Victory for the referendum looked certain.

But it wasn't.

One Republican after another said my proposal would "open the door to casinos." I assured them it would only allow for a lottery—to send children to college for free. The talk about casinos was part of an emerging political attack orchestrated by College Republican colleagues of Karl Rove: Jack Abramoff, Ralph Reed, and Grover Norquist.

CHAPTER 19

CHRISTIAN COALITION TAKES CASINO CASH

A few black preachers, legislators, and a vast majority of white clergy began to criticize our plan. They warned that a lottery would lead to casinos, sex, drugs, gambling, and sin run rampant. Blacks were told to stay home and whites to turn out en masse to vote against it. One preacher in Birmingham proclaimed the lottery an affront to God's word. One church gave $150,000 to defeat the referendum. I assumed that some of these critics had been bought off. But by whom?

The opposition ran television spots that showed a smoke-filled room, disreputable looking characters at a poker table, and stacks of $100 bills all around. A voice on the television ad warned, "Maybe a lottery, but not this lottery." The message was clear. Money from the lottery would go to sinister characters like these, not for the education of children. Alabama Lieutenant Governor Steve Windom identified himself as one of my opponents.

I asked a former AG of Nevada if he could find out where the opposition's money was coming from. He found a man who had attended a recent meeting of casino operators in Mississippi. He said they had agreed to kick in an additional $1.5 million to defeat the lottery referendum. But my question was how much had already come in?

I thought most people would see the difference between a gambling casino and a lottery to benefit education, but to the Mississippi casino operators we were just competition for gamblers' money. My political opponents, funded by the Mississippi Choctaw Indian casinos, would give millions of dollars to politicians, political consultants, and even religious leaders to defeat a plan to educate Alabama's children. It made me sick to think of their selfish greed.

The casino owners were no doubt dumping millions into the anti-lottery campaign and much of the money went to the Christian Coalition. We were told that the religious leader Pat Robinson was being paid handsomely to make robocalls against us. Ralph Reed, part of Karl Rove's network of College Republican buddies, was now the young Christian Coalition leader. He was up to his neck in this conspiracy, pouring money into the pockets of white and black clergy. Senator John McCain, as chairman of the Senate Indian Affairs Committee, would later reveal in his report to Congress that Ralph Reed, along with Abramoff, not only supported my opponent in 1998, but served as Jack Abramoff's contact with Karl Rove in the Bush White House.

Southern Baptists spoke darkly of eternal damnation. Another Karl Rove college buddy and apparent bagman, Jack Abramoff, the lobbyist for Mississippi Choctaw Indian Casinos, later admitted to illegally laundering some $20 million into the state to "stop Siegelman" whose state lottery "would have been the first breech [sic] in the Alabama anti-gambling wall."[4]

Grover Norquist, a third College Republican with close ties to Rove, was funneling the casino money through his entity, Americans for Tax Reform, to defeat me.

I also knew that this illicit use of money, purposefully raised in secret in Mississippi and passed on to Alabama preachers and politicians to influence an election, was illegal under both federal and state law. But I also knew Karl Rove's client, Alabama Attorney General Bill Pryor, wouldn't try to stop them.

On October 12, 1999, my proposal to improve public education in Alabama with a lottery was defeated, 54 percent to 46 percent.

I was stunned. Polls had showed the lottery was favored. Yet we lost. Dishonest television commercials, greedy politicians, corrupt religious leaders, and millions of dollars in casino money had persuaded many churchgoers to vote against their own children's best interests.

The Karl Rove and Billy Canary Republicans didn't care about education or gambling. It was me they cared about, the Democrat who kept winning elections. They were determined to stop me. I knew the legislature would not approve the taxes for a major initiative in education. Proposals had failed for years. It was the lottery or nothing. My dream of free college was dead.

CHAPTER 20

MAKING CHANGES

"I'm going to push for more and better jobs and improving education as best we can with the resources we have," I told my staff and cabinet. With the help of innovative cabinet members like Pam Baker, commissioner of Children's Affairs, and my Finance Director Henry Mabry, we created seventy-two early learning centers for preschoolers and removed over 3,000 house trailers, called portable classrooms, by initiating over 1,000 new school construction projects. I also funded a statewide reading initiative and much more. Our test scores rose, and our dropout rates fell. But I didn't get to provide free college. Knowing it was a step America must undertake someday, I intended to propose a national model for free higher education in 2003, when I hoped to enter the Democratic presidential primaries.

Alabama's Active and Creative First Lady

Lori was an active, creative, and compassionate First Lady. She always loved the arts, children, and reading. She created a Governor's Mansion library of first-edition books by Alabama writers and initiated a First Lady's Children's Art Festival to expose children to all aspects of art. She worked with former President Jimmy Carter to build a Habitat for Humanity house in Alabama. She hosted special events for children with disabilities and annual Easter festivals and Christmas parties for schoolchildren from families otherwise unlikely to visit the Governor's Mansion. She also frequently traveled to read to elementary school classes. The quaint log and stone cabins in Alabama's state parks, built beginning in 1929, were restored due to Lori's passion for the outdoors and her leadership.

Taking on Exxon—Beating Back Rove's Client

Still, there was much to be done. I cared about the environment and especially about our lakes, rivers, and the beautiful beaches on the Gulf of Mexico. I had grown up walking those beaches, playing in the sand, swimming, fishing, loving the warmth of the sun and the sound of the waves crashing or lapping the sandy shore. The *Exxon Valdez* spill in Alaska had shaken me and I intended to protect our natural heritage from the dangers that arose from oil drilling in the Gulf.

Throughout my career in public office, I had fought for clean air and clean water, to stop herbicide spraying of roadsides, eliminate deep-well injection of hazardous waste, and prevent at-sea incineration of hazardous waste. I filed environmental lawsuits taking on Shell Oil for disposing of hazardous waste in the Gulf, and chemical companies for illegally disposing of mercury. As governor, I made the largest public land acquisition in the United States in a quarter century, preserving 150,000 acres of the Mobile Delta for the public—protecting it from clear-cutting by paper companies.

The state had given Exxon a lease to drill for oil off our coast. I was angry when I was told that Exxon might be underpaying royalties due to the state on their profits. I called my friend John Crowder, a tough as nails plaintiff lawyer, who would know how oil companies could cheat.

"There are two types of royalty agreements," he told me. "Most provide for a net share of the profits. If Alabama has an agreement whereby oil companies pay royalties based on gross profits, there's a 100 percent certainty that they're cheating."

BILL PRYOR, CORPORATE WRONGDOER APOLOGIST

As lieutenant governor, I tried to persuade Attorney General Bill Pryor to sue Big Tobacco. Now, as governor, I asked him to sue Exxon for fraud. He was not interested. "You're on a fishing expedition," Pryor said.

"If they're so innocent, why have the oil companies offered to pay us $7 million as a settlement?" I demanded.

"Bring me evidence," Pryor countered.

We did. Soon Crowder's law partner and my old high school friend, Richard Dorman, called me in excitement. "Don, we've found the smoking gun. Exxon is both arrogant and stupid. But I don't want to talk over the phone."

"Tell me what it is, this line is secure."

"We found a memo from Exxon's general counsel to their CEO that admits they've been making illegal deductions. The CEO wanted to know the dangers. The general counsel tells him not to worry, Alabamians aren't smart enough to catch on, but even if we do they'd only have to repay what they should have paid in the first place."

With that, Pryor was in check; he had to agree for Crowder's law firm to sue on behalf of the state. As a result, Exxon was hit with punitive damages of $3.2 billion. That was second only to the $10 billion they paid after the *Exxon Valdez* disaster. Regrettably, the victory was only temporary. Here's what happened. Exxon appealed to Alabama's newly comprised, Republican-dominated, Supreme Court.

ROVE AND CANARY'S ALABAMA SUPREME COURT

Rove and Canary had focused on electing conservative, Republican, business-oriented Supreme Court justices. I had appointed a second African American judge to the court and campaigned for the Democratic justices who ran in 2000. But after an estimated $500,000 in oil company donations, Republicans achieved an 8-1 majority. Rove and Billy Canary were the architects of the takeover, which also eliminated both African American justices.

Thanks to Rove and Canary, the $3.2 billion judgment against Exxon was reduced to $147 million. This was about what they had stolen, but without the punitive damages they well deserved. It was a textbook example of why corporations supported the Rove-Canary takeover of our judicial system.

FIGHTING ROVE-CANARY FORCES ON TORT REFORM

One day Lori and I were house-hunting in Birmingham. We stopped to talk with a man who was working in his garden. He told me that I should do something about civil justice reform. I knew what he meant. Early on, Alabama had been labeled by the U.S. Chamber of Commerce as "Tort Hell."

In other words, there were few limits on the punitive damages a jury could award. Punitive damages is a monetary award by a jury to punish the wrongdoer, sometimes given in addition to compensatory damages, which are to make the victim economically whole. Most verdicts were reasonable, but some punitive damages were out of line. The man we met said that his client, Jim Senegal, the CEO of Costco, had told him he would never open a store in Alabama because of our pro-plaintiff laws.

I called Senegal, who said, "Governor, I would shut my doors before coming to your state. Your anti-business tort laws are the worst in the nation."

"Would you come to Alabama if we passed limits of punitive damages?" I asked.

"Call me if you do."

When I was lieutenant governor, I had used the power of my gavel as president of the State Senate to stop the Rove-Canary forces from eliminating punitive damage awards completely, even for personal injury or wrongful death. Now, as governor, I talked with trial lawyers, business leaders, and legislators and found support for a compromise that would protect personal injury victims. The trial lawyers were tired of fighting. My compromise, must have driven Rove mad. It most certainly angered Billy Canary.

The compromise would not limit punitive damages in personal injury or wrongful death suits but there would be a cap on punitive damages for economic losses. Trial lawyers and the business community accepted this as did Senegal and the president of Honda. They took it as an example of Alabama's emerging pro-business attitude. I hoped to bring other auto-makers to our state in my quest for more foreign investment and better paying jobs for working families.

RECRUITING FIVE AUTO PLANTS

Nothing I did as governor pleased me more than my success in bring-ing five automobile plants to Alabama in less than four years. These plants meant thousands of good-paying jobs for families and new pride and prestige for our state.

Soon after I was elected governor, my brother, Les, told me there was a possibility that we could bring a Honda plant to Alabama. Les urged me to make a film touting Alabama's great weather, skilled workers, and willingness to welcome companies from abroad. I gladly did so. We scheduled a meet-ing with Honda officials. In preparation, I had my karate instructor teach me how to say "Welcome to Alabama" in Japanese. Honda's vice president was concerned about punitive damages and excited about educational op-portunities in our state.

Bringing Honda to Alabama in 1999, to be followed by Toyota, Mercedes Benz, a division of Fiat, and Hyundai.

After landing Honda, I planned to go after a second Mercedes plant and then others.

This meant extensive travel abroad and additional infrastructure expense. I traveled to Germany, Japan, South Korea, and other countries to urge companies to come to Alabama. Typically, we handled site preparation; in one case, we added a new lane on the interstate between the plant and Birmingham, at a cost of $240 million. But our efforts paid off in thousands of jobs that paid an average of $65,000 a year.

At the end of my term, I was featured in *Automotive News* as one of the Top 25 Automotive CEOs in the world. I took pride in bringing the auto manufacturing industry to Alabama: Honda, a second Mercedes plant, Hyundai, Toyota, a division of Fiat, and a second Honda plant. We did our best to accommodate the auto companies.

CHAPTER 21

A MOTORCYCLE MORPHS INTO CRIME

On a trip to Japan, the president of Honda International took me on a tour of one of his plants. When we passed Honda motorcycles on display, I admired one that I thought looked like a Harley-Davidson.

"Do you like it?" he asked.

"Yes," I said. "It's a great-looking motorcycle. You will sell many of these in the U.S. It will compete well against the Harley-Davidson. I had a Honda 150 in college."

Upon my return to Alabama I had a call from the North American representative of Honda. "The president wants to give you a gift," he said. "That motorcycle you admired."

I was taken by surprise. "I can't accept it as a gift," I explained, "but I can purchase one." The bike was sent to a local dealership and I wrote a personal check for it.

The next morning, after our staff meeting, I told Nick Bailey that Lori was concerned about how much being governor was costing us and she

Alabama was the heart of the civil rights movement, and I worked hand-in-hand with legends of the movement for further progress. Top: with John Lewis and

President Bill Clinton at the 2000 Selma Bridge Crossing. Left: with Rosa Parks at the dedication of her museum. Above: Coretta Scott King endorsed me for reelection.

wouldn't be happy that I'd bought a motorcycle.

"Then sell it to me," he said.

"Nick, I just bought it, I don't want to sell it."

"Then sell me a half interest and she'll only be half as mad."

I agreed to that and Nick brought me a check and a bill of sale showing that he owned half of the motorcycle.

My trip helped Alabama win a second Honda plant. But the motorcycle would come back to haunt me.

September 11, 2001: the most heart-wrenching day faced to date in the new millennium by American leaders. Despite the national scramble for safety and a lack of information, I would spend the following months comforting the citizens of Alabama and ensuring the safety of all my constituents.

CHAPTER 22

TERRORISTS ATTACK AMERICA

On the morning of September 11, 2001, I took a 7 a.m. flight to Washington, D.C., in a state plane. We were near Virginia when the pilot told me that we couldn't land at Reagan National Airport and had to turn around. That sounded so strange that I told him to proceed. He made another call and told me we had to divert and land immediately or be shot down.

"What's going on?" I asked. We landed in a small airport, where I learned about the unimaginable tragedies in New York, at the Pentagon and outside Washington, D.C.

No planes were allowed to fly, so we arranged for a state trooper to drive me back to Alabama. Lori had been in New York for a meeting to build support for the arts in our state. Fortunately, she had arrived home before the disaster. I hugged her and was moved to tears that our family was together and safe at this moment of senseless horror.

In the aftermath of the 9/11 attacks, the stock market crashed, the tech bubble burst, state revenues plummeted, and George W. Bush's popularity climbed to an all-time high. Alabama along with other states faced a financial crisis. Our constitution prohibited deficit spending, so virtually all our programs would have to be cut, including a 10 percent reduction in spending on education. I, without any publicity, cut my own salary by 10 percent.

"We need $150 million to make education whole," my finance director said. I was not going to raise taxes on working people. Instead, we focused on corporate loopholes and out-of-state corporations that paid little or no Alabama taxes. New enforcement on tax loopholes could mean hundreds of millions of dollars in revenue. We proposed our new corporate tax plan to the legislature. Amid grumbling from conservatives, I moved the plan forward.

LARGEST INFRASTRUCTURE PROJECT IN FIFTY YEARS

With the new funding for education behind me, and with a federal loan of highway funds, I began a massive program to build new roads and bridges. School buses were having to detour over 14,000 miles a day to dodge unsafe bridges. New bridges were urgently needed, as were the new jobs created by their construction. I moved about the state on a "dilapidated bridge tour" that took me to isolated places where citizens and local officials appreciated the attention and the local media gave us front-page coverage.

In the end, ours was the largest road and bridge program in the state's history. About $2 billion in federal, state and local funds, leveraged by bonds, went to build new roads, pave dirt roads, and construct more than six hundred new bridges.

As my first term as governor was ending, I took pride in having brought five new automobile plants to Alabama. Those plants had provided nearly 100,000 new, good-paying jobs for working families. Starting 1,000 school construction projects and my road and bridge program put thousands more to work. I expected to be reelected and then, in 2004, to be a contender for one of the spots on the Democratic ticket that would prevent a second term by George W. Bush.

CHAPTER 23

ROVE'S FORCES & FRIENDS PLAN ATTACK

On March 28, 2001, the national business journal, *The Kiplinger Letter,* touted me as a dark horse candidate if the Democrats were "looking for a party conservative who might be able to break the GOP lock on Southern states."[5] Like Georgia's Governor Jimmy Carter and Bill Clinton of Arkansas before me, I was well positioned as a progressive. I had emerged by winning against Republicans, in a blood-red state, the home of George Wallace and the Dixiecrats. Looking back, Alabama was destined to become Donald Trump's strongest base of support.

As a candidate for reelection in 2002, I again called for an Education Lottery to provide free college tuition for deserving students. I was well-financed and faced an opponent, Republican Congressman Bob Riley, who was only notable for his poor attendance record in Congress and his failure to pay taxes for several years. I savored the prospect of a race against him.

Karl Rove with his client, Alabama Attorney General Bill Pryor.
(Courtesy Peppertree Films)

George W. Bush was in the White House and Karl Rove was his chief political adviser. In Florida, during the 2000 presidential election, his operatives had minimized the vote in Democratic areas, working to create long lines that prevented thousands of people from voting. This contributed to a statewide vote so close that a recount was needed, but instead of a recount the 5–4 Republican majority on the Supreme Court rejected precedent and handed the presidency to Bush.

Rove, who had been elevated to the Bush White House, was playing the key role in political appointments of U.S. attorneys and federal judges in Alabama and elsewhere.

My reelection campaign was going well. I had nearly universal support from Democrats. Every poll showed I was the preferred candidate of nearly 90 percent of African Americans. I had built support of mayors and county commissioners by bringing new industry, building new roads, bridges, and schools. Educators were strongly in my corner, as were environmentalists. I even had a few prominent older Republican businessmen on board. I had cultivated the NASCAR race fans through twenty-five years of attendance and I hoped the National Rifle Association would play fair with me as an incumbent.

CHAPTER 24

DODGING AN NRA BULLET

The one thing I didn't need was for the NRA to openly oppose me. The National Rifle Association always favors Republicans. However, I had worked with the NRA on gun safety issues along with restoring and upgrading shooting ranges. Jim Porter, a conservationist, admired the work I had done, and was a leader of the NRA both at the state and national level. Jim and I had developed a friendship through our mutual interest in conservation. Jim confided that a battle over the endorsement was ongoing.

It climaxed when national Republican leaders were attempting to sway the NRA to support my opponent. Richard Shelby, Jeff Sessions, and Karl Rove were names given to me by an NRA insider as those trying to get the NRA to endorse my opponent. Then I got word from this same insider, to sit tight. Charlton Heston, the NRA's national president, was coming to Alabama to endorse me. Lori and I met with Mr. Heston, who could not have been more gracious. The NRA spokesman said that it was the NRA's policy to endorse any incumbent who hadn't gone against them.

I had dodged a lethal political bullet.

CHAPTER 25

ROVE PULLS OUT HIS BIG GUN

President Bush came to Alabama twice, once raising over $4 million for my opponent and a second time to trash talk me. Some of that $4 million I suspected came from Jack Abramoff's Indian casino client, the Mississippi Choctaw Indians. President Bush's attacks were organized and advanced by Karl Rove. When I learned Bush was coming, I offered to greet him, but I was told that my greetings were not needed.

After the terrorist attacks of 9/11 President Bush's popularity went from an all-time low to a 90 percent approval rate. In a speech delivered to a packed Auburn University football stadium, the president declared, "What Alabama needs is an honest governor." I took that to be Rove's work. It was a clever statement, in that the president didn't attack me by name but still threw mud my way. Rove knew that once I won reelection my ambitions would focus on his boss. It made sense for Rove to start taking shots at me.

As the election neared, I was confident of victory but Alabama was becoming increasingly Republican. For several years, I had been the only Democrat to win statewide office. Still, my pollster, Harrison Hickman, told me on election day that I would win. As the results came in, the most populous counties kept me ahead but the race was closer than we liked.

CHAPTER 26

ROVE'S FINGERPRINTS ON STOLEN ELECTION

Election night 2002, Riley would not concede, declaring, "The votes from Baldwin County are not in yet." He seemed confident Baldwin County would give him the margin of victory.

Baldwin County, traditionally Republican, was late to report, even though it had computerized voting equipment. Voters marked a paper ballot which was then run through a machine which scanned each vote, storing the results on a cassette tape. After the polls closed, the cassettes were taken to the county courthouse where all the data on the cassettes were calculated by computer. But the Baldwin County results were late. At my victory party, we waited anxiously.

Finally, the county results were reported as 19,070 for me and 31,052 for Riley. Thanks to the lead I already had, that gave me a narrow victory. The networks declared my victory. My supporters cheered, I thanked them for their hard work, and then I went home for some rest. I was in a deep sleep when my phone rang at 4 a.m.

"Governor, wake up!" It was my chief of security. "You need to come to the office. They're trying to steal the election."

My key staff members were waiting in the Capitol. Jim Andrews, my campaign manager, said, "Governor, someone changed the Baldwin County votes after the courthouse closed and now they're saying you lost."

My press secretary added, "I had a call from the Associated Press at 2 a.m. asking if we had any comment about the 'computer glitch.' I asked what the hell he was talking about and he said someone, no one would say who, re-ran the numbers just four minutes after everyone had left the courthouse. Now they say you got some 13,000 votes, not the 19,000 that was first reported. The so-called 'computer glitch' was all in one voting box, a single precinct."[6]

"I lost 6,000 votes in one voting box?" I said. "And no other down ballot votes changed? That's impossible."

I had dealt with contested elections as secretary of state. I knew the law. "OK, here's what we do. I want a simple recount of the ballots in that one precinct. They use paper ballots in Baldwin, don't they?"

"Yes, it's an optical scan system."

"It will only take a few minutes to rerun the ballots from that one precinct. Then we want a hand count of the ballots. The ballots will tell us the truth."

I called the probate judge for Baldwin County and I told him I wanted to come to the courthouse that afternoon for a recount of the disputed votes. A state plane would fly us there. I went back to the mansion to shower and dress. When I returned to my office, I learned that Rove's client, Attorney General Pryor, and the local DA threatened to arrest anyone who touched the disputed ballots. The DA, David Whetstone, was a Democrat turned Republican. When I was attorney general, we had frustrated his efforts to execute a sixteen-year-old boy. Whetstone had switched to a Republican and wasn't my friend.

A reporter asked if my opponents were trying to steal the election. I responded, "What I'm saying is I won the election. Then the vote was changed sometime after the polls closed while no one was around. To know who won, we need to hand-count the ballots in the one precinct where my votes disappeared."

I planned to have the Baldwin County Democratic chairman ask the circuit judge to protect the integrity of the ballots and the machines themselves. All paper ballots and the cassettes would have to be taken into the court's possession for an accurate count.

Then I received the worst news. "Governor, General Pryor and the Secretary of State seized the ballots and have certified the stolen votes."[7]

"That's against the law," I protested. "Those votes can't be certified until after Friday noon. The attorney general broke the law."

After the election, a professor at Auburn University produced a study clearly showing the election was hacked and stolen. "Electronic ballot stuffing," the professor demonstrated.[8] My opponent's staffer, Dan Gans, a self-proclaimed "ballot security expert," claimed credit for "finding the votes" and swinging the election to my Republican opponent, Bob Riley. Karl Rove's associate, Kitty McCullough, was given credit by the state Republican Party. Gans went to work for a Jack Abramoff-Tom DeLay lobbying firm, the Alexandria Group. Money had been exchanged between my opponent's campaign and Texas Congressman Tom Delay and the Alexandria Group. In the mix was Abramoff's partner, Mike Scanlon, a former aide to Bob Riley.

The whole thing stank to high heaven but the news media went silent.

CHAPTER 27

JEFF SESSIONS REWARDS BALLOT THIEF

We considered going to court to demand that Attorney General Pryor be required to allow the votes to be counted but we knew we faced an implacable problem. The law said a final certification is presumed to be accurate. The burden fell upon us to prove that enough illegal votes had been counted to change the outcome of the election. But proving that was impossible without the ballots and Pryor had seized them. It was Catch-22 on a grand scale.

If we went to federal court we would be turned down by Republican judges who had been handpicked by Karl Rove. They were all buddies of Jeff Sessions and Bill Pryor. If we went to the Alabama Supreme Court we would be rejected by the Rove-Canary Republican majority.

It was a classic case of rank political corruption. We had been robbed but there was nothing to be done. Republicans insisted the results were accurate, and many newspapers supported them. The longer this went on, the more likely it was that public opinion would turn against me. Many people would see my protests as just sour grapes. With no path to victory, I decided to walk away with dignity—and run again in 2006.

On the afternoon of November 17, I told the media:

"The national media exit polls predicted I'd win and on election night I did. Votes were stolen and now those votes have been certified. The Attorney General has refused to allow a recount of the one precinct where the vote changed. Without the ballots, I cannot prove I won. Therefore, to save the people of Alabama the embarrassment of a long fight, I will step aside."

Later we would learn of another announcement that day. A conference call would take place. A call between Riley supporters led by Billy Canary telling them he had spoken to Karl and the Justice Department and his wife would prosecute me to ensure I would never be a political threat again.

With the support of Senator Jeff Sessions and the newly "elected" Republican governor, Bill Pryor was appointed a federal judge on the Eleventh Circuit Court of Appeals. Sessions told the world, "We would have appointed Bill earlier but we needed a Republican governor in place first." That was his reward for stealing an election.

CHAPTER 28

ROVE AND PRYOR AT THE BUSH WHITE HOUSE

Although robbed of 2002 reelection, I intended to continue to explore 2004 possibilities. In December 2002, Lori and I again went to Washington for the meeting of the Democratic Governors Association and to attend the White House Christmas party hosted by President George W. Bush. I wanted it clear that I was still someone to be reckoned with.

I had sent word that we were coming. Rove met us at the door with the president. I gave President Bush a hand-crafted wooden-shank golf putter for his father, George H. W. Bush, who I liked and admired. Knowing our new President Bush had trouble with words, I gave him a picture book on baseball.

I studied Rove carefully. I loathed the man, but in a strange way respected him. He was devious, dishonest, and utterly immoral but he was effective. I was determined not to appear discouraged by my loss.

The Bush Christmas party was nothing like the festive one we'd attended when Bill Clinton was in office. Few of the guests seemed happy. Rove led me to a table and sat down beside me, with Bill Pryor on my right. Lori had been taken to join the wives of other governors. Rove asked my plans and I explained that I would be practicing law. I didn't mention that I intended to remain active politically, despite the stolen election. That afternoon, at the Democratic Governors meeting, I was elected chairman of Democratic Governors Emeritus, a new national organization of former Democratic Governors. DGE would give me more national exposure and help me meet big donors going into 2004. I still had a chance to make it to the national stage.

Pryor joined in for a few minutes of awkward talk. In spite of the fact that this was the man who blocked my recount, I remained civil. I said good things about the way President Bush had performed after the 9/11 attacks. In truth, my view of Bush was not high.

That afternoon at the Democratic Governors meeting, I attacked Bush's failed war policy, as well as his economic and education policies. I had a much better opinion of George W.'s brother Jeb. I remembered a talk with Jeb at a governor's meeting during the 2000 campaign. I noted that his brother was doing well in the polls.

"Yes," Jeb said, "he's making all he can off our father's name."

I liked Jeb. Unfortunately, the wrong brother was president.

CHAPTER 29

ROVE REPUBLICANS SUCK WIND

Out of office, I had time to enjoy my family, practice law, and try to make some money, even as I looked ahead to another run for governor.

Lori and I waited for the school year to end in Montgomery before returning to Birmingham. I began practicing law again, enjoying the challenges and my growing bank account. After twenty years of public service I still had no retirement or healthcare coverage.

I was enjoying life, in part because the new governor, Bob Riley, was quickly demonstrating his political incompetence. Within days of taking office, he proposed raised the property taxes on individuals by $1.2 billion. Soon, newspapers were calling him "Billion Dollar Bob." During 2003, his first year in office, two major newspapers, the *Mobile Register* and the *Birmingham News,* both supporters of Riley, published polls showing me beating him by a two to one margin in 2006. There was speculation that the Republicans might try to persuade Jeff Sessions to leave the Senate and run against me for governor. It was reported in the *Birmingham News* that state Republican Party Chairman Marty Connors had gone to D.C. and had met with Sessions in an effort to get him to run. Political surveys were showing I'd trounce Riley, but Sessions remained very popular. Rumors were Jeff's wife was ready to return to Mobile.

THE REPUBLICAN SECRET PLAN

What I didn't know in 2002 was that the Rove-inspired Republicans weren't planning to defeat me in the 2006 by simply stealing votes. There was a much more sinister plan underway. They were now in control of the Department of Justice, the U.S. attorneys, and federal judges in Alabama.

Down the road two Republican lawyers who turned into honest whistleblowers would confirm a secret plan to prosecute me before the election. Their new plan was not to win votes, or even steal votes, but to invent criminal charges that could send me to prison. Marty Connors, the Republican Party chair who tried to get Jeff Sessions to run against me, said "Governor, I'm so sorry this happened. I told them they should drop this after the election." My friend Chip Hill was present when this confession was made.

CHAPTER 30

IT BEGINS! A POLITICAL PROSECUTION

The charges that would be brought against me were rooted in serious problems that faced a member of my staff, Nick Bailey, along with his and Paul Hamrick's friend, Lanny Young.

Back in 1994, when I was running for lieutenant governor, a county Democratic Party chair asked me to put his son, Nick, on my campaign team as a "volunteer." Nick had studied finance at the University of Alabama and had been the vice president of a bank before joining my campaign. He was bright and personable. I used him as my personal aide, someone I could count on to get a job done.

I needed a campaign manager, and Nick recommended his friend, Paul Hamrick, who had managed the agriculture commissioner's campaign. My media consultant Saul Shorr advised, "Look, if you're on the *Titanic*, you don't wait for another ocean liner. You jump in the first boat you see." So I hired Paul.

Paul was smart, tough, worked hard, and took control of the staff. It was nice to have someone who could take on responsibility.

The first time I saw Lanny Young was in my campaign office that year. Paul Hamrick introduced Lanny as his friend. Paul said Lanny wanted to contribute T-shirts and hats with my campaign logo. I thanked him, although I felt no need for hats and T-shirts. After the election, Paul asked me to say thank you to Lanny, who was waiting in the outer office. Lanny was likable, but after that I saw him only a handful of times.

Lanny and Paul had become friends and shared an apartment. After the 1998 election, Lanny became a lobbyist. I told Paul he should keep his distance from Lanny. He said he would. Soon I would hear Lanny's name involved in a scandal. The mound of Confederate soil on which the Alabama Capitol stood was called Goat Hill. I was about to hear a lot about the "Goat Hill Warehouse Project."

My finance director, Dr. Henry C. Mabry, hated paying rent for buildings the state used. One such building was a warehouse used by the Alcoholic

Beverage Control Board. Henry came to me with a proposal to save the state $19 million in rent. His plan was for us to use federal grant money to build our own warehouse. I told him to proceed.

A writer for the *Mobile Register* started to criticize the bond deal that would finance the project. Then I learned that Nick Bailey, whom I had moved to the Department of Economic and Community Affairs, had approved Lanny Young, the lobbyist, to oversee the warehouse construction. I was outraged. This was stupid and foolish. I called Nick in and asked, "What the hell are you thinking? Lanny Young's construction experience must be in Tinkertoys."

Nick's response was, "Governor, you should fire me."

I said, "Nick, I'm mad but I'm not going to fire you. But this looks horrible."

"You should fire me," he said again. But I thought I should show loyalty to someone who had served me well.

I canceled the warehouse project but the bad press continued. I saw only poor judgment on Nick's part, in hiring his unqualified friend. I would later learn that Nick was guilty of far worse than bad judgment.

An investigation of Lanny Young was underway. He had taken a plea deal, an agreement for a light sentence, in exchange for his "cooperation." Young then made allegations against me and Republicans Attorney General Bill Pryor and U.S. Senator Jeff Sessions.[9] DOJ only investigated Young's allegations against me.

Young was given a two-year sentence, serving only eleven months because prosecutors told the judge they "cannot overstate the importance" of Young to their efforts to convict me.[10] A cellmate of Young's sent an unsolicited statement:

> According to him [Lanny Young], he said whatever they (the "FEDS") told him to say. He laughs about it, and revels in the fact that he "made millions and got away with it" by becoming a "federal informant" and setting people up. . . .
>
> No man should be allowed to trade his punishment for the crimes he committed for lies against the innocent.[11]

In 2001, my family lawyer and friend, Bobby Segall, learned Nick Bailey was under federal investigation based on his relationship with Lanny Young. Attorney General Pryor, still Karl Rove's client, gave Leura Canary, the new Bush U.S. attorney who was also Rove's political partner's wife, the use of his investigators. The agents were not FBI, but were Jeff Sessions's retired FBI agents. Pryor also turned his assistant AG, Matt Hart, loose as a resource to use against me.

Bobby insisted I hire David Cromwell Johnson, a real criminal defense lawyer. I had known David for years. We had taken karate together. David discovered the U.S. attorney's husband, Billy Canary, Karl Rove's political partner, was being paid to defeat me. All hell broke loose. David held a press conference in front of the federal courthouse blasting U.S. Attorney Canary and her husband. He demanded the DOJ replace her with someone who didn't have such a conflict of interest.

David told me, "There's no way they'll bring charges against you." Over the New Year's holidays, January 3, 2003, David died.

The DOJ wrote David in reply, "No actual conflict exists."

I then hired Doug Jones as my new criminal defense lawyer.

CHAPTER 31

THE FIRST INDICTMENT

The morning of May 27, 2004, I was at the Birmingham airport waiting for a flight to New York to attend the Democratic Governors Emeritus fundraiser at the Waldorf-Astoria Hotel. We were expecting a full house of governors and big donors who still wanted to be close to the affable President Bill Clinton. I was chairman of the DGE and President Clinton was our host for the fundraiser. Then I received a call from my lawyer, Doug Jones—the same Doug Jones who, in 2017, won a close but memorable election to the U.S. Senate.

"Don, where are you?"

"At the airport, about to fly to New York."

"Don't board. Come to my office immediately. The U.S. attorney just held a press conference. You've been indicted."

"Indicted for what?" I was furious. I knew at once that Pryor and Canary were behind this, whatever it was.

"Just come. We need to make a response to the charges."

"Arrange for the press," I said.

"OK. But I don't want you to say anything about Pryor or Canary."

"I'll just say it's politics. This is all about the Republicans being afraid I'll make a comeback."

The new Bush U.S. attorney and the state AG were charging that I had engaged in a conspiracy to give Dr. Philip Bobo a Medicaid contract. Dr. Bobo, who was a popular surgeon and sideline doctor for the University of Alabama football team, had initially opposed me when I ran for lieutenant governor but became a friend and a supporter. Bill Pryor's lead assistant, Matt Hart, who we were to learn was in secret email communication with the Rileys, was now cross-designated to work as an assistant U.S. attorney with Billy Canary's wife, the U.S. attorney.

Later, the DOJ would be exposed. DOJ had copies of emails showing that Hart was in email communication with my Republican opponent's campaign manager in 2002, giving him updates on the status of my investigation.

Dr. Bobo was also the director of the Alabama Fire College, an emergency medical training center for firemen. The charge by Canary and Hart alleged that, as governor, I had money put in the education budget for the Fire College so Bobo could attempt to buy out his competition. I was astonished.

This would be Dr. Bobo's second trial on the same charge. When Matt Hart was working for Karl Rove's client, Bill Pryor, Hart approached Dr. Bobo and told Bobo he would not face charges if he would testify against me. In not such polite language, Dr. Bobo told Hart to get off his property.

Dr. Bobo was tried and convicted on phony Medicaid fraud charges which were overturned on appeal. Now, the prosecutors were going to try us together for conspiracy on the same charges. My indictment had been issued on the last day of the five-year statute of limitations. This decision we knew had to have been approved by President Bush's and Karl Rove's Department of Justice.

CHAPTER 32

PROSECUTORS' MISCONDUCT

The prosecutors, Matt Hart and Steve Feaga, both working for U.S. Attorney Leura Canary, first tried to obtain a friendly judge who'd rule in their favor. Two judges turned them down and the case went to the presiding U.S. District Court Chief Judge, U. W. Clemon. Judge Clemon was the first African American federal judge in Alabama since Reconstruction, appointed by President Carter. Hart tried to have Judge Clemon disqualified because a family member of Judge Clemon had once faced a criminal charge. The Eleventh Circuit Court refused.

After their motion had been filed and awaited the judge's order, the prosecutors commented to the media. The judge threatened to hold them in contempt for trying to poison the jury pool.

Because Doug Jones had been U.S. attorney under Bill Clinton at the time this charge was first being concocted, Judge Clemon asked Doug Jones to disqualify himself. I hired Bobby Segall and Joe Espy, two friends and "strong as new rope" advocates. I also had added two old friends from college to my legal team: Redding Pitt, former U.S. attorney under Clinton, and Jack Drake, Doug Jones's partner. Sam Heldman, another brilliant lawyer out of Washington, D.C., would write motions and briefs. I had a great team.

The trial was an absurdity and short-lived. The judge often questioned the government's witnesses, trying to find a legal basis for their claims. At one point Judge Clemon asked prosecutor Matt Hart, "What exactly are you saying when you allege 'the governor put money into the education budget' and how does the governor, who doesn't even have a vote in the legislature, do that?"

The judge pointed out that he had once served in the state senate and knew exactly how budgeting was carried out. In short: "What you have alleged is a legal impossibility. The governor cannot put money into the education budget for the Fire College. Call your next witness."

Eventually, after Hart called a witness whose testimony entirely supported me, Judge Clemon said, "Mr. Hart, do you have anything else? Because

Leaving the courthouse after the charges were dismissed in my first trial, 2004.

what I've heard your witness describe is perfectly legal."

Hart glumly said, "Judge, the government moves to dismiss the charge."

"With prejudice," the judge declared emphatically, in a tone making clear his recommendation.

"With prejudice," Hart conceded. That meant the charge against me had been settled on the merits and could not be brought again. Recognizing "his prosecution was *completely without legal merit*,"[12] Chief Judge U. W. Clemon dismissed the case on October 5, 2004, the first day of testimony.

Later the judge would tell President Obama and Eric Holder that it was the most unfounded criminal charge he had ever seen.

Although the charges had been easily rejected, I remained furious. My legal expenses had been over $900,000 and even with a victory the publicity had been harmful. Most of all, I was outraged because I knew the prosecutors, Matt Hart and Steve Feaga, had knowingly presented false evidence to the grand jury.

I asked my appellate lawyer, Sam Heldman, to help me draft a complaint to the Justice Department's Office of Professional Responsibility (OPR), which is supposed to ensure proper legal conduct. We explained that the prosecutors had not used FBI agents to build the case against me but *retired* agents who had worked for Jeff Sessions. I didn't mention that Bill Pryor was Karl Rove's client. There was no reason to assume that these men possessed the independence we expect from FBI agents. They were guns for hire.

My complaint was ignored. OPR was controlled by David Margolis, the same deputy U.S. attorney general who authorized my prosecution in the first place and ignored Leura Canary's blatant conflict of interest. Margolis was a powerful figure at Justice and was embracing false charges against me. I didn't understand why.

Still, I thought my legal troubles were over. I talked with Peter Sissman, my buddy from Georgetown Law School, about filing a Hyde Amendment motion to recover my attorney's fees. I thought the government should pay a price for their misconduct. But one of my brilliant trial lawyers and good friends, Bobby Segall, was opposed. "Let sleeping dogs lie," he said. "Don't taunt them. Just drop it." I called Peter, who said he wouldn't file the suit without Segall's approval.

Even as my lawyers urged retreat, I felt in my bones that the government would come at me again and that backing down was a mistake. Judge Clemon later told me he would have granted a Hyde Amendment motion in a heartbeat.

I couldn't understand how the Department of Justice and its Office of Professional Responsibility could approve the ridiculous case that had been brought against me. Or accept the blatant conflict of interest of a case brought by a U.S. attorney, Leura Canary, whose husband was managing the campaign of the man I was running against. The Office of Professional Responsibility, despite its lofty title, was taking orders from someone. Was it the White House or Rove?

My attorney, then Doug Jones, now U.S. Senator Doug Jones, got a call from the assistant U.S. attorney working on my case saying, "We had a meeting in Washington and we were told to go back and look at everything again from top to bottom."[13] It was confirmed by a second DOJ attorney that "'Washington' had ordered them to start over with the investigation."[14] Only a few months earlier, DOJ had insufficient evidence to bring charges: "In early July 2004," my attorneys met with prosecutors and "left convinced that the investigation would close without any charges being brought."[15]

The conclusion by local prosecutors not to bring charges was consistent with earlier findings by DOJ's career prosecutors. "Charles Niven, a twenty-six-year career prosecutor, [who] served as acting U.S. attorney supervising an investigation of the Siegelman administration from the summer of 2002 until 2003" said he "did not see evidence to link Siegelman to the investigation."[16] Mr. Niven said in 2003, "There wasn't sufficient evidence to seek an indictment against Governor Siegelman." "John W. Scott, a senior Justice Department trial lawyer helping with the case" expressed the same.[17] Mr. Scott "opposed efforts to continue the investigation of former Gov. Don Siegelman and argued to end the case in 2004" because he "felt there was not enough evidence to go forward. . . ."[18] Mr. Scott was said to be so distraught by the insistence to continue the investigation, despite a lack of evidence, that "when [Mr. Scott] left Montgomery he didn't come back."[19]

My attorney, Doug Jones, described the rejuvenation of charges against me as a directive from "Washington":

> What we saw beginning in early 2005 was much more than simply a top to bottom review . . . it appeared that *agents were not investigating any allegations of a crime, but were now fishing around for anything they could find against an individual.* New subpoenas were being issued for documents and witnesses. Anyone that was a major financial backer of Don Siegelman or who had done business with the state during his administration began receiving visits by investigators and subpoenas by prosecutors. Every bank record, every financial record, every investment record of the Governor, his wife, his campaign and his brother were being subpoenaed.[20]

CHAPTER 33

BACK TO CAMPAIGNING

Still, my 2006 campaign was going well. The polls showed me with a solid lead.

I put my campaign team together. I hired a young man named Chip Hill to work with my brother and serve as my campaign manager and hired his friend, John Aaron, an astute lawyer and an excellent researcher. I say hired; they'd say volunteered. Both did excellent work. I was traveling the state again, visiting nursing homes to talk about the needs of seniors, meeting with sheriffs to underscore my concern about crime, and touring a Hyundai plant to talk about jobs.

I had to win the Democratic primary in June against Lucy Baxley, the state treasurer, now running against me for the Democratic nomination for governor. Perhaps more importantly, Lucy was the ex-wife of Bill Baxley, who had served as both Alabama's attorney general and lieutenant governor. They had divorced after the *Birmingham News* revealed Bill's extramarital romance. Later, we learned from the testimony of Dana Jill Simpson that Karl Rove had hoped to accuse me of the same but I wasn't vulnerable on that front.

I wasn't worried about beating Lucy. Raising money was my concern. I'd beaten back the bogus charges in 2004 that robbed me of time and raised doubts in voters' minds. As the date neared for the public disclosure of contributions, I borrowed $250,000 to jump-start my campaign.

CHAPTER 34

A SCRAMBLE FOR A SECOND INDICTMENT

Then, just days after I announced I would run for governor again, more devastating news came from Bobby Segall. I'd been indicted again!

"Indicted? For what?"

"It's a RICO charge."

"RICO?"

"Racketeer Influenced and Corrupt Organizations Act."

"Jesus, now I've joined the mob? How crazy can these people be?"

Bobby said Assistant U.S. Attorney Steve Feaga said orders for this new charge against me had come from the Justice Department in Washington. Perhaps from the White House? The charge was that the $250,000 contribution from Richard Scrushy to the lottery campaign back in 1999 was a bribe I had supposedly traded for an appointment to the Certificate of Need Board. It was beyond ridiculous. I had received no money and Richard hadn't even wanted the appointment.

I drove to Montgomery to meet with Bobby Segall. We went to the federal courthouse where the U.S. marshals took my fingerprints and mug shot.

Bobby said he couldn't represent me in such a criminal charge. I needed a real criminal defense attorney. I had to decide who would be my lawyers. Doug Jones had been my lawyer but Les was troubled that Doug still considered Bill Pryor and the Canarys as friends. Pryor wasn't my friend and Les and I decided to make a change. I called a close friend from high school, Jimmy Atchison, whom I knew to be a solid anti-Jeff Sessions Democrat and a good criminal lawyer. Jimmy recommended Mobile law partners Vince Kilborn and David McDonald.

Les, Bobby, Joe Espy, and I met with them and were impressed. David declared that Vince was as good as it got on cross-examinations and would tear the government's witnesses to pieces. David said he would call in a professor from Notre Dame, Robert Blakley, who had helped write the RICO statute, and Hiram Eastland of Mississippi, who knew the law we'd be facing. I'd already hired my friend, Redding Pitt, former U.S. attorney, as a consultant. All those lawyers were supposed to be encouraging. But I'd need to hire several more before all this would be over.

Vince was tall, with coal-black hair, a moustache, and a goatee. He wore expensive suits and colorful ties. He reminded me of Paladin, the TV character whose slogan was "Have Gun, Will Travel."

David was shorter, with a bodybuilder's physique, and a mischievous smile. Vince would be the lead lawyer, with David as a writer and more the strategist. They said they were ready to fight like hell against this outrage and I decided to hire them. It was only in parting that Vince said, "This will be my first real criminal case."

What? My mouth went dry. But we hired them. We had no time for delay.

Fighting these political charges had become terribly expensive. It cost about $150,000 to part company with Doug Jones and $350,000 to hire Vince and David. I borrowed heavily, putting $850,000 into my legal defense fund. Proving your innocence takes money.

Judge Mark Everett Fuller set the trial date for May, just one month before the Democratic primary in June. That suited me. I wanted to get this over with so I could focus on my campaign for governor.

CHAPTER 35

A VENGEFUL JUDGE WITH A GRUDGE

Fuller and I had a history. He was the namesake of a Republican Congress-man, Terry Everett. In one of Everett's reelection campaigns I had encouraged a Democrat to oppose him and actively supported the challenger.

Fuller, a longtime Republican activist, had been on the State Republican Executive Committee in 1999,[21] when it opposed my Education Lottery, calling it an immoral affront to "family values." His family values apparently included denying education to the poor.

Before Fuller resigned as a local district attorney to accept the federal judgeship, courtesy of Karl Rove and Jeff Sessions, he doubled the salary of his chief investigator who had been running the office in Fuller's absence. Fuller had been busy overseeing his private company, Doss Aviation. Doss was a lucrative military defense company which Mark Everett Fuller had started with the blessings of Alabama U.S. Senators Jeff Sessions and Richard Shelby and his namesake, Congressman Everett, who was up to his neck in securing defense funding for his special projects.

As governor, I appointed Fuller's successor as district attorney. I picked his local rival, the presiding state court judge, Gary McAliley, who was asking for the job. I asked why? Gary told me, "I'm the only one strong enough to take on Mark Fuller's mess." After I made the appointment, he then questioned the huge salary increase Fuller had granted his investigator. The matter went to court, where Fuller's action was found to have improperly cost the state retirement fund some $300,000. The verdict brought bad publicity to Fuller. I doubted that he had forgotten the embarrassment. I was uncomfortable with the idea of him as my judge, but my lawyers at first liked him and were unconcerned.[22]

I became troubled about his ownership of Doss Aviation after speaking with Dana Jill Simpson, the Republican lawyer turned whistleblower. We learned that during my trial, the company was seeking a Pentagon contract that could bring it $175 million a year for ten years. A contract that would be worth billions. I assumed that Rove knew about that contract and that the judge perhaps suspected that sending me to prison might improve his company's chances of winning it.[23]

In addition to the judge, we could not forget U.S. Attorney Leura Canary was married to Bill Canary, Rove's business partner, who was managing the campaign of the man I was running against, Governor Riley. Canary claimed to have disqualified herself from the case but we found evidence to the contrary, including an email she sent to her prosecutorial team:

> Y'all need to read this. I have an email in which Siegelman says that his campaign's political survey indicates that 67 percent of the people of Alabama believe that the charges against him are political. Perhaps a reason to ask the judge for a gag order?

Prosecutors Steve Feaga and Louis Franklin followed her advice. The prosecutor's first motion was to get the judge to prohibit us from offering evidence exposing the charges as politically motivated.

CHAPTER 36

THE TORTUOUS TRIAL

As my second trial began, Judge Fuller made clear his support for the prosecution.

U.S. Attorney Canary, supposedly recused from the case, had nevertheless told her team to seek a gag order. When the prosecutors asked the judge to bar us from presenting witnesses or evidence to show "political motivation" in the charges against me, the judge obliged.

"Let me make it clear, we are not going to argue politics in this courtroom."

I just sat there, shaking my head in disbelief.

"Governor, stop it," David warned.

I thought, "How can he stop us from telling the jury that the U.S. attorney's husband is running my opponent's campaign?"

But he could and he did.

A congressional investigation conducted by then U.S. Senator John McCain showed that three of Karl Rove's closest political associates had funneled Indian casino money to my opponent, Bob Riley. In addition to Mike Scanlon, a former Congressional aide to Riley, Jack Abramoff, Ralph Reed, president of the bogus Christian Coalition, and Grover Norquist had all been illegally laundering casino money to my Republican opponent. The underlying reality was that Riley had taken all that money from the Mississippi casinos and then had done his best to shut down gambling in Alabama, to the benefit of the Mississippi casino owners.

Abramoff's goal in "Stopping Siegelman" was perhaps focused on killing my lottery plan to send Alabama's young people to college for free. That was the ugly truth. To me the lottery existed to benefit Alabama's children. To the Mississippi casino owners it was simply to keep their gambling monopoly. If I had opened up a lottery, the Alabama Poarch Band of Creek Indians could have launched a casino to draw Alabama gamblers away from Mississippi. "Stopping Siegelman" meant something entirely different to Karl Rove and Billy Canary. Getting me out of the way meant a better path to the White House for George W. and an easier path to victory for Riley.

CHAPTER 37

THE JUDGE CLOSES IN ON US

Fuller would not allow evidence that hinted to the jury that my charges were motivated by politics. He wouldn't let politics be discussed. In truth, it was all about the determination of Republicans to destroy a Democratic politician they couldn't beat at the polls. I wanted to appeal Fuller's "no politics" ruling to the Eleventh Circuit immediately. But my lawyers said we should wait.

"Look, we're gonna win anyway, so why do this now?" Vince said.

My co-defendant, Richard Scrushy, had two excellent lawyers, Art Leach, a veteran of the Department of Justice, and Fred Gray, who had represented both Dr. Martin Luther King Jr. and civil rights hero Rosa Parks. They did file a motion to disqualify Fuller. I wanted my lawyers to join in but was told we would be rocking the boat to ask the judge to recuse himself. "Let Scrushy make the arguments," Vince said. "It'd just piss the judge off and get us nowhere." Scrushy's motion for recusal did in fact go nowhere.

There were two other defendants, my former chief of staff, Paul Hamrick, and my former Alabama highway director, Mack Roberts. They also had first-rate lawyers. Mack's only crime was refusing to lie about me for the prosecution. The prosecutors rarely mentioned them throughout the trial.

THE CHARGES SHOULD BE DISMISSED

The indictment was so confusing that it was hard to know what the government was alleging. The bribery charge was unrelated to RICO but was called a RICO count. Why? Because a charge of bribery must be brought within five years and the statute of limitations for that had expired. RICO allowed them to hide the fact that the charge of bribery for a contribution for the lottery happened over five years before I was indicted. It therefore was due to be dismissed as "time-barred."

We asked for a Bill of Particulars, to clarify what the government was charging.

"Denied," the judge said, adding that "The charges will make sense as we proceed."

One allegation was that I demanded a campaign contribution to the Alabama Education Lottery campaign from Scrushy in June of 1999 to pay off the Democratic Party debt on the lottery campaign. The debt, however, wasn't created until March of 2000, making the charge void on its face. It was at that time CEO of HealthSouth, Richard Scrushy, made a second donation to retire the debt on which I was a guarantor. How could I have known in June of 1999 the lottery would have a debt in March of 2000? I had supposedly demanded this bribe in exchange for appointing him to the "powerful" C.O.N. board, on which he had already served for more than a decade and had resigned before I took office. There was testimony that he actually didn't want to serve again.

I asked David, "When are we going to ask for the bribery charge to be dismissed?"

"We'll have to wait to the end of the trial. That's when motions to dismiss will be presented. Don't worry, we'll ask for a dismissal because the charges were brought beyond the five-year statute of limitations."

After my election in 1998, Scrushy had switched from being a major Republican contributor to being a major Democratic contributor. His timing was not good. Rove liked to discourage major Democratic donors. Scrushy had been put on trial and acquitted a year earlier for manipulating the value of HealthSouth stock. Now, like me, he was being tried a second time.

Prosecutors alleged Scrushy was cooking the books at HealthSouth so he could go to Wall Street, painting a rosy projection of the company's anticipated financial growth.

The Republican-appointed U.S. Attorney Alice Martin, a cohort of Billy Canary, had indicted all the top officers, including Scrushy, and arranged an FBI raid on the HealthSouth headquarters. The publicity caused its stock to plummet. Many people lost their jobs and more lost their investments.

Five former HealthSouth executives testified against Scrushy in exchange for leniency. Yet Scrushy was acquitted on all charges. The government was humiliated and the public wanted Scrushy's head. So now the government was taking a second shot at him, along with me. Scrushy's only tie to me was the contribution he made to the lottery campaign. I was concerned his unpopularity might drag me down.

SEPARATE TRIALS WERE CALLED FOR

Scrushy's lawyer, Art Leach, argued that his client's contributions to the Education Lottery had nothing to do with the RICO charges. He was right. I pleaded with my lawyers to support Scrushy's removal from the case.

Vince disagreed. "Governor, we need him. He's got good lawyers and the resources to help us."

It didn't matter. Fuller denied the request for separate trials.

OPENING STATEMENTS

The opening statements were long and disheartening. The prosecution went on and on about organized crime, corruption, the selling of the governor's office, lie after lie. Speaking for me, Vince did all he could, but he was forbidden by the judge to talk about the underlying political basis of the case. It was heartbreaking to sit there and realize how quickly this travesty would be over if we could point out that the prosecutor's husband was running my opponent's campaign for governor.

Early in the trial, the prosecutors began bashing me in press conferences outside the courthouse. We asked the judge to remind the prosecutors of ethical requirements that prohibited them from trying to influence the jury through the media. Fuller dismissed our complaints. The attacks continued.

The lead prosecutors were Louis Franklin, diminutive and acerbic, and Steve Feaga, a large man who had helped take down Republican governor Guy Hunt for converting leftover campaign funds for personal use. Feaga had helped concoct the first false charges that were thrown out of court in 2004, the ones that Judge Clemon had pronounced as completely unfounded. I saw him as someone who wouldn't be troubled by the U.S. Constitution if it stood between him and a conviction.

The judge ordered that the jurors's names remain anonymous. This added to the drama and hype. Why would a judge do such a thing? This kind of jury was used for drug kingpins or Mob bosses, to protect jurors from being pressured or threatened or bought off. It was also to send a message to the jurors, that this was a serious trial. Our jury would also be sequestered, meaning they couldn't return home. Fuller was sending a message to the jury that we were dangerous. Those who lived outside of Montgomery would have rooms at a hotel. The jurors would have TVs in their rooms and access to newspapers, though the judge would tell them they shouldn't watch or read about the case, which of course would be ignored. The news reports mostly seemed to favor the charges against us and it would not help for the jurors to see them during the trial. But our objections were rejected.

Harrison Hickman, my pollster in several races, conducted a survey of the counties from which most jurors would come. The results, he reported, were "good news and bad news."

"Give me the good news first."

"Roughly 67 percent of the people polled believe these charges are politically motivated," he said.

"And the bad news?" I was happy about the good news.

"The bad news is that about 72 percent think all politicians are crooks, just some haven't been caught yet."

I sent the "Good News" to my email list to keep my supporters pumped up and kept the bad news to myself.

JURY SELECTION

Jury selection took a couple of days. Potential jurors came from all over the southeastern part of the state. Some counties I had carried in my elections; a couple were majority African American. I was encouraged by the makeup of the jury pool.

Potential jurors gave written answers to questions agreed upon by the prosecutors and the defense. We learned their ages, where they lived, occupations, church affiliations, and spouses. But not names. Two of them troubled me, one male and one female, because they were connected to Auburn University.

I reminded my lawyers that President Bush had told his supporters in Auburn: 'What Alabama needs is an honest governor.' That was political poison!"

I wanted to strike the two Auburn grads. As governor, attorney general, and University of Alabama alumnus, I had a history with Auburn. As Alabama's AG, I investigated an Auburn fundraiser for an ethics violation. He had allegedly induced an elderly woman to bequeath property to him rather than Auburn. I turned the matter over to a local grand jury. One of my potential jurors worked in fundraising for Auburn! Could it be that the man I investigated was a friend of this potential juror?

Then there was the matter of a wealthy Auburn alumnus Bobby Lowder, whom I'd appointed to the Auburn Board of Trustees. He turned out to be toxic on campus because he wanted to control Auburn's football program. The faculty, administration, and local community were upset by my appointment. The publisher of the *Auburn Bulletin*, the local newspaper, called my appointment of Lowder an unforgivable sin. I feared some of the hostility might have seeped down into these two potential jurors. You don't want people who hold irrational grudges against you to be in a position to put you in prison.

Vince wasn't concerned. "I like these two. So do the other lawyers. The jurors probably have never heard about this Auburn stuff."

We learned later through emails that the Auburn jurors were indeed hostile to me. The man who worked in fundraising became the jury foreman. A woman, a former gymnast who graduated from Auburn, became known as "Flipper," and lobbied other jurors for a conviction.

Still, the jury we selected looked good. Six were African American jurors, whom I thought would surely know of my longtime support from African American political and religious leaders. Most of the white jurors were working men and women. It takes a unanimous jury to convict. I told Les, "There's no way I'll be convicted. This jury will be hung at worst."

CHAPTER 38

PRESSURE TO WITHDRAW FROM THE RACE

Early in the trial, Jack Miller, a dear friend, someone I was close to both personally and politically and had known since high school, asked me to come to his office to discuss polling numbers on my race. Les and I left Birmingham and drove the eighty-mile stretch of I-65 to the state capital. My friend wouldn't tell us the source of the poll, but what it said was simple enough. Without a conviction, I would win the governor's race conclusively. With a conviction, my Democratic primary opponent, Lucy Baxley, then state treasurer, would get the nomination.

Then my friend got to the point: "Don, I'm here to ask you to withdraw from the race. Let Lucy have the nomination. I believe we can make these charges go away and have your legal expenses reimbursed."

How could he have the charges dropped? Who had that power? Or the money for my legal expenses? Angry, I told Jack, "Whoever put you up to this can kiss my ass. I'm not dropping out. But I am getting out of your office."

Les stayed to talk more. As I calmed down, I went back in Jack's office and apologized for my outburst. But I added, "I can win the case and win the race. When I beat these bullshit charges, there will be a backlash against my opponents. I'll win by a landslide."

"You might, but if you run and are convicted, you could take the entire Democratic ticket down with you."

"I'm going to win the case," I declared. "Even with a conviction, I'd be stronger than Lucy."

After Les and I left, I said, "What the hell was that all about?"

"Somebody with a lot of money wants you out of the race pretty badly if they can make these charges go away and reimburse your legal expenses."

I told Les my guess was Bobby Lowder, a bank owner, who was supporting my primary opponent. "After I appointed Lowder to the Auburn Board of Trustees, we had a falling out when I went to a Board of Trustees meeting and demanded that they not raise tuition."

There was no way I would drop out or give in to such pressure. I held my ground. The DOJ came at me in full force. The next month, I found myself fighting for my life, in Judge Fuller's courtroom, defending my name and integrity.

THE TRIAL THAT WON'T END

As the trial continued, much was made of Scrushy's contribution to pay off the Democratic Party's debt for its failed campaign for the Education Lottery. The prosecution called this donation a bribe to me, although I didn't receive a penny. Lie after lie.

They even claimed I had sold the governor's office in exchange for a motorcycle. What? I paid for the bike with my own personal check. How did they come up with this nonsense? I knew one of their witnesses must be planning to lie. These charges would have been thrown out of court, or laughed out, by an honest judge.

It made me sick every morning to hear the court announce: "The United States of America versus Don Eugene Siegelman." It wasn't my government doing this, but political partisans whose strings, I suspected, were being pulled by Rove in the White House and my enemies in Alabama. Political lies dreamed up by my political enemies.

They had stolen the 2002 election by hacking the electronic vote and stealing 6,000 votes from my total, inventing a victory for my opponent!

Now they were inventing testimony to send me to prison for the crime of being a Democrat who kept beating Republicans in every election.

I remained optimistic. Even during the trial, Chip Hill had my campaign bus there to meet me when court adjourned. My bus kept rolling until time to be at court again.

My lawyers were happy that I was out campaigning. It kept my spirits high and kept me out of their hair. Later I realized I had given them too much leeway. I should have fought them on several pivotal issues. My instincts told me I was right. I was a lawyer and I should have demanded more input.

We should have appealed the judge barring us from arguing political motivation and the judge's refusal to dismiss because the contribution in question was beyond the statute of limitations. We should have objected to the Auburn jurors, demanded a separate trial from Scrushy, and argued more clearly for the judge's recusal. Yet that was all behind us now.

There was another fateful decision ahead. The prosecutors were building their case on two felons who would lie about me in exchange for lighter sentences: Nick Bailey and Lanny Young. Nick had joined my 1994 campaign for lieutenant governor and had brought in Paul Hamrick. Lanny Young was Paul's friend. Now Paul was on trial with me.

CHAPTER 39

WITNESS LIES

Nick had been my personal assistant and I came to consider him a friend, but I had no idea that he had a serious gambling problem. During the trial we learned that Nick had mortgaged his family's cattle farm to bet on cattle futures. He lost. Then Nick had to produce $55,000 or lose his family's farm; that's when he began his illegal ties with Lanny Young. Young gave Nick the money. Nick owed him big time.

I dismissed Nick from my executive office and moved him to the Department of Economic and Community Affairs. Nick apparently had already begun extorting tens of thousands of dollars. While I had canceled the

"Goat Hill" construction project, Nick had already set in motion a corrupt scheme to get a $100,000 kickback from Lanny Young, whom Nick had anointed as the construction manager of the warehouse project. At trial, it was revealed Nick had agreed to overpay Lanny Young so he, Nick, could get the $100,000 kickback. In all, it was estimated that Nick had extorted at least $200,000. Not until trial did we grasp the full extent of his crimes. He finally confessed to shocking corruption. It was an unbelievable side of Nick Bailey, a man I had trusted. It was the most disappointing flaw in character to which I had ever been exposed.

Making a Campaign Contribution a Bribe

Nick Bailey, who had been my personal aide, was the "linchpin" of the prosecutors' case.[24] Facing possible decades in prison for extortion, Bailey agreed to a deal whereby he'd testify against me in exchange for a light-sentence recommendation.[25] Bailey at first said he'd only met with prosecutors and investigators "two or three dozen" times "during the investigation"; the meetings "typically lasted two to three hours, and some of them extended from one day to the next."[26] A paralegal for DOJ, Tamarah Grimes, described one of the meetings:

> I particularly recall one meeting in which cooperating witness Nick Bailey was persuaded to recall something that he claimed he did not actually recollect. The matter concerned a meeting between Governor Siegelman and Richard Scrushy, a check and a supposed conversation, which eventually lead [sic] to the convictions in The Big Case. Mr. Bailey repeatedly said he did not know and he was not sure. *The prosecutors coaxed and pressured Mr. Bailey to "remember" their version of alleged events.* Mr. Bailey appeared apprehensive and hesitant to disappoint the prosecutors.[27]

When Nick testified, he lied about Scrushy's donation to the Education Fund. "It was an absolute pay-for-play deal," he declared.

Amy Methvin, a mutual friend of Bailey and me, described a conversation she had with Nick, the night before he testified against me:

And then he said, you know, I really feel bad about what's getting ready to happen, I really do. He said, the Governor does not deserve this, he's a good man. I've never seen him take anything personally. And he gave and he gave and he was the best Governor we ever had.

Amy then asked, "Nick, what are you going to do if the lawyers ask you that under oath?" Amy said Nick's demeanor changed:

And he went into this long speech without looking me in the eye. And I just—my mouth dropped open because it was absolutely—it was just the opposite of what he had just said. So I let him finish. And I said, "Nick, you sound like a robot, like you have this thing memorized." And this is what he said to me, he said, *"You would have it memorized, too, if you've heard the answers as many times as I've heard the answers."*[28]

I had asked Scrushy to support the Education Lottery, as I had many other businessmen. But Nick testified that "The governor told Eric Hanson that it would take at least $500,000 from Scrushy to make things right."

Nick added "Eric Hanson called him and said . . . "

"Objection, your honor," my lawyer interrupted, "This is pure hearsay. Mr. Hanson must come speak for himself. We have a right to cross-examine witnesses who offer testimony against our client."

All that was basic. Law school 101.

"Overruled. Mr. Bailey, you may proceed to tell the jury what Mr. Hanson told you." This was the kind of ruling from Judge Fuller we were confronted with time after time.

On the witness stand, Nick told many more lies that should not have been admissible. He said that I had shown him a HealthSouth check for $250,000, signed by Richard Scrushy. He said this "showing a check" occurred in the Alabama Capitol in July of 1999.

David, in cross-examination, pointed out that our meeting occurred in June, the check wasn't from Scrushy, but from an entity called Integrated Health Systems, and was issued and delivered by Federal Express weeks after the date Nick said he had seen the check. Another physical impossibility.

"Now your story has changed," David said. "Why? Does your mind get more clear as time passes? How many times did you meet with prosecutors before the time became clear to you?"

"Maybe a dozen times," Nick admitted. He and others would later say he met with FBI agents and prosecutors as many as seventy times before he memorized the story they gave him. We asked for the notes taken by the agents at those meetings. The government claimed no notes had been taken even though agents are required to take and keep notes or transcriptions of meetings with witnesses.

Bailey acknowledged that the reports the prosecutors provided "summarize *only a fraction* of the meetings that I had with government representatives."[29] He later admitted "there were *at least* twenty-four occasions when [he] met with government representatives . . . to discuss issues related to Governor Siegelman and/or Mr. Scrushy" for which no reports were "provided to the defense team."[30]

The prosecutor, questioning Nick, asked: "What did you say when the governor showed you the check?"

Nick slipped up and told the truth. "I asked, 'What in the world is he [Scrushy] going to want for that?'" And added, "The governor said, 'The C.O.N. Board.'"

On cross-examination, David told Bailey that both his statements couldn't be true. "How can you, on the one hand, testify that you told the governor repeatedly what Mr. Scrushy was going to want for his contribution, but when he shows you the check you say, 'What in the world is he going to want for that?'"

Bailey had no answer. Both statements could not be true.

The Motorcycle Saga

The night before Nick was to testify about his purchase of my motorcycle, I had dinner with Vince and David and told them the entire story.

"This is one of those no-good-deed-goes-unpunished stories," I started.

I had gone to Japan to meet with the president of Honda International and he had taken me on a tour of their corporate office. Among a display of many of their products, I had admired a motorcycle.

When I returned to Alabama, a Honda representative called and said Honda's president wanted to give me the motorcycle. I thanked him but explained I couldn't accept such a gift but in a show of my commitment to Honda, I would buy it personally.

I thought the jury would see the truth regarding the motorcycle. The president of Honda offered to give me the motorcycle but I insisted on paying the cost, $12,500. "Doesn't that say something about my character?" I asked.

I reminded them Nick first bought a half interest in the motorcycle and later bought ownership of the rest.

The charges about the motorcycle seemed ridiculous. Was I going to endanger my governorship for sharing a motorcycle with Nick? But the prosecution made much of it, backed up by their two witnesses. Nick and Lanny Young lied in exchange for a light sentence for their own very real crimes. Nick had taken money from Lanny Young to buy his half interest, but he told the jury it was all a charade to get me money from Lanny. It made no sense. I turn down a free motorcycle. Pay for it with my own money. There was no need to be reimbursed for a motorcycle I had already paid for. At any rate, it was clear to the jury I didn't profit by a single penny.

Nick was gay. That was irrelevant to me. But we were told the prosecutors, to encourage Nick's "cooperation," stressed how difficult life in prison would be for him. Jeff Sessions's retired FBI agents had grilled Bailey to find interactions, which when bolstered by lies, could be presented to a grand jury as crimes. They did that on the Scrushy donation and again on the motorcycle.

I refused to believe such lies could lead to a conviction.

Nick, after four years of interrogations, testified that "an absolute" pay-to-play agreement existed between himself, Paul Hamrick, Lanny Young, and me, dating back to when I was elected lieutenant governor. What? Where were they coming up with this insanity?

On cross-examination, my lawyer David McDonald said, "Mr. Bailey, the government has accused the governor of being head of a criminal enterprise, yet you say Governor Siegelman didn't know you were shaking these people down and he didn't get any of the money. Wouldn't you agree that if someone is head of a criminal enterprise he should be getting the lion's share?"

Nick had no answer.

CHAPTER 40

SESSIONS AND PRYOR ACCUSED OF CRIMES

Upon reading a transcription of an interview with Young, we learned of possible crimes of both Sessions and Pryor. When Lanny Young testified, Vince asked about his gifts to Bill Pryor and Jeff Sessions. Young said, "I had my employees write Jeff Sessions checks, then I paid them back."

Judge Fuller stopped Vince. "Inadmissible. The jury is to ignore those comments."

"Your Honor, we want the record to show that we object to your ruling."

"Objection noted. Move on."

Lanny Young had given a sworn statement to the prosecutors about contributions he made to my campaign and clearly illegal contributions to Jeff Sessions and Bill Pryor. He also said he had violated campaign laws by having his employees give money to Sessions and then repaying them himself with cash. Yet we couldn't get that information to the jury. The prosecutors said Young's testimony was not credible as to Pryor and Sessions but was fine to be used against me. The judge agreed.

Vince showed the jury Young's bankruptcy records from the same time period. "Mr. Young, if what you filed in Bankruptcy Court is true, you didn't have two red cents to your name during this time, yet you testified that you were lavishing hundreds of thousands of dollars' worth of campaign contributions on Governor Siegelman's campaign and others. Which is it?"

The judge objected. Young never had to explain his perjury.

The prosecutors called a representative from Honda. It backfired. The witness testified that the president of Honda wanted to give me the bike as a gift, but I insisted on paying for it and had written a personal check for the entire amount.

Vince concluded, "So Honda offered to give the governor a gift of the bike but Governor Siegelman paid for it himself, with a personal check. Is that correct?"

"Yes."

"No further questions, your honor."

"Thank God for that," I whispered to David. It had been painful to watch innocent acts presented as crimes.

The prosecutors often overreached. They called Raymond Bell, who had been my appointments secretary, but his testimony only proved that the appointment of Scrushy was routine. They called Josh Hayes, who had succeeded Raymond. Before Josh finished testifying, the government moved to have him declared a hostile witness because everything he said supported me.

Attempting to show that I twisted arms for campaign contributions, the government called a road builder, Jim Allen, to lie for them. My highway director, Mack Roberts, wouldn't support the lie and that's why he'd been charged with improper dealings with Mr. Allen. Allen claimed that Mack and I had used the highway department to reward a contractor, Mack McCarto, whose company painted the stripes on highways. This man had given a contribution to the Education Lottery campaign. Allen alleged I had pressured him to give.

But when the prosecutors put McCarto on the stand, he told the jury that as far as Jim Allen was concerned, "You can tell he's lying if his mouth is moving." He told the jury he had given me a political contribution as he had other candidates and saw nothing wrong about it.

Allen's story was another disaster for the government.

The jury seemed to be tiring, but the government kept dragging out the trial with matters we had already stipulated to. We thought we knew why. They wanted the trial to last past the primary election, and thus perhaps ensure my defeat.

Still, Vince and David's cross-examination of the government's witnesses went well.

The government's key witness was Nick Bailey, and we had discredited his testimony.

There was no testimony of an explicit deal between me and Scrushy—because there was none. The government nonetheless offered Bailey's false testimony that Scrushy contributed to the Education Lottery to win him a seat on the C.O.N. Board.

MY LAWYERS CALL NO WITNESSES

A crucial decision—a turning point in my life—came when my lawyers advised me against testifying in my own defense. I went back and forth about it with Vince. "I need to testify; I want to tell my side of the story. Lanny Young and Nick Bailey are lying."

"Governor, we know that. The jury knows that. We destroyed them on cross. Bailey came across like a deer in headlights and Young as a liar. You don't need to say anything."

As my protests continued, Vince added, "There's too much risk. The jury is tired and wants to go home. If you testify you'll be up there a week."

"You are telling me we're about to rest? Not calling a single witness?"

"We've agreed to let Scrushy call one witness, Elmer Harris, to testify that he had to persuade Scrushy to accept the appointment. That will be the nail in the government's coffin."

My brother disagreed: "Don, it's a mistake. You need to tell your side of the story. The jurors need to hear it from you. You'll be believable. Please go back and tell them you have to testify."

It was a crucial moment, but my mind was numbed, dulled by the droning of the government's lies, and I did as my lawyers urged.

The next morning, after Elmer Harris testified that I had sent him to help persuade Scrushy to accept the C.O.N. appointment that he didn't want, Vince announced: "The defense for Governor Siegelman rests."

Lawyers for Hamrick, Scrushy, and Roberts also rested. The lawyers believed we would all be acquitted.

It was about then that Hamrick told me he had seen Lanny Young in the men's room. "I screamed at him: 'Why are you doing this to me?'" But there was no mystery about that. Nick Bailey and Lanny Young, facing serious charges, gave the prosecutors the lies they wanted and eventually served only a few months behind bars.

CLOSING ARGUMENTS

Prosecutor Steve Feaga, in his closing statement, stood behind us and told the jury, "This defendant, Governor Siegelman, is responsible for creating the criminal enterprise. Governor Siegelman is the one who attempted to corrupt his young assistant, Mr. Hamrick."

Resting a sympathetic hand on Paul's shoulder, the prosecutor pleaded, "Mr. Hamrick was only being used by the governor in a corrupt scheme to enrich himself at the expense of the state." Young must have told the government to cut his friend, Hamrick, a break.

Feaga's fabricated heartrending tale made no sense. He went on about corruption, pay-to-play agreements, and claims that I had personally benefited from donations to the lottery fund, but he had no evidence. Despite the judge's many rulings against us, we thought the jury could see the truth.

Vince, in his closing remarks, sounded exhausted and flat. He ended with a remark that made me cringe. "Are you going to send a governor to prison over part of a motorcycle?"

Good God, I thought. It sounded as if my lawyer thought the case was about me taking money from a lobbyist to buy a motorcycle. Was that what the jury would think?

JUDGE DENIES ALL POST-TRIAL MOTIONS

We moved for acquittal on all charges related to Scrushy's contributions to the lottery. They were clearly outside the five-year statute of limitations.

The government objected, saying that Scrushy's donations were part of my corrupt pay-to-play scheme. In any event, they said, I should have raised this objection earlier.

David McDonald replied that we had previously asked for a bill of particulars that the judge denied because the government said the dates would become clear during the trial. They did become clear and showed that the charges were outside of the statute. Therefore we asked for an acquittal.

The response was no surprise: "Motion denied."

Vince pushed on. "Your honor, we move for an acquittal on the motorcycle charge. Taking everything the government says as true, Governor Siegelman did not obstruct justice; he did not violate the meaning or intent of this statute. Nor did Governor Siegelman commit any crime relating to the sale of the motorcycle. It was a legitimate sale."

"Motion denied."

Fuller's instructions to the jury were predictably misleading.

Since the 1991 Supreme Court ruling in *McCormick v. United States*, every politician and political contributor had been operating under the same rules. The Supreme Court had ruled that since First Amendment freedoms are at stake in campaign settings, that for a contribution to become a bribe, there must be an "explicit *quid pro quo*," in which the terms of the agreement are asserted. To cross the line from politics to criminal behavior, there must be an "explicit" agreement to swap the contribution for some official act. That was a line no one wanted to cross. I would never have risked my future for a contribution to the lottery campaign.

We asked Fuller to instruct the jury that Nick Bailey was a felon engaged in an ongoing "cooperation" agreement and that to the degree he cooperated, he would be given a reduction of sentence, perhaps no prison time at all.

"Denied."

When the judge read his proposed instruction, my lawyers objected. "Your instructions must tell the jury that to convict Governor Siegelman, they must find beyond a reasonable doubt, that there was an 'Explicit Quid Pro Quo.'"

"Denied."

As I listened to the jury instructions it seemed that the judge was ordering the jury to give him the guilty verdict he clearly wanted.

CHAPTER 41

JUDGE INSTRUCTS JURY FOR CONVICTION

The judge told the jury that they could consider a contribution to the lottery as a thing of value because the Education Lottery was my proposal. I couldn't believe what I was hearing. He was saying because I supported the referendum for free college a contribution to pass, the referendum was a thing of value to me personally.

In other words, someone could be sent to prison for accepting a campaign contribution that involved no personal benefit! Which would mean that every politician in America would have to weigh the legal dangers before accepting routine donations.

Still, as the trial ended, I believed I was going to win the case and my race for reelection.

TRIAL ENDS, JURY DELIBERATIONS BEGIN

The jury began deliberations on June 18, 2006. After six days, the foreman reported a breakdown in deliberations. They seemed unable to reach a verdict. The judge tried to break the logjam with an *Allen* charge, a so-called "dynamite" charge, insisting that the jury keep trying.

Then, Friday, as a new day in court began, Judge Fuller announced a security threat. The nature of the threat was unclear but it gave the jury another weekend to wish they were home.

By then, the prosecutors knew they had allies on the jury, the two jurors from Auburn. The delay would give these two more time to put pressure on other jurors for a guilty verdict. We suspected that the one FBI agent assigned to my case had something going with the female juror from Auburn. Later it was proven he had been having more than a casual relation with the Court's clerk as well.

The one juror other jurors and the prosecutors called "Flipper," we learned, had been emailing other jurors urging a conviction. The foreman, who worked for Auburn University, told the judge that some jurors were no longer willing to participate in the deliberations. So there were holdouts. It meant a hung jury. No conviction. These jurors believed in my innocence. The judge called the jury back in and made it clear he wanted a decision.

On Tuesday, June 27th, after nine days of deliberation, the jury was still deadlocked. Hopelessly, it seemed. The judge demanded more deliberations.

By June 29th, the jury had not been home in ten weeks. They missed their families. They wanted to be home for the Fourth of July. But the judge wouldn't recognize a hung jury. The ones who were desperate to go home would have to agree to a conviction. It was that simple.

JUDGE TELLS JURY TO BRING A VERDICT

Fuller, speaking emphatically, not hiding his desire for a guilty verdict, told the jury: "Look, I've been appointed for life. I can keep you here until next July if I want to. Bring me a verdict or a partial verdict."

WAITING ON A VERDICT

I couldn't believe what he said. He was bullying the jury, demanding a verdict they were unable to reach. I was sure that some jurors wanted to set me free, but at a certain point, their need to go home would bring excruciating pressure on the holdouts. The judge seemed to be saying they must return a guilty verdict or risk being his prisoners forever.

That afternoon I needed breathing space. I walked from the courtroom down the long marble corridor toward the elevators. Looking out the floor-to-ceiling windows, television crew trucks were parked in their usual spaces at the back of Troy University's parking lot. Then I looked down at the front entrance. Trees and pink and red petunias lined the entrance. A good place to sit in the shade, I thought, and headed downstairs.

I took the marble stairs down to the first floor. The security people would wave me back in when it was time. Outside, I joined a couple of reporters. As we chatted, we heard a new voice.

"Are you guys talking about me?" said a reporter who approached us, a pen stuck behind her left ear and a spiral notebook in her hand. We all broke out laughing, as she and I gave each other a high five. "I'm Susie Edwards, Channel 48, Huntsville."

"Well, I guess you know who I am . . . "

We talked for a few moments. Her smile eased my anxiety. I breathed in fresh air, trying to smell the flowers, realizing that this young woman's friendliness had brightened my difficult day.

When court was out for the day, I watched through the third-floor windows as prosecutors and paralegals made their way out the front entrance of the courthouse toward the cameras gathered on their side, stage right. Ours was stage left. We always waited for the government to hold their news conference before we made our way out to confront the reporters.

I felt that most of the electronic media was fair, or even friendly, while much of the print media didn't care about the politics of the case. The possible conviction of Alabama's governor was the story. I'd rather talk to TV reporters. They would ask reasonable questions and many times use what I said.

It was June 29, 2006, three weeks after the Democratic primary election, which Lucy Baxley won.

With the jury still out, Vince and David invited my friend Maze Marshall and me to join them in a visit to a nearby men's clothing store. Vince wanted to get my mind off the jury deliberations. There wasn't anything we could do to speed it along, so we all got into Maze's van and drove to the clothing store.

Maze Marshall, in his wheelchair, had been at my side throughout the trial. Many people took him for a lawyer, but he wasn't. Maze had been an Army Ranger, and while serving in Korea he fell fifty feet from a helicopter to the ground. That accident had cost him the use of his legs.

Maze made a comeback. He was part of the 2000 U.S. Olympic Paralympics team in Australia. Maze won three gold medals for the javelin, discus, and shot-put. Maze got his name from singing with Frankie Beverly and the Maze. He's a remarkable man.

Maze, also a sharp dresser, accompanied us to the clothing store as we awaited the jury's verdict. Vince insisted that I be fitted for a suit. He picked out a beautiful blue one, along with three ties and two shirts. Then Vince got word: "The jury has reached a verdict." We quickly left the store.

Driving back to the courthouse, my cell phone rang.

CHAPTER 42

JUDGE ROY MOORE

"Don, this is Judge Roy Moore." I put my hand over the phone and whispered, "It's Roy Moore."

"I just heard the jury was in. Wanted to wish you good luck. I know where your problems came from. We have common enemies. God is with you."

"Chief, thanks so much," I said.

Roy was the former chief justice of the Alabama Supreme Court, "The

Ten Commandments Judge," and the darling of the Christian Right. Roy was a political maverick; in 2004, if he had run as a third-party candidate for president his following among Christians might have attracted enough Republican votes to have elected a Democrat.

Roy had been forced off the bench by Rove's underling, Bill Pryor, because Roy refused to remove the marble engraving of the Ten Commandments he had placed in the state Supreme Court building. We did have enemies in common. This was the same Roy Moore who became the focus of national media in 2017, labeled as a "pedophile" for his alleged interest in young women. He still nearly defeated Democrat Doug Jones in a race to fill the U.S. Senate seat left vacant when Jeff Sessions became Donald Trump's U.S. attorney general.

Back in the courtroom, I sat anxiously, trying to look calm and confident as the jurors returned.

CHAPTER 43

THE JUDGE AND JURY'S VERDICT

"Has the jury reached a verdict?"

"Yes, Your Honor."

"Read the verdict."

The foreman began reading: "The jury finds the defendant Mack Roberts not guilty on all charges." Great relief came to Mack and his lawyers. The foreman from Auburn continued to read the verdicts. "The jury finds the defendant Paul Hamrick not guilty of all charges." Paul started to cry and was embraced by his wife and lawyers.

I couldn't breathe.

"The jury finds the defendant Siegelman not guilty of . . . "

The foreman read off all the RICO charges. I glanced over at the prosecution. The look on their faces remained confident.

The foreman declared: "We find the defendant Siegelman guilty of bribery and obstruction of justice."

I sat stunned.

Because Fuller's instructions to the jury allowed contributions to the lottery to be considered a "thing of value" to me, the jury found me guilty of bribery. His instructions allowed a conviction based only on an "inferred" or "implied" agreement without evidence of anything approaching the explicit or express agreement that the law required. His instructions created a dangerous precedent, as legal experts across the country would soon point out to the U.S. Supreme Court.

Richard Scrushy was convicted on all charges.

I was convicted on the contribution to the lottery referendum! The jury returned the partial verdict against me as Fuller had commanded. Perhaps some jurors thought those were lesser charges, and they were doing me a favor. They gutted the prosecution's main case, finding me not guilty of all the RICO charges.

I was found guilty of obstruction of justice on the motorcycle charge. I recalled Vince's closing words to the jury: "Are you going to send Governor Siegelman to prison for part of a motorcycle?"

Now we knew.

After the jury was dismissed, most walked out quickly, glad to be headed home. But the two Auburn jurors had looks of satisfaction and I saw a smile on the face of "Flipper." We later learned that she had an amorous crush on the agent who sat at the table with the prosecutors. During the trial, she asked a U.S. marshal to find out if he was married. Flipper seemed to have more on her mind than justice.

Judge Fuller said he would let us know when the trial transcript would be ready and he could set a date for sentencing.

How could I have been convicted of bribery for a contribution to the lottery referendum campaign? There was no self-enrichment and no evidence of a quid pro quo. As Alabama's attorney general, I had been careful and cautious, erring on the side of defendants. I had angered some prosecutors, making them turn over exculpatory evidence and pushing for racially balanced juries. I thought all of us, even the prosecutors, should be on the side of truth, on the side of justice.

Facing the Media

I had to face the media. The big-story headlines would be "Governor Guilty." By the time we emerged from the courthouse, the media was eager to fire questions at Vince and me. I faced the reporters, flanked by my wife, Lori, and lawyers Vince, David, Professor Blakey, Redding Pitt, and Hiram Eastland. My ole buddy, Maze Marshall, was there by my side.

Reporters shouted questions and pushed microphones in my face.

"To say that I am shocked and disappointed is an understatement. As you ladies and gentlemen know, this verdict is not what I expected. I expected to win the case and win the race. Now we will appeal and there I remain hopeful this wrong will be set right."

We would appeal, but I faced the possibility of prison. I had to summon all the strength I possessed. I had to face my friends, neighbors, karate buddies, and countless people who had believed in me. I was disappointed, but positive we'd turn this verdict around.

My campaign for governor was over. My political future was at best on hold. So much that I had dreamed of and worked for had been destroyed. I was heartbroken for my family, especially for Dana and Joseph, who would have to live with this, and heartbroken because our system of justice had failed. I hoped my friends would see the truth.

CHAPTER 44

CONGRESS TO THE RESCUE

As Les and I discussed what could be done, we thought Congress could be the key. We needed a congressional investigation of Rove's involvement in my prosecution and of White House manipulation of U.S. attorneys.

I thought our best hope was the U.S. Congressional Black Caucus. Congressman John Conyers of Detroit was chairman of the Judiciary Committee.

I knew many prominent civil rights leaders. One was the Reverend Fred L. Shuttlesworth, the Alabama civil rights icon. Reverend Shuttlesworth's Bethel Baptist Church, and his parsonage, had been bombed three times. I had worked with Colonel Stone Johnson, Reverend Shuttlesworth's friend and bodyguard. Colonel Johnson's mission was to protect Reverend Shuttlesworth from the many dangers a civil rights leader in the South faced on a daily basis. Once, Colonel Johnson picked up a dynamite bomb and carried it away from a church and across the street to place it in a ditch.

Colonel Johnson and I would often see each other on Sunday mornings at the Fellowship Breakfast Forum, a civil rights organization formed to bring like-minded people together. The Forum met at a different black church every Sunday morning. They didn't want to be an easy target.

The Sunday following my conviction, the Breakfast Forum met at the 16th Street Baptist Church, in the same basement that had been bombed by the Klan in 1963. I asked Colonel Johnson how to find Fred Shuttlesworth.

"He's here this weekend," he said. "He's staying at the Redmont Hotel. Call the hotel and they'll put you through, he'll take your call."

I called, and Reverend Shuttlesworth invited me to his room. He was a gentleman and a kind soul. He was also a strong man, determined to fight injustice. He had faced death so many times that he seemed to fear no one.

When I told him my story, his response was, "They stacked the deck against you. Let's pray." We held hands and Fred prayed for me, for justice, and for the wrongdoers to be exposed. I asked if he would write a letter to members of Congress and specifically to Congressman John Conyers and members of the U.S. House Judiciary Committee.

"I know John well. You draft a letter and I'll make my changes," he said. Excitedly, and with optimism, I did as instructed.

The letters were in the mail by the next day.

He invited me to join the Congressional Civil Rights Pilgrimage. We would start in Birmingham, travel by bus to Montgomery, then on to Selma for a walk across the Edmund Pettus bridge in honor of the historic march of 1965. The leaders of the pilgrimage were civil rights leaders from the early 1960s and members of Congress.

ENTER GREG CRAIG

I had gotten a call from my old friend, Greg Craig, now a prominent Washington, D.C., lawyer, asking me to support Barack Obama against

Hillary Clinton. I asked, "Greg, do you really think a black man named Barack Hussein Obama can be elected president of the United States?"

Greg said, "Don, just go to Selma and hear him speak. Then call me back."

I met Congressman Steny Hoyer, the Democratic Majority Leader, for breakfast in Montgomery. He said he would do anything he could to help. I sat with him and other dignitaries at Brown Chapel A.M.E. Church that Sunday morning in Selma. My friend, A.M.E. Bishop T. Larry Kirkland, introduced a young politician, Senator Barack Obama, whom some were calling "the black John Kennedy."

Obama entered with youthful supporters from Alabama colleges wearing "O-Bama" T-shirts. His speech offered hope and change and was rewarded with excited applause. I called Greg, "I think he may be able to go all the way." Later President Obama would push Reverend Shuttlesworth's wheelchair during the symbolic march across the Edmund Pettus Bridge.

CHAPTER 45

JUROR MISCONDUCT EXPOSED

Back home, David McDonald called. "Don, I have good news," he said. "A juror has come forward with an affidavit expressing his remorse and saying that extraneous materials were brought into the jury room. Scrushy's team and Vince and I will be filing a motion with the court today."

"Will Fuller set a hearing?"

"We believe he'll set one quickly. This could be explosive. This can get us a new trial. "

The judge set a date. Les and I met Vince, David, Redding Pitt, and Maze Marshall. We entered the courthouse together. We noticed the juror and his lawyer also entering. An angry Judge Fuller awaited us. His face matched his reddish hair. It was unprovoked anger. He wasted no time in attacking us. This was to be an inquisition of my lawyers, as well as of the juror who had something to confess.

"How did you, Mr. McDonald, come into possession of this affidavit?"

David said, "I received a phone call from the juror's lawyer."

Fuller put the juror's lawyer under oath and quizzed her about her contacts with the juror and our lawyer.

"This is going the wrong way," I told David. "He's trying to discredit us and the juror before even hearing what the juror has to say."

"I thought he was going to have the marshals come for me," David whispered back.

Fuller called the juror to the stand, had the oath administered, and began asking insulting questions: "Did you get paid for writing this affidavit?" he demanded, waving the document at the juror.

"No, sir," said the juror, visibly shaken.

"Well, how did you come to write this affidavit? What education do you have? Did you finish high school?"

"No sir, I stopped at the third grade."

"Well, let me break this question down where you can understand it."

I almost lost it. This rich, arrogant, bigoted judge was talking down to a brave soul who came forward because his conscience was bothering him, only to be insulted by a white racist hiding beneath a black robe.

The juror told his story: "My conscience was bothering me. I couldn't sleep. My wife told me I should talk with our preacher. I did. I told him I had made a mistake. I felt pressured when you said, you'd keep us until next July. I wanted to be home with my family. My preacher said, 'Well, if you feel you made a mistake, you need to speak with a lawyer.' I told the lawyer about the stuff that was done in the jury room and she started writing everything down. That's where my affidavit came from."

"What 'stuff' are you talking about? What did you see in the jury room?"

"This female juror, the one they called 'Flipper,' she'd do flips to entertain us. She brought documents into the room and opened her coat and showed us things."

"What things?" Fuller asked.

"There was something she printed off her computer. She read from it. It had all the charges and she had news from one of the TV stations or newspapers that sort of told us what was going on day-by-day."

The judge told us he would hold a second hearing with all the jurors to see if anything came into the jury room that might have been prejudicial.

While waiting for the judge to rule, Les and I worked at his office every day. Often, we'd meet at ZaZa's, a small cafe on the Twentieth Street, a flowered boulevard with trees on both sides, in downtown Birmingham. We would walk to ZaZa's with Bou, Les's adopted shelter "puppy." Bou, short for Bouchet, our paternal grandmother's maiden name, was a sixty-five-pound fluffy mix. We considered Bou the world's best dog. We all loved him.

After getting our coffee at ZaZa's, we sat at an outdoor iron table, eating our unbuttered toasted bagels, over-easy eggs, fruit, and grits. Bou settled near Les's feet. Les tossed him small pieces of his toasted bagel. As soon as we returned to the office, my cell phone rang. It was David McDonald.

CHAPTER 46

MORE JUROR MISCONDUCT

"Don, I need to speak with you. You can't tell anyone."

I didn't keep secrets from Les. I put my phone on speaker.

"Vince and I just received, by mail, copies of what appear to be an email exchange between three of our jurors. The foreman, the juror called "Flipper," and one other, we think the tall African American woman who sat in the back. We believe these emails will bust this case wide open and get you a new trial."

"David, what do they say?" I asked impatiently.

"Flipper says in her email to the foreman that 'all politicians are crooks' and refers to Richard Scrushy as 'scum.' Don, these emails are dated before the case went to the jury. She was trying to persuade other jurors to go along with a conviction! Before the government had finished presenting their case. We're preparing a motion asking for Judge Fuller to set a date for a hearing and a new trial based on these inflammatory emails."

I hung up and Les said, "This is the break we've needed. Bill Canary's wife is your prosecutor; the judge hates you, and now a prejudicial jury, too. This can be the breaking point."

The day of the hearing, Les and I met with Maze, Vince, and David, so we could all arrive at the courthouse together, a show of unity and determination for the media.

The judge warned us, "I'll ask the questions of these jurors. You are to have no contact with these jurors. Anyone that does will be held in contempt."

"Your honor, we would also like to question the jurors," David said.

"Denied," said Fuller. "I'm the only one asking the questions."

The judge first called the foreman and then "Flipper," the female juror from Auburn. He asked the foreman, "Did you see anything in the jury room that was not authorized? Did any juror do anything which you feel was improper? Were there any improper communications between jurors?"

Unsurprisingly, the foreman said he'd seen nothing improper.

Fuller asked the jury foreman, "Did anyone bring anything into the room other than what I had given you?"

The foreman admitted, "Only the original indictment. It was printed off the internet. I also printed the jury foreman instructions from the court's website to show the other jurors."

The judge then called Flipper, who admitted to bringing in a reporter's blog of what happened in court each day, which included discussions outside the presence of the jury.

When the jurors were gone, David said, "Your Honor, with all due respect, you never asked these jurors about the emails. You didn't show them the emails or ask if they had sent them."

"I had determined what was legally sufficient. The jurors said that there were no improper materials brought into the jury room."

"But your honor, that's not the same as asking them point blank, 'Did you send this email?'"

Fuller said court was adjourned.

"We got screwed on the emails," I whispered.

There was only one reason why Fuller wouldn't ask the jurors the appropriate and obvious legal question: "Did you send this email? Did you try to influence other jurors to vote for a conviction? Did you say that Don Siegelman is a crook?" The Judge didn't ask because he knew that truthful answers would force a new trial.

My appellate lawyer, Sam Heldman, even without the transcript was already at work on my appeal to the Eleventh Circuit. The primary issues were: Improper jury instructions regarding what constitutes bribery involving a campaign contribution, insufficient evidence, the statute of limitations having run on the bribery charge, and juror misconduct.

CHAPTER 47

FIRST REPUBLICAN WHISTLEBLOWER

It was late April. Les and I returned to his office after lunch at Gus's Hot Dogs. As I was leaving for the day, my cell phone rang as I started my car. It was Mark Bollinger, a friend who'd been a campaign volunteer for me in north Alabama. Mark wanted to talk about his friend Dana Jill Simpson, a Republican lawyer he said had worked for Bob Riley to defeat me in 2002. He said Jill had been doing research on Judge Fuller and his company, Doss Aviation, a Defense Department contractor. Mark said, "Jill thinks there's a connection between your case and Doss." She wanted to talk with me.

Mark insisted it was stunning news. I quickly called her.

"Is this Jill Simpson?"

"Yes. This is Jill," she said.

"This is Don Siegelman. Mark Bollinger asked me to call."

Jill told me she'd done research on Doss Aviation and the $175 million renewable contract it received from the Defense Department during my trial. All this data Jill was giving me was better suited for my friend, John Aaron, Chip Hill's partner, who I knew was more research-oriented than I was. I asked if I could get John to give her a call. Then she dropped an unsuspected bomb. Not only had Jill worked against me, she told me she'd been hired by Karl Rove to do negative research on me and that Rove had been involved in my prosecution. She then laid out in shocking detail a connection between Governor Bob Riley, his son Rob, Billy Canary, and Karl Rove.

Jill had graduated from the University of Alabama law school and had begun a solo practice in north Alabama in 1989. In college she had known Rob Riley and had done legal work for him. They remained friendly and had done campaign volunteer work together.

"I worked in Riley's campaign against you," Jill said. "I worked for Billy Canary and Karl Rove, doing negative research on you. I was on a conference call with Rob and Billy Canary. Rob said you were 'like a cockroach, you hit him with your shoe at night, think he's dead, then wake up the next morning, and he's crawled off.' Canary told us to stop worrying about you. He said stop worrying about Siegelman, I've talked to Karl and Karl had the Justice Department going after you. Billy said his girls would take care of you."

Canary's "girls," his wife Leura and Alice Martin, were Karl Rove vetted Republicans who had been appointed U.S. attorneys in Alabama by President George W. Bush. Martin, along with Leura Canary's assistant, Steve Feaga, and Matt Hart, from the state AG's office, had prosecuted the first bogus case against me before Judge Clemon in 2004.

Jill said that Rob Riley called me the biggest threat his father faced and "a kind of Golden Child of the Democratic Party in Alabama" and "an incredible fundraiser." She said "Rob told me that they decided to try you and Scrushy together and could do it by using the lottery issue, claiming Scrushy had given you a bribe. Rob said Scrushy was so unpopular he would drag you down with him."

Jill said Rob told her that Billy Canary and Governor Riley had gone to Rove and had gotten him to influence the Public Integrity Section of the Justice Department late in 2004. She said they talked about what a mess Alice Martin had made of the first case against me and that they were going to bring a new case. They would bring the case in the Middle District so Leura Canary could be the prosecutor and Mark Fuller could be the judge.

Jill also said Rob told her that Fuller hated me and would "hang" me because I had caused him trouble over the excessive raise he'd given his investigator when Fuller was a district attorney.

Later another Republican whistleblower, Tommy Gallion, a respected Montgomery lawyer and former counsel for the National Republican Committee, would confirm everything Jill said.

My worst fears about the Republicans' determination to destroy me had been confirmed.

Request for DOJ Documents Denied

In 2006, John Aaron filed a Freedom of Information Act (FOIA) request for Leura Canary's recusal documents. We were hoping the DOJ would release the documents proving Canary's conflicts of interest and support my new trial motion. The Department of Justice first denied having such documents. Then they said they wouldn't release them.

The Justice Department had ignored its own policy by not even questioning Leura Canary's blatant conflict of interest. Or had she lied to DOJ? Her husband was being paid to defeat me. But Deputy U.S. Attorney General David Margolis said there was "no actual conflict." WTF! We wanted to know Margolis's justification. Something was clearly wrong.

Jill said that she had become troubled by the determination of Rove, the Rileys, and the Canarys to invent a criminal case to send me to prison. She contacted the Alabama Bar Association and spoke to an expert on legal ethics, who urged her to write an affidavit about what she knew and present it to authorities. But, fearing retribution, she went to Georgia in May 2007 to write her affidavit and have it notarized.

In time, Jill went to several lawyers including Greg Craig (later White House Counsel under Obama), whom I had asked to help guide her through the process. She hired a lawyer and headed to Washington. In September 2007, she testified for four hours before the House Judiciary Committee, recounting the specifics of what Rove, Canary, and Governor Riley had said about their plan to destroy me.

Jill's testimony would inspire articles and editorials in the *New York Times, Time, Washington Post, Harper's,* and elsewhere.

Simultaneously, furor erupted over charges that Rove, with others in the Bush White House, had arranged with DOJ for several Republican-appointed U.S. attorneys to be fired for refusing to bring phony charges against Democrats. Obviously, Leura Canary was not among those fired, nor was I the only Democrat targeted. It was exposed that the DOJ tried to entrap Wisconsin's Democratic Governor Jim Doyle in a scandal.

The renewed media and public support Jill's testimony won me was heartening but, as my sentencing date neared, I feared it would have little impact on the hanging judge, Mark Fuller, who awaited me.

CHAPTER 48

PREPARING TO BE SENTENCED

In June, Lori, Joseph, and I were off to California. Dana was graduating from California State University in Long Beach. We were excited for her. Seeing Dana's dorm room, meeting her classmates, professors, and university staff made us feel closer to her California adventure. It was heartwarming to hear the accolades from the university president, her professors, and her classmates.

Everyone loved Dana and for good reason. She's a kind and giving soul. She loves humanity and humanity loves her.

With my sentencing coming on June 28, Lori and I wanted Dana and Joseph to be spared the ordeal.

Dana had graduated with a degree in communications focused on religious rhetoric. Joseph had just finished high school. The charges against me caused emotional harm to them. Dana was in California, where almost no one knew or cared about my case. She kept quiet about me at first, then became my PR machine, making radio and TV appearances and putting out daily calls for action on the internet. Joseph had to deal with his high school classmates, some of whom had heard from their Republican parents that Joseph was the son of the governor who was a crook. That's part of why we wanted our children far away from the sentencing. We never told them my sentencing date.

It happened that both Dana and Joseph planned to be in Israel. Dana had entered Haifa University's Peace and Conflict graduate program. She wanted to learn Hebrew and Arabic so she could translate old manuscripts. Joseph was making a "Birthright" trip to Israel, something many Jewish children do after high school. Both were excited about being in Israel together. My sentencing would take place when they were halfway around the world.

I told Joseph and Dana, once they were both there, about the sentencing, and asked them not to worry. Dana called me on the 27th, the night before sentencing, saying, "God has got your back, Daddy. Everything will be OK."

CHAPTER 49

MY SENTENCING CIRCUS

When I arrived for sentencing the morning of June 28, 2007, I still hoped for community service, but the reality was that the prosecutors had asked for a prison term of twenty-five years to life. My trial lawyers weren't comfortable with the federal sentencing guidelines, so I needed to hire an expert in that field. I hired the best. My sentencing lawyer, Susan James, made an impassioned case for clemency. My other lawyers were not encouraging.

"The judge wants a confession of guilt and an expression of remorse," they reminded me.

That I would not provide. I wouldn't lie to justify the prosecutors' lies.

My friends and I met my lawyers near the massive new federal courthouse, then went together to greet the media.

"We hope Judge Fuller will show mercy," Vince told reporters. "We hope he will see that this was an unintended consequence. Governor Siegelman did not profit by a single penny and has already suffered greatly."

"Good luck, Governor," said one television reporter. She had not been friendly in the past, but she seemed sincere.

I thanked her and held Lori's hand as we headed toward the courthouse. It was already a hot, steamy, summer day. I held the door for Lori and Maze as we all entered.

Since being charged, I never liked going into this place. Once, years ago, when I worked for Bob Vance as a lawyer, we had many pleasant meetings, discussions and social events with federal judges, even Republican-appointed judges. But now it was different. Today, I would face a Republican judge who hated me.

"Hello, Governor," said one of the marshals. Another marshal wished me luck. I couldn't help taking their greetings as a good sign.

Inside the courtroom, Vince, David, and Susan took seats at the defendants' table, and I sat between Susan and David.

Seeing the judge gave me a sick feeling. The black robe, and that damn patriotic coffee cup he was so proud of, with its red, white, and blue eagle, turned my stomach. "Some patriot," I thought to myself.

Here I sat, targeted by my political enemies, the victim of a plot that reached to the White House, framed by prosecutors seeking right-wing glory. Steve Feaga, who helped frame me by presenting misinformation to the grand jury in 2004, had brought his daughter to see her daddy at work. To him, this was a game, a way to balance out his professional scorecard—one prosecution of a Republican, Governor Hunt, and now a Democratic scalp for his office wall. Steve Feaga was smart and tough. He knew right from wrong but chose to be nothing but a "professional" political whore.

The judge began with pious remarks about American justice. "Bullshit," I thought. "You've fought justice at every turn."

Then it was time for my character witnesses to speak.

Maze told how he, as a wounded U.S. Army Ranger, was down-and-out and hungry, I gave him food, along with my friendship and encouragement. His words brought tears to nearly everyone's eyes. Fuller wasn't moved.

Bobby Segall said, "It makes no sense to put this man in prison," and asked for community service.

Helen Vance, Bob's widow, spoke of how her late husband, my dear mentor, a judge on the Eleventh Circuit Court of Appeals, had respected and trusted me.

Bob Abrams, my dear friend and former New York attorney general, cited my unprecedented support from state attorneys general both Democrats and Republicans, and said it would serve no purpose to put me behind bars.

Then it was the government's turn. Louis Franklin, Leura Canary's stand-in, spoke first. He should not have prosecuted this case. He had embarrassed himself before the jury calling Fred Gray, who had been Dr. Martin Luther King's lawyer, an "Uncle Tom" and had nearly started a fight in the courtroom with another lawyer for Scrushy. Clearly, he was too invested in getting a conviction. When Leura Canary supposedly recused herself because her husband was working for my opponent, DOJ should have brought in another U.S. attorney from another state to try the case. Instead she gave it to Franklin and continued to give him encouragement and make decisions for him about the case.

"Judge, don't be swayed by all this sweet talk," Franklin began. "This man is guilty of corruption, of destroying public trust, of selling the governor's office to the highest bidders. Remember, we sent a drug dealer's mother to prison. You don't need to be soft on this crook."

While it was undisputed that I had not received a penny, nor could I have contemplated any benefit, the prosecution nonetheless had originally asked the judge to sentence me to twenty-five years to life in prison.[31]

Finally, it was my turn to speak.

MY PLEA FOR LENIENCY

"Your Honor, I was raised by two loving parents who taught me the difference between right and wrong. My parents worked hard to see that my brother and I had a better chance at life then they did. I wouldn't do anything to bring shame upon them.

"I was seeking higher office. I wouldn't have done anything intentionally to have jeopardized all my years of hard work. I have been in public service for twenty years. I have raised millions of dollars from thousands of people. If I had been doing the kinds of things with which I was charged and convicted, those bad traits would have shown up before now."

The government wasn't finished. Then Feaga and Franklin called for a longer prison sentence because I didn't show remorse. It was true that I blamed the prosecution on politics, on Leura Canary, her husband, Billy, Karl Rove, and the White House. They submitted newspaper clippings to prove that I had protested my innocence many times. I was proud of those clippings. The prosecutors were determined to get Fuller to add more prison time because I had spoken out about my innocence.

The judge declared that I had besmirched the prosecutors and the United States government. He was adding time for my having spoken out about the politics of the case and for all the matters for which I was acquitted—the criminal RICO charges for which the jury found me not guilty!

Susan James spoke up. "Your Honor, you've heard me make this argument before, and one day the Supreme Court will agree with me. It's unconstitutional to add time for acquitted conduct. Your action violates Governor Siegelman's Sixth Amendment rights to a trial by jury and violates his First Amendment rights."

Fuller ignored her, tripling the federal sentencing guidelines based on matters for which the jury had found me to be innocent. He then proudly pronounced my sentence.

"Governor Siegelman, please stand. Mr. Scrushy, please stand. Mr. Scrushy, I sentence you to eighty months in the federal penitentiary. Governor Siegelman, I sentence you to eighty-eight months in a federal penitentiary."

"Your Honor . . ." David began, wanting me to remain free on bond pending appeal. Before he could rise, the judge said, "Take them away, marshals."

CHAPTER 50

PRISON, A POLITICAL GAG ORDER

Richard and I were taken out of the courtroom. With handcuffs, chains around our waist, and shackles around our legs, we were driven to the Atlanta maximum security prison.

After stripping and being searched, we were given well-worn prison jumpsuits. Then we were locked in a small cell in solitary confinement in the basement of the oldest maximum-security federal prison in the country. We had a sheet and a small blanket.

SOLITARY CONFINEMENT

We were now in our prison orange jump suits, with light shining through the bars of the door, and the chatter of other inmates coming in like surround sound.

"Don, pray especially hard tonight that we get out of here soon," Richard said.

I had taken the top bunk. As I stretched out on the cold, iron bed, I gazed at the ceiling. My mind began to dart from one thing to another. I gave thanks for those who came to my sentencing, for everyone who believed in me. I wondered how reporters would tell the story. Wondered if hauling me out of the courthouse in chains and shackles would create an outrage and backfire on Judge Fuller.

My sleep was troubled. I awoke to sounds of inmates screaming high up on other levels, then footsteps and unfamiliar noises. Was it morning? Two trays had been pushed through the slot in the bottom of the door. Coffee, a half pint of milk, and a small box of cereal. I tasted the coffee and after I saw Richard drinking his, I offered him mine. We swapped. My coffee for his milk.

I was living on prison time now. I had no control. No contact with anyone outside these walls.

I started doing push-ups in the six feet by twelve cell that had a metal table, our bunks, a stainless steel toilet, and a sink that provided small spurts of cool water. We had two tiny bars of soap, a ragged washcloth, and a small towel. Two paper cups. Richard scrubbed penciled obscenities off the walls.

He prayed several times a day. I stopped whatever I was doing and joined him. We prayed for our families and friends. I prayed to make a phone call. Richard prayed that his medications would come soon.

Lunch was a bologna sandwich, brought by other inmates. They didn't say much, but they were friendly. Others gave us extra crackers, an old newspaper, and a roll of toilet paper.

A guard told us we'd be given some time to shower and to turn in our jumpsuits, T-shirts, socks, and underwear for clean ones. He pointed to a pile of clothes on the cement floor outside our cell. "Find something that works. There's only enough for you inmates in solitary."

The door swung open. Shower time. It was a one-man shower, with a floor of rotten wood. I picked out clean clothes, as did Richard.

A guard arrived as Richard was trying on a pair of the pants.

"These pants are baggy," Richard said, then tried another pair that were too snug. He asked the guard for advice.

"All I can tell you is, I'd go for the baggy ones. You might get the wrong kind of attention around here with those tight ones on."

The rest of the morning, Richard worried about his medicine. He rapped on the door until a guard came.

"I need my medicine," he said. Soon a man who might be a nurse stopped by.

"Here, take these aspirin." He turned and walked away. Was that all the medicine available? We were learning about our new home.

Back in Sweet Home Alabama

Immediately after I was hauled out of the courtroom, Les and Chip wasted no time. With the help of Reverend Shuttlesworth and Bob Abrams, coordinating many former state attorneys general from both parties, as well as many outraged friends, Les started a letter-writing campaign to urge members of Congress to investigate.

Dana dropped out of Haifa University to devote full time to freeing her dad. Joseph, who was in finance at the University of Alabama, struggled with the thought of his dad being in prison. Later, when he graduated *summa cum laude* from the Honors College, he started considering law school as an option so he could try to help me. Their personal and professional desires and careers were put on hold and changed forever. My family was irrevocably changed, something I can't forgive or forget.

While Jeff Sessions's retired FBI agents were investigating me and questioning large contributors to the lottery ballot initiative, they also subpoenaed all of my wife's, my brother's, and my children's financial records, looking for anything. They found nothing. Not one penny out of place. But in the course of their dragnet approach looking for a crime, they questioned my brother's out-of-state business clients, scaring them away and shutting down his income.

CHAPTER 5 I

JUDGE FULLER'S CONFLICTS EXPOSED

The full story of Judge Fuller's involvement with Doss Aviation and its impact on my trial emerged quickly. On August 6th, 2007, just a little over a month after I was sentenced and sent to solitary confinement in shackles, *Harper's* published a detailed look at my judge. It was titled "The Pork Barrel World of Judge Mark Fuller," and was written by Scott Horton, journalist and law professor at Columbia.

These are highlights:

. . . We've been examining the role played by Judge Mark Everett Fuller in the trial, conviction, and sentencing of former Alabama Governor Don E. Siegelman. Today, we examine a post-trial motion, filed in April 2007, asking Fuller to recuse himself based on his extensive private business interests, which turn very heavily on contracts with the United States Government, including the Department of Justice.

. . . On February 22, 2007, defense attorneys obtained information that Judge Fuller held a controlling 43.75% interest in government contractor Doss Aviation, Inc. . . . Quoting from defense counsel's motion for recusal:

"Doss Aviation, Inc. has been awarded numerous federal military contracts from the United States government worth over $258,000,000, including but not limited to: . . . a February 2006 contract with the Air Force for over $178,000,000 for training pilots and navigators, and a March 2006 contract with the Air Force for $4,990,541.28 for training at the United States Air Force Academy. The February 2006 contract with the Air Force for over $178,000,000 is for 10 ½ years, **but is renewable from year to year . . .**"

Doss Aviation and its subsidiaries also held contracts with the FBI. This is problematic when one considers that FBI agents were present at Siegelman's trial, and that Fuller took the extraordinary step of inviting them to sit at counsel's table throughout the trial. Moreover, while the case was pending, Doss Aviation received a $178 million contract from the federal government.

The Public Integrity Section of the Department of Justice intervened, saying almost nothing about the merits of the motion, but attacking the professional integrity and motives of its adversaries. . . .

Judge Fuller denied the motion for recusal. His decision raises three issues:

First, Fuller suggests that he is merely a shareholder in an enterprise. In fact, Fuller's 43.75% interest in a company with a handful of shareholders makes him the controlling shareholder in a tightly held business.

Second, Fuller derides as a "rather fanciful theory" that he would be influenced by the fact that his business interests derive almost entirely from Government contracts, including from the litigant before the court. It seems that Fuller would have us believe that the process of issuing these contracts is divorced from the political world in Washington. That's absurd . . .

Third, Fuller states that he "made several rulings in favor" of the defense. I looked through the record, attempting to find the rulings to which Fuller is alluding, and I can't . . . Fuller was relentless in his support for the prosecution and his rejection of defense claims.[32]

There's more to Horton's devastating expose of the dishonesty of Fuller, the prosecutors and the Justice Department. I recommend the report to law professors and students.

CHAPTER 52

WORKING FOR FREEDOM

Les and Chip pressed the media to pursue my case. One day, while I was still in solitary confinement in Atlanta, a *New York Times* article reached my cell and filled me with hope. Les had inspired a story based on Jill Simpson's 2007 affidavit in which she connected Karl Rove to my prosecution. The *New York Times, Time,* and *Harper's* would all write about my case and Rove's connection to it.

I asked the guard for paper and something to write with. I was given lined paper and small pencils, like golfers use. I wrote Les and urged him to tell my friends I was strong physically and spiritually, but needed them to pray, act, and write the Judiciary Committee.

Soon, Les and Lynne Ross, former director of the National Association of Attorneys General (NAAG), were in touch with Bob Abrams, who pulled together three former AGs to be on a coordinating committee. My champions were Republicans Grant Woods of Arizona, who served as national co-chair of U.S. Senator John McCain's presidential campaign, and Bob Stephan of Kansas, and a Democrat, Jeff Modisett of Indiana, who was practicing law in California. They soon had forty-four former state attorneys general who called on Congress to investigate the irregularities which raised questions of selective prosecution and government misconduct. Over time, the number grew to 113 former state attorneys general.

Les worked with Chip to devise a national press strategy in which my daughter would play a major role. Dana took off under her own power, capturing the news media wherever she could find it and creating a Free-Don.org campaign online with emails going to the White House. She also involved Mimi Kennedy, president of the Progressive Democrats of America. Les recruited Anita Darden and her husband, Claibourne, who was Jimmy Carter's pollster early in Carter's career. They all signed on to help. Anita worked on the Free-Don website and issued emails in coordination with Les. Claibourne helped Les and Chip on media strategy. My supporters were now writing members of the Congressional Black Caucus and John Conyers, chairman of the House Judiciary Committee. Many of my good friends, like Pam Miles, a women's issues activist from north Alabama who was wired into the DNC, were already screaming mad and doing all they could. In prison, it was hard for me to grasp what was happening outside the walls of my cell. News was slow reaching us. No daily newspapers. No phone calls, except one to my lawyer. No contact with Lori or my children.

Back in 2004, from the grand jury transcript, it was plain as day that witnesses had been induced to flat-out lie. Prosecutors Matt Hart and Steve Feaga, both tied to Karl Rove's client, Bill Pryor, got witnesses to lie so they could get an indictment against me. In the secrecy of a grand jury, there's no judge watching, no lawyer to object, and no bars against prosecutors who want to lie, present false testimony, or withhold exculpatory evidence.

Dr. Bobo had told me what Matt Hart did to try to get him to lie. Les told me that one of Jeff Sessions's former FBI agents had tried to get Gary White to lie about the timing of my meeting with Scrushy at the Capitol so they could make the date of the meeting match what Nick Bailey had lied about. I had personally spoken to Gary's wife, Judy, who confirmed it. Nick Bailey had said he'd seen a check for $250,000, but the check wasn't even issued until weeks after my meeting. Sessions's FBI agent wanted Gary White to help them by lying about when that meeting took place. Gary refused, then he was indicted on unrelated charges.

Not until we were in prison together did I learn from Richard Scrushy that the government had offered to drop charges against him if he would testify that I committed the crime of extortion, demanding a contribution from him.

Richard and I were not close. We rarely spoke before we were charged and never after we were indicted. All conversations were through our lawyers. After sentencing, of course, we were thrown together by circumstances. The afternoon of this revelation, we were in what were supposed to be solitary cells, but because of overcrowding, some "solitary" cells had two or even three inmates. Richard and I were in one together.

"I talked it over with my wife," he told me. "But I couldn't lie." He added, "You won't believe this, but they even came back to me and my lawyers during the trial, asking if I would change my mind and help them convict you. They're the criminals, not us."

Richard and I spent much of our time praying or exercising. Richard did more praying, me more exercising. Sometimes he exhorted me to pray more.

"Don, you've got to get right with God. Do you believe? Do you really believe in Jesus Christ as our Savior? Until you get right, we're never going to get out of here."

We must have done something right, because after about thirty days we heard through the prisoners who brought us food that we were about to be transferred. I took that as answered prayers. I was ready to leave the dungeon.

My Transfer Out of Solitary

We woke to a guard approaching, his boots hitting against the cement floor making a heavy thud, thud, thud. His large ring of jingling keys startled us. It was early. We had no way of knowing the time.

"Siegelman, get your shit together."

I grabbed the two Bibles sent to me by my friend Amy Methvin and the few letters I'd received. I was cuffed and taken from the cell, headed for an unknown destination.

Later I learned that Richard was sent to a prison in Texas; we didn't meet again for nearly ten years. I regretted his fate then, as I do now. In this case, Richard was a pawn in the government's scheme to put me away. There was no bribe.

The corrections officer held tightly to my elbow as I clutched my Bibles and correspondence. I joined a growing line of inmates, waiting in a long hallway. We were told to strip, turn around, bend over, then were given a jumpsuit to wear during transport. Shackles were added and chains were connected to my handcuffs so that my arms and hands were tightly restricted to my waist. Our personal property was taken. To be returned later, they said.

Each of us was handed a brown paper bag containing an apple and a baloney sandwich. We were led to a holding cell, packed like sardines in a can. After standing for four and a half hours, we were led to a bus and driven to the Atlanta airport. We stepped from the bus to the tarmac, greeted by marshals. They had automatic weapons and encircled the buses and the well-worn Boeing 737, waiting to take us to only God knew where.

When my name was called, I shuffled carefully behind other prisoners up the stairs to the plane's door, our chains singing out a melancholy tune against each aluminum step as we boarded. I made my way through the narrow aisle and squeezed between other prisoners.

"Anyone needing to use the restroom, raise your hand. There will be no movement whatsoever on this flight."

I still had my sandwich. As others opened their brown bags, I couldn't get into mine because my wrist and fingers couldn't maneuver to open the bag. Finally, with my head bent down so my chin rested on my chest, I was able to take a bite of my baloney sandwich. There was no way to eat the apple while cuffed and chained.

I dozed as we started our descent.

"Any idea where we are?"

"Harrisburg." Some inmates departed and more boarded.

I slept again.

"New York," I heard as I woke. More inmates came and went.

"Any idea where we're going?"

"Detroit, I think, then Oklahoma City," some prisoner familiar with the route said.

When we finally landed in Oklahoma City, we exited the plane directly into the prison. We shuffled down the hall and were told to step up onto a long, low platform so the U.S. marshals wouldn't have to bend over as far to unlock our shackles. We remained cuffed as we were put into holding cells. Once again we stripped, went through the inspection for foreign objects, and were given some old prison clothing.

After an hour or so in a holding cell, I was questioned about physical and mental health issues, then, with my elbow held tightly by a marshal, taken to solitary. The door slammed. I knew the routine, I bent my knees, backed up to the door and put my arms through the slot. The correctional officer—we called them "COs"—unlocked my cuffs. It felt good to be free. Even just free in my tiny cell. I asked for a Bible or a book. Susan James told me, "They have to give you a Bible. At least you'll have something to read."

I asked for a Bible every time a CO walked by. They ignored me.

I started doing pushups and squats. Up to 1,200 a day. While on the floor exercising, I noticed a book under my bunk. A biography of Hubble. I thanked God for delivering me from boredom and read until what I assumed was the wee hours of the next morning.

A CO told me that the federal prison in Texarkana rejected me because I was too high-profile. "They don't want the publicity."

After more days went by, a guard came to cuff me.

"Am I being transferred?"

"No, you have a legal visit."

I was taken to a large room and there was Susan James. My hands were uncuffed from behind my back and recuffed in front.

Susan is a self-made defense lawyer. A dang good one. The last time I saw her, at my sentencing, she was crying. She was now in Oklahoma for her son's rodeo, here to see me, and she was all business.

"Governor, we are all working to get you out on bond. It's not going to happen fast, so get ready for more rough treatment. 'Diesel therapy' they call it. You may spend days on a bus. You'll be transferred soon, but we don't know when or where."

Back to my cell. One long slender window had been frosted so it was translucent. One dime-sized hole had been scraped by some previous inmate, at the very top, and allowed a peek at the sky.

After two weeks in solitary, my transfer finally came. That meant I'd be out of isolation until I arrived at my next prison. Handcuffed, shackled ,and chained, I was led to the plane. After making several stops to drop off other prisoners, it landed. The sign over the small hangar read Alexandria, Louisiana. We loaded a bus destined for the Oakdale federal prison complex. The prison was built on old swampland in central Louisiana. I was going to a low-security facility.

CHAPTER 53

PRISON LIFE IN LOUISIANA

Once again I was told to strip, turn around, bend over. I put on other prison garb and was processed in. The case manager told me I was going back to solitary.

"Sir, I've been in solitary in Atlanta and Oklahoma City for over a month."

"Let me see if I can find you a bunk at the camp."

He found one, and an inmate drove me to the camp in a white Chevy van. "Now this is freedom," I thought. The camp counselor showed me my bunk.

Inmates offered toothpaste, a brush, a comb, and crackers.

"Just something to hold you over for the night. Breakfast at 6:30."

Thus began my life in a prison camp.

In many ways, Oakdale was a breath of fresh air. Soon after I arrived, a prisoner in his seventies greeted me with, "Welcome to Oakdale, Governor. I'm Governor Edwards." Edwin Edwards laughed and added, "I was the governor of Louisiana for four terms, so people call me Governor. There's only room for one governor here, so you're G-2." That became my name at Oakdale, G-2.

Edwards had a remarkable political career. He served several terms in Congress, then four as governor, a total of sixteen years, close to the national record. Unfortunately, near the end of his fourth term he was convicted of accepting several hundred thousand dollars in bribes for his decisions on the awarding of riverboat casino licenses. He denied the charges but served about eight years in prison, before being released in 2009 at age eighty-three. He was a good-natured man whose company we all enjoyed.

I soon met Kenny Wall, from Orange Beach, Alabama, who not only became a friend in Oakdale but remained so later. Kenny had been jailed on questionable charges. His business partner had given the local mayor gifts and helped the mayor get a good deal on the sale of his home. The government called that a bribe. When Kenny didn't help convict his partner, they indicted him, too. There was no evidence or testimony to link Kenny to a crime, but he was convicted and given a year in prison. His judge had apologized for having to send him to prison.

It was my first day. I immediately headed outside to the track and started walking in the quarter-mile ellipse, wearing my new prison camp green uniform and blue canvas made-in-China slippers, breathing deeply and looking around. Looking at the clouds slowly moving in the blue sky. I tried to discern north from south, searching the trees for life. I saw birds! Flying, chirping. I gave thanks for this taste of freedom.

All this openness and the beauty of nature was a gift. I had been in solitary confinement for more than thirty days. Each time around the track, I passed a concrete block building with a tin shed roof where inmates were working out with weights. Some of them helped me get settled. I was invited to join Oscar Torres for dinner later. "I'll fix a little soup," Oscar said. "You are welcome to share."

Soon Oscar, Kenny, and I had a routine. I would bring a can of tuna and saltine crackers I purchased at the commissary and we would find a tomato and onion if possible. Some inmates on special diets, such as Muslims or Jews, were given fresh vegetables. Sometimes they would share their vegetables and Oscar would make soup. Governor Edwards might join us. He was full of life in his mid-seventies. I wondered if it was equal justice to give a seventy-year-old and a twenty-year-old the same sentence. Weren't years more precious near the end of one's life? Or the other way around? Freedom is always precious.

I tried to keep a positive frame of mind. It helped that I believed I would be out soon. My lawyers were appealing Judge Fuller's gaveling down of their attempt at an oral motion for me to be free, pending the outcome of my appeal. Such behavior by a judge couldn't be tolerated. Or so I liked to think.

My spirits were lifted by letters of support from all parts of the United States and by the spotlight focused on my case by the national media and pending Congressional investigations. I had visits from Lori, Joseph, Dana, Les, Maze, Chip, and my lawyer, David McDonald. All brought news of progress.

CHAPTER 54

WAITING IN PRISON

My appeal had been filed. The list of former state attorneys general who asked Congress for an investigation kept growing, and Scott Horton kept writing updates on my case for *Harper's*, questioning the fairness of the judge and the trial and laying out the prosecutors' political and financial conflicts and their links to Rove.

I knew progress was being made, yet my life remained frozen. Every day was the same. I woke, exercised, ate breakfast at 6:30 a.m., and worked around the dorm sweeping and mopping floors. Then ate lunch at 10:30, walked the track, went back to work. The last meal was at 2:30 p.m.

Often I would have a salad, sometimes with tuna purchased from the prison commissary. I had stopped drinking coffee while in solitary. It was so disgusting, I couldn't get it down. Now I stopped eating meat—while working in the kitchen, I saw one case of frozen chicken marked for the San Diego Zoo with a label showing it had been expired for three years!

Tuna or peanut butter on graham crackers were my meals of choice. After work I wrote.

I had the freedom to think and time to write. I focused on justice issues, what was wrong, and what could make things right. I saw the injustice that sent black youths to prison for longer terms for using crack cocaine than whites who used powder cocaine. The laws seemed to have been drawn with an unconscious racist intent. There were guilty men in prison, but also some I believed were innocent, and many who had been given unreasonably harsh sentences.

We all passed around books worth reading. One, Stephen Hawking's *A Brief History of Time*, reinforced my belief in a God, a Creator, a power with more meaning than a "Big Bang." I walked around the track with fellow inmates Oscar and Kenny. We searched the heavens nightly. We found consistency and solace in the North Star, Polaris, and the Big Dipper and other constellations that hinted at the mystery and wonder of God's creation.

The subjects we discussed mattered less than our friendship. We were brought together by fate. We looked to the heavens and spoke of God and the universe. And sometimes about our own lives and uncertain futures.

I watched the leaves change. From the summer greens and leaves dried brown by scorching heat, to the oranges, yellows, reds, and browns of autumn. Then winter arrived, followed by the welcome verdant greens of late February and early March. Same trees, larger branches, different leaves.

CHAPTER 55

NATIONAL MEDIA AND CONGRESS

Les and my family were on alert to tell me of an MSNBC segment about my case. Dana had become a tireless advocate for my cause and for holding Rove accountable.

A correctional officer, whom I cannot name because he might still get into trouble, printed out and gave me an online story of Dana's appearance. This CO let me see her interview with Dan Abrams of MSNBC. Chip had sent word the *New York Times* had called on Congress and the Department of Justice to investigate my case. The *Washington Post* also questioned Rove's involvement.

The House Judiciary Committee began an investigation and demanded answers from the Department of Justice. Jill Simpson's affidavit and her testimony before the Judiciary Committee had convinced several members of Congress of DOJ's misconduct. Jill had placed Rove at the scene of the crime and center of my case: "Billy Canary, the U.S. attorney's husband, told us to stop worrying about Siegelman. He said, 'I've spoken to Karl and he has the Department of Justice pursuing Siegelman.'"

Jill testified under oath that the conference call with Billy Canary and other key Republican operatives took place on November 17, the day I was to announce that Karl Rove's client, Bill Pryor, had prevented a recount of the disputed votes and therefore I would walk away and run again in 2006.

The Judiciary Committee confirmed Jill was indeed on that call. This was backed up by telephone records. Was Karl Rove a part of a conspiracy to fabricate a criminal case against me? His client sure was. Jeff Sessions's retired agents were in up to their necks. Who else? David Margolis had approved of U.S. Attorney Leura Canary's involvement in my prosecution even though her husband was being paid to defeat me. No conflict? Come on!

Rove and Margolis were linked to the firing of Republican-appointed U.S. attorneys, those who refused to do Rove's dirty work. To me, those were crimes. But could a man so valued by President Bush be punished? Or was he above the law? Could the Judiciary Committee get to the bottom of what Rove and his allies at Justice had done? I knew that Chairman Conyers and his staff wanted the truth. They wanted Karl Rove's head on a platter and didn't trust David Margolis. Now, Rove was refusing to give testimony under oath. It was obvious. He intended to lie.

Les had told me he was sending a visitor Saturday morning. I ironed my prison uniform. Oscar had given me a haircut the night before. I was presentable.

The visitors' room was a trailer with a wooden deck and some wooden tables and benches. My visitor was Susie Edwards, the TV reporter I had met during my trial. She had moved to New Orleans for a new job. Not only was Susie kind and cheerful, she was not part of my previous life, the world of politics, or the hateful people who put me here. Her face did not reflect pain, heartache, or disappointment, as did the faces of my family.

Les had asked her to visit. I asked how that came about.

"He called me in New Orleans and asked if I could come to see you. He passed on news that he wanted to get to you in person and quickly, so he gave me the assignment."

"So, what's the news?"

"CBS is doing a *60 Minutes* piece on you. Governor, this is great news."

Maybe, during the worst moments of our lives, we need to escape reality to maintain our sanity. Having this incredibly good news gave me a high that surely exceeded that of the drug that brought so many people to this prison.

Susie added, "Les said John Aaron is coming tomorrow to give you the details." Then she whispered, "CBS's request to interview you was turned down, so they hope to get you on film tomorrow. They'll be shooting from inside a van or car."

I was grateful for both the message and the messenger.

Out in the free world, the Judiciary Committee was investigating the Justice Department for both selective prosecution and government misconduct. A *New York Times* editorial declared: "There is still a lot of questionable Justice Department activity for Congress to sort through. The imprisonment of Don Siegelman, a former Democratic governor of Alabama, should be at the top of the list."

Chip Hill, fighting for national media attention, thought my legal team should be more aggressive. "I think our team should be raising holy hell about the transcript and about Fuller thumbing his nose at the Eleventh Circuit on the appeal bond issue," he said. "We can't count on the media alone to free Don. Reporters are asking what we're doing on the legal side."

After Susie's visit I called Les, who confirmed John Aaron was coming to see me the following morning. "When you go to meet him, stand behind the flagpole in front of the camp. Take a look at Old Glory. Just do what I say for once. And shave, damn it. No one will recognize you with a beard. OK?"

"Got it, Les. Shave. Before 9 a.m. go stare at the flag."

It was my first beard since Oxford, but I agreed to shave.

Sunday morning, clean-shaven and carrying my mop bucket, to add realism to the scene, I visited the American flag as directed. John Aaron arrived and told me that *60 Minutes* cameras were concealed up the road. "The warden refused permission to film you, but they should be filming us now."

But could I watch the program? The TV sets were jealously guarded and the older inmates ruled. I went to Kenny Wall for advice. "You'll have to get Governor Edwards to agree," he said. "They watch some reality show on some other channel."

There were four TV rooms: one for Spanish-speaking inmates; one large room where African Americans watched; one room for sports, which were interracial; and one small room where white guys gathered. Governor Edwards held sway over that room. I explained to him that *60 Minutes* was doing a segment on my case and asked if he would help convince others to let us watch. The Governor agreed.

CHAPTER 56

CBS 60 MINUTES MOVES MOUNTAINS

One Sunday passed, then my birthday, February 24th, rolled around. I was told my segment would run on the 24th. News of my case on *60 Minutes* drew a crowd. As six o'clock neared, the small TV room for white guys filled up. The black inmates offered their room, which was much larger. I took one of the last seats.

Scott Pelley laid the story out with devastating clarity:

> Ten years ago, life was good for Don Siegelman. After he was elected governor, many believed he was headed to a career in national politics. In 1999, Siegelman's pet project was raising money to improve education, so he started a campaign to ask voters to approve a state lottery. He challenged Republicans to come up with a better idea.

Pelley pointed out that the government's key witness, Nick Bailey, was a "crook" who testified that I had shown him a check from Scrushy immediately after Scrushy left my office. Pelley pointed out that couldn't be true because the check didn't arrive until days later.

He interviewed Grant Woods, the former Republican attorney general from Arizona, who said:

> I haven't seen a case like this with so many red flags that point towards a real injustice being done. I personally believe that what happened is that they targeted Don Siegelman because they couldn't beat him fair and square. This was a Republican state and he was the one Democrat they could never get rid of.

Pelley also interviewed Jill Simpson. She explained that she had been hired by Karl Rove to do negative research against me and had come forward because her conscience bothered her. She told how Bill Canary, who was both Rove's business partner and the husband of my prosecutor, had said on a conference call that "his girls"—one of them his wife, Leura, the U.S. attorney—"can take care of Siegelman."

The report explained that Nick Bailey, fighting for a lighter sentence for himself, admitted that he had been interviewed over seventy times by the prosecutors, who made him write his testimony over and over to get his story straight. Pelley added, "If Bailey's telling the truth, his notes, by law, should have been turned over to the defense." We never knew those notes existed.

The *60 Minutes* segment continued:

> PELLEY: Richard Scrushy did make donations totaling $500,000 to that education lottery campaign, and after serving on the hospital board under three previous governors, Scrushy was reappointed by Siegelman. But Woods says "that's politics, not bribery. You do a bribery charge when someone has a real personal benefit. Not 'Hey, I would like for you to help out on this project which I think is good for the state.' There's been no allegation that Don Siegelman profited by a single penny."
>
> PELLEY (to Woods, on-camera): After two months the jury deadlocked twice, then voted to convict on its third deliberation. Many legal minds were

shocked when the Federal Judge Mark Fuller, at sentencing, sent Siegelman directly to prison without allowing the usual forty-five days before reporting.

WOODS: He had him manacled around his legs like we do crazed killers. And whisked off to prison just like that. Now what does that tell you? That tells you that this was personal. You would not do that to a former governor.

PELLEY: Would you do that to any white-collar criminal?

WOODS: "No. I haven't seen it done.

PELLEY: Help me understand something. You are blaming the Republican administration for this prosecution. You are saying it was a political prosecution. You are a Republican. How do I reconcile that?

WOODS: "We are Americans first. And you've got to call it as you see it. And to stand up for what is right in this country.

PELLEY: Karl Rove and others at the White House were subpoenaed to testify before Congress but refused to appear. And the Justice Department has refused to turn over hundreds of documents in the case.

Pelley's report was everything I could have asked for. When the program ended, I asked Governor Edwards: "What did you think, Governor?"

Edwards said, "Well, I had assumed you were guilty. Now I'm thinking you got screwed."

Les thought it was a home run, as did Chip, Lori and our kids. Everyone thought the piece would inspire more support in the media.

Incredibly, *60 Minutes* had been blacked out across the most densely populated part of north Alabama. My supporters raised hell, but they could not prove who was responsible. They believed that powerful Republicans had arranged the blackout.

Still, the impact of the *60 Minutes* report was huge. Joseph wrote: "Dad, people I don't even know or ever met, come up to me saying that now they know what happened to you was a 'political hit.' People know the truth. Dad, I love you and think about you way too often. I hold my head high. I am proud of who I am and damn proud of you."

Tears filled my eyes. I hated the bastards who caused this pain for my children.

Dana made me cry again. "Dad, you are my hero. Whenever I start to feel down, I hear your voice telling me to think positively. You are coming out 1,000 times stronger than you went in. The best days are yet to come. Can't wait to see you."

CHAPTER 57

GOING HOME

On March 27, a month after *60 Minutes*, the news I had hoped for came. "Siegelman, pack up. You're going home."

I was freed by unprecedented support from former state attorneys general, two Congressional investigations of Rove's involvement, entitled "Selective Prosecution and Government Misconduct," editorials in the *New York Times*, consistent exposes by *Harper's*, powerful reports by *Time* and *60 Minutes*, and tireless efforts by family, friends, and lawyers.

"The court has ordered your immediate release," the prison's case manager said. "I spoke to your lawyer this morning. The Eleventh Circuit said there were substantial questions of law and fact that will likely result in you going free. I'm awaiting word that the Bureau of Prisons has received the court's order."

"What do I need to do?" I asked.

"Keep it quiet and make sure you have a ride home tomorrow morning. Congratulations."

I called my brother. "Les, did you hear?"

"Yes! Finally! I feel like a new man. Lori and Joseph will pick you up. They're on their way now."

"I've been thinking about what to say to the media," I said.

"Don't say anything to the media until you've spoken to Chip. He's trying to get you back on *60 Minutes*. Now you can handle your own defense. I'm going to the beach."

He deserved a trip to the beach.

The state attorneys general had petitioned the Eleventh U.S. Circuit Court of Appeals for my release and Chairman Conyers made plans for the House Judiciary Committee to hold hearings. Conyers questioned U.S. Attorney General Gonzales about misconduct in my case. He also had questions about the involvement of Karl Rove and the Justice Department's David Margolis in the firing of U.S. attorneys.

The Judiciary Committee also wanted to question Noel Hillman about his possible misconduct. He had been head of the Public Integrity Section of DOJ during the time I was charged and afterwards was nominated for a federal judgeship. The White House, rather than have Hillman questioned under oath about the firing of U.S. attorneys and my prosecution, withdrew his nomination for the Circuit Court of Appeals.

On March 28th, the day I was released, the Judiciary Committee called on Rove to testify. He claimed he would be in Russia on the day they specified. He said he would talk, but not under oath, and only if he could see the questions in advance. He claimed executive privilege, although it was far from clear that such a right existed. Conyers wanted Rove arrested.

The Judiciary Committee issued a subpoena for Rove's emails. The White House claimed millions of emails had been destroyed. It was then I learned Rove used a private server, computers, and cell phones paid for by the Republican National Committee to conceal their calls and messages. It was said that Rove went to meet on street corners with lobbyist Jack Abramoff, his close political associate, who would later serve forty-three months in prison for bribery and mail fraud in a case involving an Indian casino in Florida. Abramoff, Ralph Reed, and Grover Norquist were never so much as charged with the $20 million in Indian casino money illegally laundered into Alabama to "stop Siegelman."

On the night before my release I spoke to my family.

"Hey, Don!" Lori said. "What do you think of the news?"

"I think it's about time the bastards let me out."

"Are you happy?" Joseph asked.

"No," I said. "I'm just venting. I'm pissed that I had to be here at all."

"Dad. Cheer up. We're driving eighteen hours to get your butt back home. Be nice or we'll leave you in Oakdale," Joseph said.

"Sorry. But I've been keeping a happy, positive attitude for nine months," I said. "Thanks for coming to pick me up. I'll see you guys at 8:30."

I thought about what to wear home. It was a tradition at Oakdale to leave in a pair of prison blue jeans and a shirt. I opted for the prison garb I'd worn every day. My black rubber-soled slip-on shoes I had inherited from another inmate. My gray sweat pants. White long-sleeved thermal with my old ragged cutoff T-shirt given to me by a departed bunkmate.

I went through my locker. I planned to give everything to prisoners who needed it. I waited until late in the evening to announce my departure and make bequests, lest I have to deal with congratulations all evening.

The next morning, March 28, 2008, the prison counselor said a driver would take me a few blocks away to meet my wife and son. They didn't want the news media near the prison. Neither did I.

My reunion with Lori and Joseph was a thrill, despite all the frustration I had built up over my imprisonment. Joseph jumped out, gave me a tight embrace, and told me to sit in the backseat. "Keep your head down, we want to bypass the media," he instructed. "We need to get out of here unless you want to be interviewed. There's a TV truck from Montgomery just around the corner." I ducked down as we started the long drive home.

"You have to call Chip Hill, then call Dana," Lori said.

"I know, I spoke with Les," I said.

"You'd better call," Lori said. "Chip says it's critical that your first interview be *60 Minutes*."

That sounded like a demand. For months I had been told what to do every minute of every day by guards, administrators, and prison rules.

"I need some space," I said. "I've been in prison for nine months. I would like to make my own decisions."

I called my daughter first. I knew Dana had been working endlessly for my freedom. She had contributed significantly to my being home. "Hey, Dana, how are you?"

"Dad, I'm so happy you're going home. Please call Dan Abrams right now. He wants to do an interview tonight. Dan has been the most supportive of all the national media."

Even Dana was telling me what to do and her plan conflicted with those of Chip and Lori. I spoke to Chip for the first time in nine months. He said, "If you go on any major network, *60 Minutes* will drop the follow-up.

CBS reaches millions of people. MSNBC is cable. *60 Minutes* is by far the best vehicle to get your message out."

I called Dan Abrams at MSNBC. "Dan, I appreciate all you have done but I have to go with CBS as my first interview." He was extremely disappointed. Dan had been my champion. I felt I should do his show but in deference to Les and Chip, I went along with the CBS decision.

Then I told Chip, Les, and Dana I had changed my mind. "I'm doing a press conference at Liberty Park as soon as I get to Birmingham."

It was a spur of the moment decision. The others begged me not to do this. I told them, "It will look like I am hiding from the media if I don't say something tonight. And they'd be camped at our doorstep until I gave each one an interview. CBS will have to give on this."

PRESS CONFERENCE: LIBERTY PARK, ALABAMA

The park was just around the corner from my home. It featured a replica of the Statue of Liberty, a reminder of my freedom. Perhaps I just wanted to decide something for myself.

Chip put out the word that I would speak at Liberty Park. After a quick stop at our house, Joseph and I drove to the park. I was wearing my prison clothes, ready to make my case.

I told those gathered there, "I prayed each day, giving thanks for my family and friends whose letters, thoughts, and prayers kept my spirits lifted. I gave thanks each day for Chairman John Conyers and the House Judiciary Committee for their investigation of Karl Rove's involvement in my case.

"And I gave thanks each day for the national media which has put a spotlight on the government misconduct involved in my prosecution. I remain hopeful and positive that I will win in the end, the truth will come out, and those responsible will be held accountable."

It went smoothly. Great coverage.

The next day Les and I began to plan a trip to D.C. We wanted to keep the pressure on Congress to hold Rove in contempt and to urge the media to pressure the Department of Justice to stop its persecution of me. But my trip was suddenly put on hold. The government's hand was firmly planted over my mouth so I couldn't speak.

GOING LIVE

My probation officer told me I couldn't travel without first getting permission from the U.S. attorney in the area to which I wished to travel. "What? Why?" I asked. I was told Judge Fuller had categorized me the same as a "terrorist" would be categorized. So my travel was severely restricted. That meant I'd have to get permission from the U.S. attorney in Washington in order to travel to D.C. to speak to members of Congress. I imagined how hard it would be to travel to D.C. if I was categorized as a "terrorist."

I said screw it and made an appeal on Thom Hartmann's national radio show. He blasted Fuller and asked listeners to call and protest. Two days later, Fuller changed my classification. I was still restricted but not as a "terrorist."

Another *60 Minutes* piece was being readied. Scott Pelley would be in Birmingham. Les and I met Chip and my lawyers at the Tutwiler Hotel in Birmingham. Congressman Artur Davis, a smart, politically ambitious African American, was there. Vince and Congressman Davis urged me, begged me not to blast Karl Rove, the prosecutors or Billy Canary, now head of the Alabama Business Council. They did not want me to announce I would be testifying before the Judiciary Committee about Rove's involvement. They didn't want me to lay out how my prosecution had been politically motivated by Rove and Jeff Sessions's FBI agents. Vince was perhaps giving his best advice, but he seemed enamored with Congressman Davis. Les was immediately suspicious of Davis's motives.

Vince said, "Why risk anything? Hold off."

They said their concern was about Republicans on the Committee trying to destroy my credibility. Yes, of course they would try, but I believed the truth would be convincing. Nevertheless, I caved to Vince and the Congressman.

As soon as I finished my interview with Scott Pelley, I knew I had made a mistake. My gut told me. I felt empty. I should have hit Rove hard. Instead, I pulled my punches and my interview was worthless. I had wasted a great opportunity because I didn't talk about Rove's vendetta or my prosecutor's conflict of interest, how the prosecution was clearly linked to Rove. My heart sank as I suddenly realized I should have followed my instincts.

In later interviews with Dan Abrams, Chris Hayes, and Rachel Maddow, I did explain Rove's web of involvement in my prosecution.

"It's time to hold Karl Rove accountable for his abuse of power and his use of the Department of Justice as a political weapon," I said. "It's time for Congress to hold Rove in contempt. He can either lie under oath or take the Fifth. Either will satisfy me." That's what I should have said to the much larger audience of *60 Minutes.*

Les's suspicions of Congressman Artur Davis's motives for opposing my testimony before the Judiciary Committee were valid. Soon we heard rumblings that Davis himself might run for Governor of Alabama. Thus, he wouldn't want to see my reputation restored. That might mean that I'd return to politics. We learned Davis had taken donations from Billy Canary and the Alabama Business Council, which Canary ran. Davis wanted Canary's and the Business Council's support for a run for Governor. It was clear to us, Davis had sandbagged me. Les had been right to suspect him.

Les was my partner and adviser throughout my battle to prove my innocence. He had a deep understanding of the destructive and vicious game they were playing with my life. It was impacting Les's life as well.

Les had achieved great success with a company that published books that honored outstanding American high school students. He maintained that company for seventeen years and then became a business consultant working with companies to achieve higher levels of productivity. After the political attacks on me began, government agents, often Jeff Sessions's ex-FBI agents, harassed his clients around the country, and his business plummeted, but he never faltered in his support for me. He worked tirelessly for my exoneration, contacting congressmen, seeking the right lawyer to represent me at the Supreme Court, speaking to national media figures and political leaders. No one could have done more, nor been a better brother.

CHAPTER 58

MEETING MY WARRIORS

North Alabama Democratic political activist Pam Miles had helped organize a symposium on prosecutorial misconduct. It was to feature Scott Horton, the Columbia law professor who had written extensively for *Harper's* about my case. It was just one month after my release.

Without fanfare, but with my probation officer's permission, I went with my friends, Pam and Jeff Miles. Pam had been tireless warrior. It was my first public appearance since Liberty Park. I was grateful for what Scott had written and curious about his intense interest in my case.

He spoke eloquently on political prosecutions, then turned to my case. We were sitting behind a reporter from the *Mobile Register*. The reporter had written so many negative stories about me, it seemed like a vendetta or he was being paid. He repeatedly interrupted Scott until Jeff told him to be quiet. When the reporter persisted, Jeff told him, "If you don't shut up, I'm going to kick your butt." It worked.

When Scott finished, he took questions. To my delight, whistleblower Jill Simpson was present. She raised issues about Rove and Canary and explained how she had learned firsthand how Rove and Canary were involved in my prosecution.

I was grateful to meet two people who had spoken the truth about my case. Jill had risked so much by breaking with fellow Republicans to support me. Her economic ties to Republicans were gone.

I learned that Scott's interest had begun with his brother. He reminded me that when I was secretary of state, his brother had asked me to intervene with the state archives so he could access a document for his thesis. Good deeds sometimes have good outcomes.

Scott added, "My grandfather was James E. Horton, the judge from Florence, Alabama, who ordered a new trial for one of the Scottsboro Boys. He was nearly tarred and feathered by the Klan. So I have an interest in people who behave honorably."

The case of the "Scottsboro Boys," nine African American teenagers falsely charged with raping two white women on a train in 1931, is one of the darkest chapters in Alabama's long history of racism. His grandfather had been an honest judge who gave the youths a fair trial, as other judges had not during a time of statewide hysteria. Scott said he and his wife would be vacationing at Gulf Shores, Alabama, soon. We made plans to meet.

With permission from the senior probation officer, Les and I drove to Nashville to see Al Gore. After having the presidency stolen from him eight years earlier, Al had become a tireless advocate for worthy causes. He knew all about my case and agreed to send an email to my supporters. His message said:

> Don is engaged in two important fights: One for his own freedom and the other to save our democracy by seeing that Karl Rove is brought to justice. As Americans, we have a responsibility to protect our democracy from those who would take advantage of it and abuse their power. By making sure Don has the support to keep up his fight for justice, we can do just that.

Al Gore may have seen parallels between my case and the decision of the Republican majority on the U.S. Supreme Court to hand the disputed presidential election to George W. Bush in 2000. Rove was up to his neck in the mess that led to Gore's defeat. Most Americans assume that anything the Court decides must be right—but not everyone agreed with that decision.

Harvard law professor Alan Dershowitz had this to say:

> The decision in the Florida election case may be ranked as the single most corrupt decision in Supreme Court history, because it is the only one that I know of where the majority justices decided as they did because of the personal identity and political affiliation of the litigants. This was cheating, and a violation of the judicial oath.

For better or worse, my story was far from over.

CHAPTER 59

DOJ'S ONE-SIDED INVESTIGATION

Despite Karl Rove's denials and ranting about Dana Jill Simpson, he still refused to give sworn testimony to the House Judiciary Committee.

Chairman Conyers wrote the U.S. attorney general about my case and renewed his call for Rove to testify or face arrest. Both the House and Senate Judiciary Committees were demanding that Rove answer questions, under oath, about his involvement in my prosecution and his role in the firing of several Republican-appointed U.S. attorneys for the sin of refusing to do Rove's political dirty work. Rove was also being investigated for his involvement in the "outing" of CIA agent Valerie Plame. It was speculated that the public cries for Rove's scalp became too much for the White House, and Rove, perhaps hoping to dodge the controversies, resigned from his White House post in August 2007. But that didn't stop the calls for Rove's testimony.

From my perspective, if he could finally be brought before the committee, that would be cause for rejoicing. "Rove can lie, tell the truth or take the Fifth; any of those will satisfy me," I told MSNBC.

But Rove had no intention of answering questions about my case or anything else. March 25, 2008, on ABC's *This Week*, George Stephanopoulos asked Rove, "Did you contact the Justice Department about this case?"

Rove replied, "I read about it. I'm going to simply say what I've said

I was interviewed on MSNBC when Karl Rove refused to testify before Congress, 2008. (Courtesy MSNBC)

before, which is I found out about Don Siegelman's investigation and indictment by reading it in the newspaper."

Stephanopoulos: "But that's not a denial."

Rove fumbled his words, stuttered and repeated that he had "learned about it for the first time by reading about it in the newspaper."

Could anyone believe that? Rove was also playing games with the Judiciary Committee. He said he would speak to the committee but not under oath. He wanted the questions in advance. In short, he wanted freedom to lie with impunity.

On May 5, 2008, the Justice Department notified Chairman Conyers that the Office of Professional Responsibility would investigate my case. But with David Margolis in control, the House Judiciary Committee staff was skeptical. "OPR is known for protecting its own," they said. "Margolis covers for everyone and everyone depends on him to keep the Department out of hot water."

During this critical period, when Congress was seeking answers to Karl Rove's involvement in my case, the *New York Times* published seventeen editorials with headlines like: "The Strange Case of an Imprisoned Governor," "Questions About a Governor's Fall," and "A Case of Politics." All raised questions about Rove's involvement and demanded Congress "put a stop to it."

In June 2008, the *New York Times* ran another editorial: "Congress should keep investigating the prosecution of Don Siegelman and what crass role politics may have played in his conviction."

A Break With Bloggers

I had a call from Brent Blackaby, an Internet whiz-kid from Berkeley, who urged me to attend NetRoots Nation, a convention of bloggers in Austin in July.

"Governor, these are your people. They'll be all over this story. I'll set up interviews for you. Just tell your story." He also organized a national petition "HoldRoveInContempt.Com." A blitz of calls and emails asked members of Congress to hold Rove in contempt.

I met Brent in Austin. I was overwhelmed by the enthusiastic reception

I received. In Alabama, I usually faced skepticism from the media. Here, reporters and bloggers were informed and friendly. It was a new media world. I also spoke to countless bloggers, radio talk show hosts like Thom Hartmann and Stephanie Miller, and the Progressive Democrats of America. Its president, Mimi Kennedy, star of "Mom" on CBS, welcomed me. It was reassuring to meet so many people who believed in my cause and wanted Rove to face Congress.

FORMER STATE ATTORNEYS GENERAL

Lori and I went to the annual Conference of Western Attorneys General. I had been a bit reluctant to attend. I feared some of my former AG friends might see me just as an ex-convict. Bob Abrams, my friend from New York whom I had first met at a National Association of Attorneys General meeting in 1986, urged me to go. He had testified at my sentencing. His law firm wrote the amicus brief that the former state attorneys general filed with in support of my motion to be freed on appeal.

Lori and I met with Democrats Bob Abrams and Jeff Modisett of Santa Monica and Republicans Bob Stephan of Kansas and Grant Woods of Arizona—who had testified so eloquently on *60 Minutes*. We wanted to recruit others to join in another amicus brief. We ended with more than a hundred former state AGs who would sign the brief saying my case involved not crime, but politics. After months in prison, it was heartwarming to see all these men and women, whose lives were dedicated to justice, who still believed in me.

Back in Alabama, I attended a fundraiser on Mobile Bay to help Hillary Clinton pay off her debt from her primary campaign against Barack Obama. It was a small event. Bill Clinton was collecting contributions. Bill greeted me and our mutual friend Redding Pitt warmly and offered to help recruit people to my cause. Redding had worked in Bill's first campaign and had been a U.S. attorney under Clinton. President Clinton said he didn't realize my case was still going on. Later, in Selma, Bill promised to do everything he could to help.

Chairman Conyers was also at the DNC. We were interviewed together on Free Speech TV's "Democracy Now, with Amy Goodman." In a private setting, we had a candid talk about Alabama Congressman Artur Davis's conflict of interest. Davis, wanting to run for governor, needed the support of the Alabama Business Council, controlled by Billy Canary. I told Chairman Conyers about Davis getting a campaign contribution from the Canarys. Davis, as a member of the Judiciary Committee, was supposedly helping the Judiciary Committee's investigation into the Canarys' role in my case. Another conflict of interest.

"Do you have proof of that?" Conyers asked. I handed him copies of documents from the offices of the Alabama Secretary of State and the Federal Elections Commission documenting the contributions to Davis from the Canarys.

"Davis has been acting like he was the chairman of the Judiciary Committee," Conyers said. Soon, Davis was no longer on the Judiciary Committee.

Conyers gave me his word he would not let Karl Rove escape.

On July 30, 2008, big news: the House Judiciary Committee voted to hold Karl Rove in contempt of Congress. Chairman Conyers released a statement saying: "Our investigation has revealed Mr. Rove to be a key figure in the firings of the U.S. attorneys, and the questions about his role in the Siegelman case only continue to mount."

Redding Pitt and I discuss my case with President Bill Clinton, 2008.

In August, Dana and I went to the National Democratic Convention in Denver to see Senator Obama become the first African American nominated for president by a major party. While there, I visited the Wisconsin delegation and was greeted warmly by Governor Jim Doyle. Jim and I would later regroup to discuss the similarities in our attacks.

The Justice Department, meanwhile, claimed it was investigating U.S. Attorney Leura Canary. But it was an in-house, OPR investigation, so it meant David Margolis was in control. We knew nothing was being done because none of the principals named by Jill Simpson were being interviewed.

On November 7, 2008, Chairman Conyers wrote to Attorney General Michael Mukasey, "In a matter where it is the prosecution's own conduct that is at issue, such a one-sided investigation seems incomplete."

CHAPTER 60

ROVE PROSECUTORS ATTACK DOYLE

Governor Jim Doyle, like me, had been his state's attorney general before becoming governor. Unlike me, in 2006, he survived what appeared as a Karl Rove-inspired prosecution to defeat his reelection, an attack much like the one Rove's U.S. attorney launched against me that year.

Doyle had not been charged. Instead a fifty-seven-year-old civil servant named Georgia Thompson was accused of helping steer a state contract to a company whose two top officials had donated $20,000 to Jim's reelection campaign.

Ms. Thompson was prosecuted by U. S. Attorney Steven Biskupic, a Republican appointee. He first tried to persuade her to testify falsely against the governor. When she refused, Biskupic made her the defendant. A jury convicted her but the decision was quickly and soundly overruled.

New York Times reporter Adam Cohen wrote on April 17, 2007, of the higher court's action:

> The United States Court of Appeals for the Seventh Circuit, which heard

Ms. Thompson's case this month, did not discuss whether her prosecution was political—but it did make clear that it was wrong. And in an extraordinary move, it ordered her released immediately, without waiting to write a decision. "Your evidence is beyond thin," Judge Diane Wood told the prosecutor.

. . . Opponents of Gov. Jim Doyle of Wisconsin spent $4 million on ads trying to link the Democratic incumbent to a state employee who was sent to jail on corruption charges. The effort failed, and Mr. Doyle was re-elected—and now the state employee has been found to have been wrongly convicted. The entire affair is raising serious questions about why a United States attorney put an innocent woman in jail.

. . . The prosecution proceeded on a schedule that worked out perfectly for the Republican candidate for governor. Mr. Biskupic announced Ms. Thompson's indictment in January 2006. She went to trial that summer, and was sentenced in late September, weeks before the election.

The article cited the ongoing controversy over the Justice Department's firing of Republican U.S. attorneys:

Most of the eight dismissed prosecutors came from swing states . . . Wisconsin may be the closest swing state of all. President Bush lost it in 2004 by about 12,000 votes, and in 2000, by about half that. According to some Wisconsin politicians, Karl Rove said that their state was his highest priority among governor's races in 2006, because he believed a Republican governor could help the party win Wisconsin in the 2008 presidential election.

The trial of Georgia Thompson in Wisconsin, along with my trial in Alabama, also in 2006, make crystal clear how Rove was inventing crimes and arranging dishonest prosecutions to defeat Democrats and boost the chances of electing a Republican president in 2008. Fortunately for Jim Doyle and Ms. Thompson, the scheme failed in Wisconsin. I was not so lucky.

Although Doyle and I did not know it at the time, the phony charges that were brought against me and against him, via the charges against Ms. Thompson, were the opening salvos. So began what appeared to many as a corrupt scheme by Rove and the Bush White House to appoint partisan

U.S. attorneys to attack Bush's perceived enemies under the cover of law.

Planning for the scheme began soon after Bush won reelection in 2004. In January of 2005, Kyle Sampson, the chief of staff to U.S. Attorney General Alberto Gonzales, wrote a White House aide about the budding plan to replace U.S. attorneys who were not sufficiently partisan. He warned that there would be political pushback from senators who had supported the ousted U.S. attorneys, but purportedly said if Rove thought they could ride out the political storm, he was game for the firings. In other words, this corrupt scheme was laid at Rove's feet.

The implementation began in December 2006, when the Bush White House carried out unprecedented midterm dismissals of seven U.S. attorneys. These were Rove and Bush's own Republican appointees, fired for what they claimed were "performance-related" issues. In truth, they were purely political firings.

Those dismissed had either brought charges against fellow Republicans or refused to bring dubious charges against Democrats. To Rove and other partisans in the White House, they were clearly not "loyal." The prosecutors who brought charges against me in Alabama and Doyle in Wisconsin were among those willing to do Rove's dirty work. Others refused and were fired.

The scheme's targets included Bud Cummins in Arkansas who was forced out to create an opening for Timothy Griffin, a Rove aide and protégé. In the Congressional investigation of the firings, an email was found in which Sampson, the attorney general's chief of staff, said Griffin's appointment was "important to Harriet, Karl, etc." This meant important to Rove and White House counsel Harriet Miers.

We wanted the other emails relating to my prosecution.

U.S. attorneys are supposed to enforce the law without fear or favor, not railroad political opponents into prison. Neither Rove nor Bush was a lawyer. Rove's passion was not the law, but political power. The Department of Justice was turned into a political weapon. But the firings were too blatant, and they inspired angry resistance in Congress.

The Justice Department's Inspector General in October 2008 found the firings to be "arbitrary," "fundamentally flawed," and "raised doubts about the integrity of Department prosecution decisions." David Margolis was reprimanded by the Senate Judiciary Committee and Attorney General Gonzales resigned. With the support of President Bush, Karl Rove refused to testify under oath before Congress.

The resulting scandal may have led to Rove's resignation in August 2007. His prestige had already been diminished by the Republicans' loss of their House majority in the 2006 midterm elections. But even as the Republican duplicity was exposed, I was still fighting to stay out of prison.

In 2008, after greeting Jim Doyle and other Democratic governors, Dana and I watched as Obama delivered his speech accepting the Democratic nomination. His words gave us hope, as they did many others. My specific hope, of course, was that an Obama Department of Justice would treat my case more fairly than Bush's had.

Whistleblower Gets Blown Away

In November, *Time* broke another story. This one was about Tamarah Grimes, a Department of Justice whistleblower. She exposed massive misconduct and prosecutorial corruption she had personally witnessed in my case. Grimes was a Republican. She worked on my case as a paralegal for the prosecutors. She charged that Leura Canary remained actively involved in the case against me, long after she claimed to be recused.

Grimes produced emails from Canary to back up her testimony. Grimes said she was present when Jeff Sessions's retired FBI agents, now working for the state attorney general, along with federal prosecutors Feaga and Franklin, pressured Nick Bailey to memorize the testimony they wanted him to give. She said Bailey was coached and cajoled to say what the prosecutors demanded.

She produced emails from an assistant U.S. attorney showing that a female juror wanted to know if the FBI agent sitting with the prosecutors was married, saying, "The prosecution team jokingly named the juror 'Flipper' because she was a gymnast who entertained other jurors by doing back flips in the jury room."

Ms. Grimes raised the question: "How did members of the prosecution team know what this juror did in the jury room?"

On July 8, 2009, the *New York Times* broke the story. Tamarah Grimes, for her honesty, was fired.

David Margolis, who was supposed to keep the Justice Department honest, continued to ignore Canary's role in my case. Rather than investigate Grimes's allegations, he backed Canary's firing of the whistleblower and signed the order firing her.

Judiciary Committee Chairman Conyers raised questions about Canary's failure to recuse herself from my trial. He cited emails in which the juror "Flipper" was trying to convince other jurors of my guilt before the case went to the jury. Conyers warned that the juror's messages "raise serious issues of fairness" in my case.

CHAPTER 61

BARACK HUSSEIN OBAMA ELECTED

On Election Day, 2008, I drove to meet Lori at St. Vincent's Hospital, where she was visiting the Reverend and Mrs. Fred Shuttlesworth.

Reverend Shuttlesworth, the civil rights icon, had been admitted to the hospital after a possible stroke. Lori and I wanted to be with Fred as Barack Obama was declared the winner. As we awaited the election results on TV, I told Fred, "This will be the night that an African American is elected president of the United States. Fred, you made it possible."

When the outcome was clear, I said, "Fred, did you ever think you and a white governor of Alabama would be cheering on a black man named Barack Hussein Obama who was just elected president of the United States?"

"No," Fred said, smiling but speaking with difficulty.

Days later, Fred was settled in a nursing home. My love and respect for this man brought me to his side often. At first, he was lucid but later less talkative. When he was able, we discussed politics and professional football. Other times, I just held his hand.

On January 20, 2009, I was in Washington to observe the historic inauguration. But first, I had my own business to take care of. I knew John

Conyers's staff were with me in my cause. I had a meeting set with the staff to argue that Nick Bailey and Billy Canary should be questioned by the Judiciary Committee. After I made my case, I proceeded to a viewing stand near the White House with my friend Tom Goodwin. Tom and I worked together in the McGovern campaign in Birmingham in 1972. Tom had settled in D.C. after working in the Carter White House.

Our new president declared, "I'm looking forward, not back."

Looking forward is good, but not looking back? I wondered what that meant. What about fixing all the old problems in America? Bush and Cheney taking us to war with lies? Illegal wiretaps? Torture? Water boarding? Assassinations? Jails overflowing with people who didn't belong there? Rove's abuses of power? What about my case? Would the new president, looking forward, turn his back on injustices in America? Or was I worrying too much about rhetoric?

SPIRITS LIFTED, HOPE RISES

My hopes rose when Obama made Eric Holder his attorney general. Holder was African American, and he soon dropped the corruption charges against Republican U.S. Senator Ted Stevens. This was a very good omen. The government misconduct in the Senator's case was perpetrated by two of the same DOJ prosecutors who were tangentially involved in my case. The prosecutorial misconduct in my case was far more severe than that in Stevens's case.

Still, I learned that during a previous stint at Justice, Holder had worked with David Margolis and that they had an unbroken bond of mutual respect. Holder, before being appointed attorney general, had worked in the politically powerful law firm of Covington & Burling. The firm boasted on its website of having represented Rove and the Republican National Committee. The firm also protected Rove when the Judiciary Committee subpoenaed emails related to the firing of U.S. attorneys and my case. Lord, I just needed someone who was unbiased to look at what had been done to me.

Bob Abrams had tried to speak with Holder about my case when they were face to face in New York. Bob was rebuffed. Governor Jim Doyle, with two other governors on the phone, attempted a conference call with Holder.

Questions remain about why President Obama ignored the prosecutorial misconduct against me. A picture is worth a thousand words.

He refused to take their call. The Reverend Tommy Lewis of Alabama was also rebuffed by Holder. Why couldn't we penetrate this shield around the government's misconduct? It was like an umbrella of protection being held by someone, but whom? Margolis? Or did it go higher? All this was profoundly discouraging. It enraged and fired up Chip Hill and Les and kept my son and daughter heartbroken. Lori would persevere, working in the arts community and involving herself with her elderly mother.

THE MYSTERIOUS DAVID MARGOLIS

David Margolis was no doubt central to all misdeeds of the Justice Department, including the Alabama prosecutors. He let Canary stay on my case even though her husband, a Rove operative, was being paid to defeat me. Margolis had written that there was "no actual conflict." No fair-minded person could say that. Margolis approved all charges against high-ranking public officials. That was his job. Margolis had to have approved the first frivolous charge in 2004. He had to have ordered or approved the bogus RICO charge in 2006 that brought me to trial one month before the Alabama primary election. DOJ hid the fact that the statute of limitations had run out on any bribery—had there been any—relating to Scrushy's contribution to the lottery referendum. Margolis would have had to have known of that legally subversive act. He approved or edited all OPR investigations or complaints against DOJ prosecutors. He had to be the one responsible for stonewalling the House Judiciary Committee's demands to investigate my case. He stalled the OPR investigation some eighteen months. Chairman John Conyers ultimately described it as "one-sided." Margolis approved the firing of the DOJ whistleblower, Tamarah Grimes, who accused the DOJ of pressuring their witness to lie. Margolis was involved in the cover-up, but was he the mastermind or a complicit political puppet?

Scott Horton, writing in *Harper's*, summed up the problem: "Margolis has demonstrated repeatedly that he places more value in the vanity of institutional prestige than he does in the duty to do justice."

On April 25, 2009, another editorial in the *New York Times* spoke out on my case:

> Attorney General Holder should investigate the case against Don Sie-gelman, the Alabama governor convicted in 2006 on dubious corruption charges, for prosecutorial misconduct.

On May 1, 2009, Professor Bennett Gershman of Pace Law School, author of the book *Prosecutorial Misconduct*, said of my case:

> I can think of no better illustration of the abuse of the prosecutorial function than the prosecution of Don Siegelman. I can say that among the thousands of cases of prosecutorial misconduct I have studied over the years, the Siegelman case stands out starkly. Indeed, I have never encountered another prosecution in which it appears so clearly that the prosecutors were zealously bent on pursuing an individual, rather than on a crime that needed to be prosecuted. As an example of a bad faith prosecution, the Siegelman case may be without parallel.

Not until July 2009 did Rove finally talk before a Congressional com-mittee. Then he answered questions posed by Congressman Adam Schiff, but in a closed session, not under oath, and with so many restrictions that almost no one cared. There was no oath and no cross-examination. He could lie without consequence. He also suffered from exceptionally poor memory.

"I do not recall," was Rove's constant refrain.

He was asked if he had spoken to U.S. Department of Justice officials about prosecuting me. But Mr. Rove did not need to speak with "any Justice Department official" because he could speak to his old buddy, Billy Canary, the U.S. attorney's husband.[33]

Some detractors feared that my long time friend and future lawyer, Greg Craig, as President Obama's first White House Counsel, might have cut the deal that let Rove off the ropes. I never believed a word. Greg and I had been friends since 1967. Greg told me that he had been "sickened" by what had happened to me. Chairman of the House Judiciary, John Conyers, had been outspoken on holding Rove in contempt if he wouldn't testify under oath. But Rove never did.

On September 25, 2009, John Conyers wrote Eric Holder urging him to take a personal look at "the extensive allegations of prosecutorial misconduct and politically influenced prosecution" in my case.

No one knew what impact, if any, these personal appeals were having.

CHAPTER 62

LEGAL APPEAL BEGINS

In May 2008, I was home with my family, enjoying the blessings of freedom. It was hard adjusting to normal life after so many months behind bars, but I didn't have time to acclimate; there was work to be done on my appeal.

Our brief to the Eleventh Circuit Court of Appeals was due soon and my lawyers, Sam Heldman and David McDonald, were working on it non-stop. A three-judge panel of the Eleventh Circuit had released me from prison because "there were substantial questions of law and fact likely to result in a reversal." Those were encouraging words.

Our brief argued that trial judge, Mark Fuller, had been wrong on the law and wrong on the facts.

Wrong, not to have thrown out the bribery charge, because the statute of limitations had run.

Wrong, to ignore the Supreme Court's *McCormick* standard, which ruled that the legal standard for bribery in a campaign contribution case required an "explicit" and an "asserted" quid pro quo.

Wrong, to ignore juror misconduct when emails from jurors surfaced proving they were seeking a conviction before the trial was over.

Wrong, to increase my sentence for criticizing the prosecution's motives and protesting their political prosecution. Fuller said I had demeaned the executive branch of government. In truth, he had demeaned the judicial branch. Later, his habitual domestic violence helped the United States Judicial Council prove this to be true. Judge Fuller was the real criminal and a violent one.

I knew that if I could face unbiased judges I would be acquitted.

My legal team met in Atlanta. I wrote another check for $25,000 to cover Sam's argument to the Eleventh Circuit. Lori, Les, Maze, and other friends came to Atlanta for my hearing. I watched as three old white men in long black robes slid into their chairs. These weren't the three who'd set me free pending my appeal! We faced three new judges! All Republicans! They came at Sam from the start.

The presiding judge declared, "Mr. Heldman, you can argue the McCormick standard if you want but . . ."

Sam did his best but it was clear they had already made up their minds. Despite what the United States Supreme Court had said, despite the clear law governing campaign contributions, despite the opinion of all the attorneys general, these judges didn't care. On March 6, 2009, their ruling came.

Convictions upheld. They agreed with Fuller on every issue except for two counts for which the Eleventh Circuit had admitted there was "absolutely no evidence."

The Eleventh Circuit had eleven judges. Three had voted to free me from prison while I appealed my case. That trio had included only one Democrat. But these three Republicans were there to reject me. My nemesis, Karl Rove-connected Judge Bill Pryor, was on the court, thanks to Jeff Sessions. Pryor wasn't one of the three who ruled against me but I suspected he had a hand in their selection and their decision.

ON TO THE SUPREME COURT

We again looked to the Supreme Court to set things right.

We tried to get Walter Dellinger, solicitor general under Clinton, to take my case. Then I went to Ted Olson, Bush's solicitor general. Both were supportive but unavailable. No matter, I was happy with Sam. He knew my case, he knew the law, and he cared about me.

Now, we had ninety-one former state attorneys general on an amicus brief to the Supreme Court and the list was soon to top one hundred. Jesse Choper, a law professor at Berkeley, a wonderful man whom I had met in 1987 at a Conference of Western Attorneys General, recruited the top constitutional law scholars to file an amicus brief. We had powerful legal arguments written by highly respected legal scholars. We all were hopeful.

After several months, Sam called. "Governor, good news. The Supreme Court reversed Fuller and ordered the Eleventh Circuit to look at the case again."

"What? We won?"

"Sort of. We didn't lose. It was vacated and remanded back to the Eleventh Circuit."

"So we have another shot at it. Will we have a different panel this time?"

"No. Probably the same three Republicans."

The Supreme Court had vacated the Eleventh Circuit Court's ruling, telling the three Republican judges to look at my case again "in light of our ruling in *Skilling*." The Court in the *Skilling* case defined bribery as kickbacks, cash, tangible corruption, some kind of self-enrichment scheme. None of this applied to me.

The ruling lifted our spirits. The next day, I spoke to Sam about the "Honest Services Fraud" statute. I was the first public official ever charged with an "honest services" violation for accepting a campaign contribution to a ballot referendum where there was no allegation of self-enrichment. I had been the first to be sent to prison on a new legal standard, created by Judge Fuller just for me, whereby juries can convict for bribery based on an "implied" agreement rather than an "express" or "explicitly asserted" agreement required by the U.S. Supreme Court.

BACK TO THE APPELLATE COURT

In Atlanta, before the Eleventh Circuit, home of my political nemesis Bill Pryor, Sam reminded the three Republican judges "*Skilling* pared down 'honest services' to self-enrichment schemes of kickbacks and bribery. The definition did not include any cases involving campaign contributions, much less contributions to an issue advocacy campaign. Governor Siegelman took no money."

Sam chastised the government, "The prosecutors have resorted to the use of loose language. The government described the campaign contributions as 'payments . . . to Don Siegelman' or as being money 'paid to Siegelman.' The contributions were not payments to Don Siegelman. They were contributions to a campaign regarding a lottery referendum. This is undisputed."

MY CONVICTION UPHELD, ON TO THE SCOTUS

My conviction was upheld again. Now in 2012, ninety-one former state attorneys general argued to the Supreme Court, "The Eleventh Circuit's decision creates extreme uncertainty regarding the breath of criminal liability in campaign contribution cases, and the potential for arbitrary and discriminatory enforcement raises serious First Amendment concerns."

Law professors, in a separate amicus brief, admonished the Eleventh Circuit's ruling as "especially dangerous because of the great danger of abuse of power in prosecuting political opponents."

Sam noted that the Eleventh Circuit itself agreed "this is the first case to be based upon issue-advocacy campaign contributions . . . Based on *Skilling*, a contribution to an issue-advocacy campaign is just not a bribe."

He added, "A person in Governor Siegelman's position could not have known or understood in advance that this court would accept an 'implied' agreement inferred as a 'state of mind' to be an 'explicit' agreement."

Sam's logic seemed beyond dispute. We had made a strong appeal to the Supreme Court.

Pulitzer Prize-winning writer George Will, a Republican, wrote in the *Washington Post*, "Until the Supreme Court clarifies what constitutes quid pro quo political corruption, Americans engage in politics at their peril because prosecutors have dangerous discretion to criminalize politics." The *New York Times* agreed.

We waited for the Supreme Court decision that would surely grant oral arguments or outright reject the charges against me.

Then Sam Heldman called.

"Don, I'm sorry. The Court has denied *certiorari.*"

I felt sick. "How could they not even hear our case?"

"We'll never know. They just said 'Denied'. I don't understand how they could refuse to hear your case."

I told Sam he had done a phenomenal job.

"You need to prepare for sentencing. Governor, I'm so disappointed I just can't talk about this," Sam said.

The Supreme Court had spoken. I was going back to prison.

My lawyers agonized over the Court's unexplained rejection of my appeal. They cited various precedents that they thought demanded a ruling in my favor. The law was clear, they said, and the ruling simply made no sense.

I saw it differently. The ruling made perfect sense if you saw it as pure politics, much like the 2000 ruling in *Bush v. Gore.* The court, or at least a majority of it, chose to ignore the law and the facts, because it was unwilling to open a political can of worms that would embarrass the Department of Justice and the White House. The court, by ruling in my favor, would be agreeing that I had been imprisoned for purely political reasons.

The court's majority gave the White House, Rove, Pryor, and Republican leaders in Alabama what they had sought for so long, my removal from political life and a gag order that would last for years. I was going back to prison so that powerful people's contempt for the law and greed for political power wouldn't be exposed.

CHAPTER 63

THE JUDGE GETS HIS POUND OF FLESH

It was now six years after my conviction in 2006. Going back before Judge Fuller would be humiliating. I still had to deal with my lawyers telling me that for me to get "mercy" from the judge, I had to be remorseful. I would not lie just to please this judge. I would not, under any circumstances, tell him I was guilty. I would go down with my integrity, with my sense of honor. I knew my sentence would be Judge Fuller's final "pound of flesh."

I started to outline my allocution, my statement before I'd be sentenced.

Les said, "Why not tell the judge, I hope you believe me when I say if I had known I was coming anywhere close to the line separating politics from crime, I would not have come one step closer." I agreed with Les, it was a good place to start.

My son was writing his version, declaring my innocence. I appreciated what he'd written, but my lawyers were adamant, begging me to, at least, try to appear remorseful.

"Dad, this is your last chance to set the record straight."

I started writing, wanting to do what Joseph suggested. I cited each inconsistency and lie the government had spoken against me. I couldn't admit guilt. What the bastards said were all lies and they knew it. I was innocent of breaking any law.

I ran my proposal by Bobby Segall. "Say you are sorry," he replied.

Joe Espy said, "Don, if you say that, Fuller's going to give you more time in prison."

Bob Abrams warned, "Don, the judge isn't going to like this at all."

At lunch the day of sentencing, I talked with Grant Woods, the former Republican attorney general from Arizona, about what I'd written. Grant was the national co-chair of Senator McCain's presidential campaign, the one he lost to George W. Bush. He knew Rove was behind the plot to take me out of politics and told *60 Minutes* as much.

"Don, you have to apologize," he said. "You have to say you're sorry, to ask for mercy. Fuller may not show you mercy, but this judge holds your life in his hands. You cannot say things that will set him off."

So we rewrote my statement. I had hoped someone would agree with my son's approach, but no one did.

My wife, children, brother, lawyers, Maze, and I, walked into the court together to face my sentencing judge. Some members of the press wished me luck. I missed my dear friend Fred Shuttlesworth, who had been with me every day of my sentencing in 2007, up to the very second Fuller had me hauled off in chains. Fred had died at age eighty-nine. Mrs. Shuttlesworth, Maze, Grant Woods, and Jackie Gamez, my Hispanic friend from karate classes, came as character witnesses. My daughter was chosen to represent the family. "I cannot imagine my dad going back to prison." Her emotional appeal drew tears from many.

In the end, I did say I was sorry. Sorry for the embarrassment my actions had caused the state, my friends and family, and for the pain and suffering my acts caused my children. It was true my conviction brought bad publicity on the state, even though it was all politically motivated, and it was true my friends and family had suffered greatly. For that, I

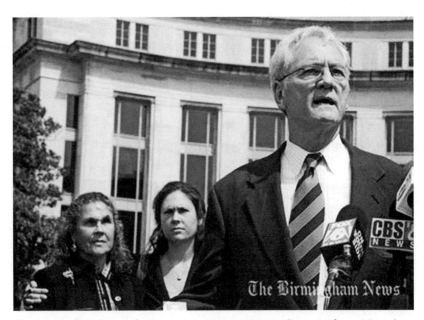

Dana comforts Lori after my resentencing, 2012. (Birmingham News)

really was truly sorry. I could say that.

I apologized for "my acts that have brought us here today." I had hired Nick Bailey, who had brought in Lanny Young. I could apologize for my bad hires. I was certainly sorry for that.

But I wasn't sorry for accepting Richard Scrushy's contributions to the lottery referendum. I wasn't sorry for asking him to rejoin the C.O.N. Board. I wouldn't apologize for buying the motorcycle.

What I said mattered to me, but not to the judge. Fuller had his mind made up before he walked into the courtroom. For the two counts for which the Eleventh Circuit had said there was absolutely no evidence, he took ten months off my original sentence of eighty-eight months.

I wondered if I should've bothered to say anything at all.

CHAPTER 64

THIRTY DAYS OF FREEDOM TO FIGHT

Fuller gave me thirty days to self-report.

As we headed out of the courtroom to meet the press, Les immediately said, "Fuller just screwed up. We get thirty days to raise hell before you go off. We'll keep fighting. Fuller should've sent you straight back to prison. We start to work tomorrow morning."

Les, Dana, Joseph, and I went to work.

THE DEMOCRATIC NATIONAL CONVENTION

Dana wanted to go to the 2012 Democratic National Convention in Charlotte, North Carolina. "Dad," she said, "I'm going whether you go or not." Joseph agreed. We agreed to tell my story to the media and to seek the support of as many influential people as possible.

I was to be interviewed by Neil Cavuto on Fox from the convention floor. Eric Spinato, Neil's producer, wanted to help. "Don, when you go to prison, we won't be able to speak with you. You'll no longer be able to get your message out. You need to be out there now every chance you get." Dana was fired up about an online petition urging the president to "Pardon Don." I announced it on Neil's show. Neil denounced the judge's bias in my case.

KARL ROVE RUNS FROM DANA

Then Dana found Karl Rove lurking in the halls. She acted quickly.

"Mr. Rove, I'm Dana Siegelman," she said, her hand extended.

Before she could say another word, Rove stuck his finger in her face and snarled, "Tell your father if he doesn't stop using my name, I'll sue him." He fled when he saw cameras approaching.

Dana, stunned by his rebuke, was interviewed by Current TV. I was proud of the way she stood up to this dangerous and dishonest man.

Most of our time was spent with the media and old friends. Congressman Steny Hoyer hugged me and then Joseph, his former legal intern, who introduced Dana. Steny brought over the Congressman and civil rights leader John Lewis, who said he would speak out on my behalf.

Political conventions are at best chaotic. Even when I was governor, getting around had been a challenge. On Wednesday night it was pouring rain. No transportation was available. No taxis or buses. People walked in the downpour trying to shelter under awnings. We all huddled together

Dana telling Current TV reporter about Rove running from her at the Democratic National Convention, 2012. (Courtesy Peppertree Films)

in long lines, soaked, awaiting entry to the convention. As we approached security, we saw people were shouting insults at columnist George Will, a man I greatly admired. Our common link was William F. Buckley Jr. Will had bonded with Buckley as an intellectual conservative. My national political mentor, Congressman Al Lowenstein, had brought me in contact with Buckley back in 1968.

"Mr. Will, I'm Don Siegelman, thanks so much for your column." His young aide was trying to cover him with a plastic bag. Dana, Joseph, and I were huddled under one tiny umbrella. George was a gracious companion in the rain. Later we met Joe Scarborough of MSNBC's *Morning Joe*, who talked with Joseph about his days at the University of Alabama and Joseph's "Crimson and White" tie. Scarborough had graduated from Alabama in the 1980s.

CHAPTER 65

A 'HAIL MARY' PARDON PASS

Back home, Les hoped to seize President Obama's attention. "Don, you've got to have a few key people write the president asking for your commutation. Have them send two originals to me. I'll put the package together."

Les wrote a cover letter on my behalf, saying, "I am asking the president to commute my sentence in the interest of justice and to draw attention to the need to clarify a crucial area of the law. Unlike others charged with bribery, I was never accused of taking any money personally."

Notre Dame law professor Robert Blakey told the *New York Times*, "It's a joke . . . find as much trash as you can, then dump it in. The shakiness of the case forced prosecutors to adopt the 'garbage-can theory' of RICO."

Mrs. Fred Shuttlesworth wrote President Obama hoping her husband's national reputation as a civil rights icon might catch his eye. She said, speaking of her husband's hospitalization:

From the day we arrived to the final week of my husband's life, Don Siegelman stood by his old friend. Week in and week out, usually on a Sunday morning, Don Siegelman visited Fred Shuttlesworth. It was not uncommon to find them holding hands, sitting quietly or watching each other sleep. Oftentimes, as Don prepared to exit, he'd kiss my husband on the forehead and remark something about him being kissed by an old white man. The two of them would part in warm laughter until the next time. Fred Shuttlesworth loved, trusted, believed in and respected Don Siegelman.

A total of 113 former state attorneys general signed a letter to President Obama pleading for my release: "The pain, anguish and disgrace imposed upon Don Siegelman and his family already constitute a severe penalty."

Former chief justice of the Alabama Supreme Court Mark Kennedy said, "I write to ask for justice for a man who the system has failed."

Retired U.S. District Judge U. W. Clemon put it plainly to Obama, "In my thirty years on the federal bench, I have never seen a federal prosecution with such a glaring lack of substantial justification."

Civil rights attorney Fred Gray wrote, "I had the honor of representing Mrs. Rosa Parks and Dr. Martin Luther King . . . I recognize injustice when I see it. I see it in the case of the criminal prosecution and trial of my friend, Don Siegelman."

Columbia Law professor Scott Horton wrote, "Don Siegelman's case presents perhaps the clearest modern example of what Robert Jackson, our greatest modern attorney general, foresaw might happen when prosecutors, motivated by their baser motives, wield the immense power granted them to take down a political rival."

There were many such letters to President Obama, but they drew no response or even any indication that he had read them.

Dana and her team of warriors generated nearly 100,000 calls, emails, and letters to the White House on my behalf. Various petitions called on President Obama to take a look at my case and grant a pardon. At times, they created so much traffic the White House personnel asked them to back off.

CHAPTER 66

BACK TO PRISON

September 11, 2012, was my date to report to federal prison. Nothing had changed my legal status. The petitions to President Obama, the tens of thousands of calls, emails, and letters to the White House had made no impact. My plea for commutation of my sentence was ignored. September 11th had been selected by Judge Fuller as his last not-so-subtle message.

After more than four years of freedom, it was time to go back to Oakdale federal prison, over nine hours from my home, nearly five hundred miles one way. I had hoped to be closer to home, perhaps at the facility in Pensacola, Florida. U.S. Representatives Terri Sewell of Alabama and Steve Cohen of Tennessee wrote to the head of the Bureau of Prisons asking that I be sent there. He refused.

Lori, Dana, Joseph, and I drove to New Orleans the day before I was to report. I wanted to have a good dinner and breakfast with my family, then head to Oakdale for my 2 p.m. return to captivity. We checked into the Monteleone

Lori took this picture of Joseph and Dana with me in New Orleans the night before I returned to prison, 2012.

My tenacious daughter, Dana, established the FREE DON national network to fight for her dad's freedom. (Courtesy Liesa Cole, Studio GoodLight, Birmingham, Alabama)

Hotel in New Orleans, then walked to stretch our legs and see the city.

I had places to share with my family. I knew they would enjoy the food and ambiance of Stella's for dinner. First, I wanted Joseph to experience a Monsoon, a stout rum drink, from Port-O-Calls. We turned off St. Ann to Canal and headed to Esplanade, then a couple of blocks further to get "Monsoons" to go. Laughing and walking arm-in-arm like in the Wizard of Oz, we headed down St. Ann to have a "Voodoo" lager at Lafitte's Blacksmith's Shop. The old pirate hangout was dark and mystical.

At Stella's, I had a wonderful soft-shell crab and the tastiest filet ever. Joseph and I had a Manhattan, since it would be five years before I could have another. After dinner, we walked back to our hotel, a little tipsy and replete. We all snuggled in for a good night's rest. We had a busy morning ahead.

We woke early for my morning interviews, one with Amy Goodman on *Democracy Now!* and then with a TV station from Mobile. On to breakfast at Stanley's on Jackson Square and then a view from the balcony of Muriel's across the street. We were near the Cafe du Monde, so we went by for coffee and their celebrated beignets before heading to Oakdale.

Knowing this would be the last time I'd be with my family for nearly five years was heartbreaking. Yet, somehow, we managed to laugh and enjoy these final moments together. We discussed who would do what to win my freedom. We still had hopes for a successful appeal to President Obama.

We pulled over at a small country church. The weeds surrounding it were worn down by the cars and trucks that would park there during Wednesday and Sunday services. We got out of Lori's Trailblazer. First, a strong group hug, then individual embraces with Lori, Joseph, and lastly, Dana. I tried to remain strong during this last chance to be with them as a free man for several years. In a quarter mile, we turned into the Oakdale Federal Prison Complex.

REENTERING OAKDALE PRISON

"Recognize it, Don?" Lori said.

"I don't think I'll ever forget this place."

As we passed the visitors' trailer, I saw the wooden patio where I would sit on weekends when friends and family came to visit. Those memories could make things easier. Those memories had helped me survive this place the first time. Maybe they would again.

"Joseph, pull in over there," I said pointing toward the detention center, a clearinghouse for new inmates, a place that also held the Special Housing Unit. "That's 'The Hole,' solitary confinement intended to whip us into submission. Hadn't worked so far."

We stared at the high barbed wire fences with strands of razor wire rolling along the bottom and top. The thought of one's skin being ripped and bleeding was enough to discourage inmates from climbing over the two twenty-foot high galvanized steel fences. It was an agonizing sight that made me weak. I secretly loathed the bastards who sent me here. Now, I must enter this cruel, senseless place for a crime I didn't commit. I thought fleetingly of the lying witnesses, the politicized prosecutors, and my vengeful judge.

We parked. What could I say to my family I loved so much? I had to be strong for them.

"Well, this is where we end our journey. Take care of yourselves; I'll be fine. I know my way around. I have no fear of this place. And besides, you guys are going to get me out."

Dana used a nickname she had given me when she was a child. "Yes, Dadally, we'll get you out before Christmas, and then we'll take a family vacation."

"British Virgin Islands, here we come," Joseph said.

"You guys best stay in the car. I'll walk over and check myself in. If I'm not in the right place, I'll be back shortly."

I climbed out of the car, wearing what I had worn out on May 29, 2008, my gray sweat pants, white thermal shirt, and a well-worn short-sleeved white T-shirt over it. And the same black "Totes" that I had worn in prison. I wanted myself acclimated. Once more, I looked like an inmate.

I walked around to Joseph in the driver's seat. He had his cell phone out to take a video of my return to prison. I gave him another hug through the window. Dana took her phone out, too. I looked once more at Lori, my beautiful wife, who had endured so much.

"Take care of yourself," she said.

"Dadally," Dana called, "we'll see you soon."

As I made my way toward the razor-wire fence and the prison door, I looked back one last time.

Once I stepped inside, I knew I wouldn't see them for a long time.

Inside, a guard sat before an imposing desk. I tried to remember this setting but couldn't. After I was processed out in 2008, I quickly shed memories of this god-awful place.

"Siegelman, are you back again?"

I turned to see a guard covered in tattoos. I remembered Mr. Bird. Who could forget him? Tattoos everywhere. Tattoos all over his neck, cheeks, forehead, nose, and down his arms to the tips of his fingers. Why would anyone do that?

"Mr. Bird. Yes, it's me, back again," I said and tried to smile. I felt dazed. In prison again, unable to leave, unable to see my family. Even the second time it was surreal.

Pointing to a bench, he said, "We'll get you checked in, just have a seat."

A pleasant enough welcome. Kind and surprisingly respectful.

Joseph came in.

"I'm in the right place," I told him, standing to greet my son.

"We wanted to make sure," he said.

I gave Joseph another hug, conscious of the guard watching. "Dad, we love you." His voice started to weaken. Damn, this was hard on my kids.

"I love you, too," I said, trying to suppress my own emotions.

He turned and walked out the door. Loneliness washed over me. I sat and waited until processing began.

CHAPTER 67

PRISON . . . AGAIN

"Take everything out of your pockets," the guard said. I had nothing but a box of contact lenses and a letter from my orthopedic surgeon explaining the surgery I had in my right leg and ankle, from the tibia and fibula I broke in a karate tournament in 2009.

I was told to sit again and wait. After what seemed like hours, another guard came. I was handcuffed and led to another room. A guard said, "Take everything off," as he took the handcuffs off. "Turn around, spread your cheeks." I did. Then he gave me some old green prison uniform and I dressed and was eventually led to another room. More guards. Fingerprinted and photographed. I brought my old federal prison ID with me and the card with my medical records.

"What's that?" the guard asked.

"A letter from my surgeon and my old ID," I said.

"Keep your ID with you. Give me the letters. What's in the box?"

"My contacts."

"Medical will make a decision on these." The guard took them, never to be seen again.

I was taken to another room and told: "Sit." Now I knew how my dog, Kona, must feel. I had gotten Lori a six-week-old male chocolate Labrador Retriever in March before my departure.

It was a small cell, with thick iron bars and an iron bench. I waited maybe two hours. I was given a baloney sandwich. After another long wait, a guard handcuffed me. I was led down a long corridor of cells in the Special Housing Unit. Back to solitary.

SOLITARY, "THE HOLE"

I had spent over a month in solitary in 2007, so I knew what to expect. When a new inmate arrives, he's put in the slammer, "The Hole," officially called the Special Housing Unit. It's small, cold, and uncomfortable. The food is nasty, just enough to keep you from starving. But the worst is the isolation. Never knowing the time of day, or weather, or seeing anything but four walls, is almost more than the human mind can bear.

The guard led me to an open cell. "You'll be here until space opens up at the camp. I'll bring you some sheets and a blanket."

He shut and locked the cell door. It felt good to have the cuffs off. Freedom is relative. I looked around. The bottom bunk had been slept in. A small metal stool swung out from the wall next to the bottom bunk. Nothing to do but wait.

I heard talk, two voices, and keys clanging together. Guards were coming. A big key, I knew, would be used to unlock the iron door. The cell door opened. Another inmate came in wearing only shorts and holding soap and a towel behind his back in his cuffed hands. He had been to the shower. My cellmate. He stuck his hands and wrists through the slot. I heard the click of the handcuff being released.

"I'm Don."

"My name is Hobbs. I'm called Hump."

We shook hands and started getting to know each other, settling in for the long haul. No one really knows how long he will stay in "The Hole" before a bunk opens up. Even if a bunk is available, it doesn't mean you'll be moved right away. Sometimes they like to give you a taste of what they can do to you. They can leave you in "The Hole" as long as they like.

I asked Hump how long he'd been there. "Four days," he said. He told me where he was from and, eventually, why he was there. During the next few days we shared stories of our fortunes and misfortunes, our families and work. Hump was there for pirating music.

We had no idea when we'd be out of solitary. Then the jangling of keys. A guard kicked the door. "Siegelman, get your shit together. I'll come back for you later this afternoon."

I was thinking, if they are about to take me, a white man, before they take this black man who's been here longer than I have, that's not good. I'm going to be living with this guy for a while. I shouldn't be treated differently. When the guard came back, he was with the camp counselor, Mr. Hill, a fifty-year-old black man not known for his pleasantness.

"Siegelman, I didn't think you were coming back."

I was getting tired of hearing that.

"I thought I was out for good, too, Mr. Hill," I said.

"I'm moving you to the camp."

"Mr. Hill, Hobbs has been here four days longer than me."

"Don't start telling me how to run my business, I'll leave you both here." He walked off.

Hump said, "Man, thanks for trying."

In about an hour, Hill came back.

"Hobbs, get ready. You're going to the camp, too."

Victory. Maybe I could still do some good.

Later that afternoon, we were both taken out in cuffs, told to strip, and searched again, then given green prison pants and shirts. We were told a driver would meet us out front to take us to the camp. I remembered the routine.

CHAPTER 68

FROM SOLITARY CONFINEMENT TO CAMP

Just like that, freedom, relatively speaking. No cuffs, and we're trusted to stand outside by ourselves where my family had dropped me off. I could still feel their presence as I waited for an inmate-driven van to take us to the camp's entrance.

We were driven to the dorm, a metal warehouse. We were put in tight quarters that had been a small TV room in 2007. Now it had ten bunks, ten lockers, ten inmates. One fan. We were welcomed by the others: three African Americans, three Hispanics, one Asian, and one other white guy. In that small space, we came to know each other quickly. The entire dorm was built for eighty but now housed 175, with four toilets and urinals, eight showers on each side, and a cafeteria that seated only forty. There were lines and waits for everything. Patience and respect were essential.

After two months, I was moved from the ten-man cell to a cell for twenty-one. It was another former TV room where inmates once watched sports. Now, with more people behind bars, space was tight. It was called the "21 room," about twenty-one by twenty-one feet with five rows of beds stacked three high and twenty-one lockers. It was like being in the crew quarters of a submarine. I had a middle bunk. There wasn't even room enough to sit up. After two more months, I was moved to the north wing of the dorm. Compared to the submarine space, it was like a merchant marine vessel with space between the seventy-four bunk beds and lockers to move more freely.

One night we set a camp record. We snagged six mice using sticky paper. Not a pleasant sight, but I was glad to be rid of them. Lenny, our resident cat, had a feast.

Two puppies came and went. A black and white one, and a black and tan. The black and white pup never barked. The black and tan dog learned to bark at the guards. Only the guards. They won lots of attention and shared our food. Soon, because of the dogs' knack for treeing squirrels, guards who were squirrel hunters took the dogs home. All the guards got time off on what they call "National Squirrel Day."

The "rec yard," short for recreation, was the same as before except minus some of the equipment. A room which had housed a pool table was now the main TV room. There were two more TVs high on the wall outside, under the tin roof that covered the iron dumbbells. We still had the old quarter-mile oval track.

Our days were carefully planned. COs counted us at 5 a.m., 11 a.m., 4 p.m. (lights out at 10 p.m.), midnight, and 3 a.m.—day after day. Nothing changed but the faces of inmates who came and went. Breakfast was at 6:30, lunch at 10:30 a.m., and dinner at 3 p.m. Usually, after I finished my job in landscaping, I'd hit the library, to make notes in my journal and send emails to friends and family or to hear words of encouragement from Les or Chip. I was blessed with mail, embarrassingly so. I guessed Dana and others had been encouraging everyone to write me. Some inmates seemingly never received mail.

The library was a small two-room facility. Maybe a thousand books, mostly paperbacks, old inmate hand-me-downs. The computers were a new feature from the first time I was at Oakdale—computers but not connected to the Internet in the usual way. No "Word" or "Google," but when you sent an email it would arrive, although hours later. Everything could be censored or read. I usually spent much of my day on a computer. It was contact with the outside world. We had one printer that dated to the prehistoric era. This was prison.

My Prison Mates

Black inmates made up about 60 percent of the prison's population, mostly here for crack or cocaine, some just marijuana. Some were Africans, Pakistani, Palestinian, and a couple from Syria. There was a sizable Hispanic population, maybe twenty, mostly for marijuana or cocaine. The white inmates were in for a mix of white-collar fraud, meth, or parole violations. The races tended to stick together but, for the most part, everyone got along.

I learned from my fellow inmates how they were convicted. Often, it was false testimony by a government informant who was repaid with money or a shorter sentence. Soon, Hump left after agreeing to be a government witness. Some sentences had been "enhanced," made longer, for "acquitted" or "relevant" conduct or for having a firearm. Evidence of prosecutorial abuse was frequent. In recent years, over 1,500 inmates had been freed because of DNA or evidence or testimony that proved their innocence; over one hundred and fifty of those were inmates on death row. I recalled my time as attorney general when I worked to get Johnny Harris off Alabama's death row. Mr. Harris had been accused of killing an Alabama prison guard during a riot. I had found that the prosecutors had withheld exculpatory evidence showing that it was impossible for Harris to have committed the crime!

Christmas is Coming

I had to stay sane and focus on a positive future. As Christmas approached, I recalled my family Christmas vacations. They were our best times together as a family. Now, the local radio station played The Eagles, "Bells will be ringing this sad, sad news, Oh, what a Christmas to have the blues . . . "

Most inmates tried to forget. It would be just another day down for us.

I tried to concentrate on my blessings. I had family and friends who supported me. I always named them in my prayers, day-after-day. Morning and night. I had my health. I could walk, talk, exercise. I could see and hear, taste and feel. I felt with my heart as well as with my hands. I had friends here, too. People to work out with and talk to, who were genuinely good people. I had food, a bed, and clothes. I had good lawyers. Most of all, I had my family. I prayed for God to keep them safe and happy. I had far more than many others who were here. I had a lot to be thankful for.

I increasingly believed that my mission was to expose and change this cruel and senseless system of justice. God had seemingly said to me, "Ok, Governor, now you've seen what's wrong. Go fix it."

CHAPTER 69

WHITE HOUSE COUNSEL AS MY ADVOCATE

Greg Craig, whom I first met in 1968, was coming to see me. Joseph told me Greg hoped to talk me out of pursuing my appeal for a new trial, so I could seek a formal commutation. Les, Joseph, and I thought this was useless, since President Obama had ignored our pleas thus far. Greg was President Obama's first White House counsel, now a partner in one of the most successful law firms in the world. We met years earlier, in September of 1968, through Al Lowenstein. We worked side by side on Al's congressional campaigns, on voter registration and delegate selection, on the excessive use of force by police and the National Guard in Ohio where four anti-war student protesters at Kent State were gunned down in 1970. Greg, a Yale Law School graduate, had worked for U.S. Senator Ted Kennedy and powerful Washington law firms. Greg knew his way around and through the power elite in D.C. Now I was asking him to confront this legal mess of mine.

Greg was accompanied by my son Joseph, now a lawyer himself. Joseph had gotten a full scholarship to Alabama's law school so he could learn the law and help extricate me from this legal quagmire. Joseph spent the better part of ten years working to free me. Greg had told me that President Obama would only consider a commutation if all appeals were finished. My appeal for a new trial was pending. It had been filed by my Georgetown classmate, Peter Sissman, who was now suffering from cancer.

I met Greg and Joseph in the sterile visitation trailer. I had been sent to mop and wax the floors the night before. I knew I had to convince Greg not only of my innocence but also of the viability of our motion for a new trial. He listened patiently for nearly two hours as I told my story, in detail, about how Karl Rove's client, Bill Pryor, had started the investigation and helped steal my 2002 election, about Leura Canary's conflict (her husband working for my opponent), the whistleblowers, my vengeful judge and corrupt trial. When I finished, after hearing our plea, Greg agreed to take over my case.

Greg said, "My firm and I will represent you . . . pro bono."

"Greg, thank you so much," I said. "This is the best news possible."

We shook hands, all of us smiling and me relieved. I gave Joseph a bear hug, thankful for this chance to see him and all he had done. As they left, I smiled again, this time only to myself. Feeling confident, I thought, "We'll win this appeal. What a blessing, to have a lawyer who is one of the best in the world and a friend, too."

I was content and confident once again, with Joseph working the legal side, Dana doing public relations, Les working on the presidential pardon with Bob Abrams and Lynne Ross, Chip Hill working the media, and now Greg Craig as my lawyer! I had a great team. Anita Darden kept my Free-Don website up with posts from Dana and the boundless energy of my foot soldiers on social media. I also had a new-found friend, Barbara Tarburton, with whom I had daily contact through the prison computer system.

CHAPTER 70

INMATE STORIES

The camp reminded me of an inner-city boys' club where I once volunteered in Mobile. There was an outdoor basketball court, the quarter-mile oblong asphalt track, and its infield that doubled for tag football, softball, and an occasional soccer match. A volleyball net, set up in a sand pit, was used by the feral cats who lived under the education trailer.

There were many inmates at Oakdale who didn't belong there. One was a cardiologist who I felt had been wrongfully convicted of Medicaid fraud. Mostly I knew good people, people who loved their wives and children, who wanted to do an honest day's work. Few were there for violent crimes or anything that justified years of imprisonment.

I made interesting friends. James Pumpelly played classical pieces on the chapel's old upright piano and read at least one book a day—not thrillers, but biographies or other nonfiction, or the classics. Jim brought me books like the biography of Margaret Fuller, the first female war correspondent for the precursor to the *New York Times*. He brought books he thought I should read or would enjoy.

Nick Collado had read every book ever published on trade and currency and kept track of every change in gold and oil. Nick also read interesting writers from Hunter Thompson to Mark Twain. Nick convinced me to buy an MP3 player on sale at the prison commissary and afterward recommended music he knew I'd enjoy. He helped me write to the Library of Congress, to President Obama, and the director of the Federal Bureau of Prisons urging them to allow prisoners to access free online courses offered by prestigious universities. No response, of course.

Steve Jamieson, a bright PR guy, was very supportive of my telling this story. Steve was approached by the FBI. Sequestered, Steve was accused of being a part of a multi-million-dollar telephone scam. He was scared and requested a call to a lawyer. He tried calling, but his lawyer didn't answer right away. By the time the lawyer called him back, Steve had been questioned for hours until he agreed to enter a plea deal. He was sentenced to prison based on what the FBI said Steve had said during the interrogation, while Steve had no lawyer to protect him. Steve went to prison; the CEO fled the country.

My inmate friends, Kenny, Steve, James, and Nick should never have been in prison.

Some prisoners have nicknames. When I first arrived in 2007, Louisiana's

Governor Edwards was "Governor" and I was G-2. Now, Governor Edwards had been released—in January 2011, after serving eight years—so I was either "Gov" or "Governor." Most inmates had a nickname: Dice, Ace, Deuce, FoFo (short for four-four), and Seven. There was World, Curly, Whisper, Big Phil, Doogie, Rico, Scrap, Cut, Shorty, Panda. The nicknames were memorable and endless.

Along with creative nicknames came crazy sounds. One inmate liked to imitate a screeching cat, another a cooing dove, and one whistled like Curly of the Three Stooges. Some sounds may have arisen from mental illness.

Voices were often raised. Many inmates thought the louder they talked, the more likely their views were to prevail. Topics were most often sports, such as how the Saints should have run the ball or how the Cowboys should have caught the pass. When Governor Edwards was an inmate, I kept quiet whenever LSU played Alabama. Now, with Edwards gone, I bellowed "Roll Tide" when appropriate.

Life skills were in short supply so sometimes I would open doors and hold them for others. Now and then I saw someone catching on.

CHAPTER 71

PRISON GUARD CRUELTY, SAVING LEROY

One of my best friends at Oakdale staggered into camp in the summer of 2015, a frail, half-starved mutt who weighed about forty pounds.

Many of us were drawn to him and his plight. Someone, probably one of the Southern white boys, said he looked like a Leroy and the name stuck. We fed and bathed the poor guy. He would stay for a while, wander off, then come back. One morning he looked as if he'd been in a fight with a fierce raccoon. His face had been bitten from his left eye to his mouth. His ear was bleeding and I feared he would lose the sight in his left eye. He looked all but dead.

We nursed and loved him back to health. I put antibiotic cream on his wounds and started feeding him every day. Others pitched in. Soon I was saving the food I rarely ate for Leroy—potatoes, chicken, hamburgers, pasta, and hotdogs. At breakfast, guys would feed him doughnuts.

After a couple of months, Leroy's ribs weren't showing. Once he'd been fed decently, cleaned up, and had recovered from his wounds, he was a handsome fellow, white with brown splotches, brown ears, and the body of a very large Basset hound, or close to it.

Leroy was a gentle companion. We had a tomcat called Bob who grew up at Oakdale. He and Leroy were curious about each other. Leroy would wag his tail at Bob cautiously, then go back to whatever he was doing. The tomcat was more dangerous than Leroy.

But prison can be hard on animals as well as on people.

Back in 2007, I saw a correctional officer named Williams, who we called "Showtime" because of his ego, viciously kick a pregnant beagle who had made the camp her refuge. Animal cruelty can lead to inmate brutality and shouldn't be tolerated. When I was lieutenant governor I had a law passed, the "Gucci Act," which made animal cruelty a felony. I had hoped this guard had retired, but soon it was "Showtime" again.

He came in at night for what was supposed to be a routine check but he was blasting his radio so everyone was rudely awakened. He went from bunk to bunk shining his three-Mag flashlight in each inmate's eyes, and he tore down anything hanging from a bunk to shield sleepers from unwanted light. Most COs did the night checks quietly and pointed their flashlights at the floor.

I saw Williams the next morning and when he saw Leroy, he yelled, "I ought to kick that dog in his f---ing head."

I filed a formal complaint against Williams, based on him kicking the pregnant beagle. When confronted by the camp counselor, Williams denied it all. Then he went into the kitchen and screamed, "Who was the inmate who wrote me up? I'm coming back here and tear this place up." He did come back one night and tear the place up, threatening an eighty-six-year-old inmate, whose crime was wanting to use the restroom; Williams broke the man's reading light on the floor.

Wardens came and went at Oakdale, but many of the guards were there until they retired. Many COs were decent people who lived in or near Oakdale and had family members who had worked at the prison camp. But a few were thugs or simply crazy COs we had to be careful around.

Williams was one of the crazy ones. He was not liked or respected by the other guards. He was a sick bastard who used his authority to bully inmates. I had to draw attention to this dangerous, violent man.

The warden declared, "Get rid of these animals." Two cages were brought in and several pets taken. Leroy ran and escaped. They said, "We'll come back for that one."

The guards would take the animals to the Oakdale city pound, where dogs were given one week or so, then put to sleep if no one claimed or adopted them.

I reunited in 2017 with Leroy, the hound who also found his way to freedom, now at his forever home in south Alabama.

I was determined to save Leroy. I spoke with my friend Carolyn Haines, an animal lover and respected fiction writer living in south Alabama. She agreed to keep Leroy. Carolyn and Barbara Tarburton, my friend from Minnesota, joined forces. Barbara, a retired airline employee, had helped American families adopt children from Asia. She flew with the children to the states if new families couldn't afford the trip. Barbara agreed to fly from Minnesota to Mobile, meet up with Carolyn, and drive to Oakdale to transport Leroy to Carolyn's farm.

The night before Leroy was to leave, three of us gave him a six-hand bath and re-bath. Between his toes and under elbows, everywhere. He was such a calm dog, he just stood and enjoyed the experience. We hand-picked every visible flea. There were no ticks. He would still need the Frontline flea treatment between his shoulders but he was cleaner than any dog west of Alabama and was towel-dried after shaking and spraying bath water on three nearby inmates. Everybody wanted to feed him because they knew it was his last supper in prison. I then took him out for a late-night walk.

After much planning, Leroy was ready to start the trip to his new home in rural Alabama. Amid fierce rain from a hurricane brewing in the Gulf of Mexico, and after just a few hours of sleep, Barbara arrived to pick up Leroy. Two inmates brought Leroy prancing through the hallway of the dorm out the front door. He was wagging his tail and seemingly smiling as Barbara helped him into the back of the rented van for the long drive to Semmes, Alabama, where Carolyn lives with her family of rescued cats, dogs and horses. Leroy enjoys his freedom to this day.

CHAPTER 72

SAVING INMATE GARCIA

I began to discover inmates with legal problems and others discovered me. I would call my son and ask him to do research to help. Someone would need a petition to the appellate court for a reduction of sentence, a petition to the Supreme Court, a quickie divorce, a claim for damages. One inmate had paid his lawyer for a polygraph test which never happened. I drafted a letter to his lawyer demanding a return of the inmate's $1,000, with a copy to the Louisiana Bar Association. A check came quickly.

One prisoner, Gavin, was arrested while he was living in a house on his mother's farm. He was charged in a drug conspiracy. The Sheriff seized a pistol from his nightstand and all of his father's and grandfather's firearms. The sheriff had also seized his mother's farm, home, and farming equipment. I constructed a motion for discovery to get his mother's property back and to find out what had happened to the property and the antique firearms. Some of the firearms were missing, but she got back her house, property and most of her farm equipment.

Defendants were often hammered at sentencing. Gavin, a first-time nonviolent offender, had four years added to his sentence for the handgun found at his home, even though it was legally purchased, not used in the commission of a crime, not charged in the indictment, and not raised at trial. Gavin was sentenced to fourteen years and wasn't eligible for a reduction in his sentence because of the gun charge.

First-time offenders were sometimes given additional time for exercising their constitutional right to testify on their own behalf. If they pleaded not guilty and testified on their own behalf but were convicted, judges rationalized that this constituted perjury or obstruction of justice because the jury had not believed the testimony.

One first-time offender, Sonny Breckenridge, was charged in a drug conspiracy. At the time of his arrest, he had eleven dollars to his name, lived in a duplex, and drove a leased truck. He pled not guilty and testified to deny the charges. He was convicted. Additional time was added for perjury, and he was sentenced to life plus twenty-five years for conspiracy to possess with the intent to distribute crack and marijuana. He was twenty-six years old. He had no crack or marijuana, no money, and no possessions of any value. What he had was a bag of seeds in his truck. The U.S. attorney charged he had "marijuana in his personal vehicle." A friend of Sonny's used the Freedom of Information Act to procure the DEA lab report on the bag of seeds found in Sonny's truck. The lab report read, "Not a controlled substance." Unbelievable! The prosecutors knew all along that it was not marijuana. I helped Sonny construct a motion for a reduction in sentence. He was released at the age of forty-two and now plans to marry his high school sweetheart, who was waiting for him.

Juan Garcia was given twenty-five years as a "career criminal" for three felony charges. Juan slept above me for a while and we became friends. I asked why he was in. He replied, "Marijuana." I asked Juan if he had applied to have his sentence commuted. He hadn't, so I went to work. I read every legal document he had. One conviction in 1994, "½ oz. or more of marijuana," probation; 1997, "½ oz. or more of marijuana," probation; 1999, a conspiracy involving marijuana, no amount specified. I prepared his application for President Obama to commute his sentence. He was released after nineteen years. So many of those I tried to help remained in prison, but here was a clear victory.

Marquel Riley, known as "Seven," was about six feet seven and powerfully built. He might have played professional ball, but instead, at the age of twenty-five, he was sentenced to twenty-seven years in prison. Marquel was a gentle man, kind, and generous. He didn't want to tell me his story at first, but he did over time. He had started selling pot to pay his mother's water and electric bills. He didn't come out and say but I knew his mother had problems of her own. He was put on probation at the age seventeen for marijuana, and again on probation at twenty-one.

When Marquel was twenty-three, a few grams of cocaine were found at his house, and he was charged with conspiracy to distribute crack. Government witnesses with long felony records testified they had bought drugs from Marquel, no doubt in exchange for lighter sentences. These are called "ghost drugs" by inmates. Drugs that never existed. No video tapes or paper trails, just felons giving false testimony for a lighter sentence. At twenty-five, Marquel had four children under eight years old when he went in. He finally got out at age forty-two.

Inmates told about lies that put them in prison. I met inmates who had been sentenced to ten years or more on their first federal drug charge. Many prosecutors would close their eyes to perjury, or even encourage it, to rack up more convictions.

Why are drug treatment programs not court-ordered for first time nonviolent drug offenders? Who thinks prison is a substitute for drug treatment? Why not drug treatment first?

CHAPTER 73

GOVERNMENT WITNESS CONFESSES LIES

There is not much difference in "ghost drugs" and a "ghost bribery" charge. They both come about by the government encouraging a felon to lie in exchange for a lighter sentence. Nick Bailey's deal with the devil was easy to figure out: Say what the government wants and they'll recommend "No time in prison." He did what they pressured him to do and they held up their end of the deal. He went free after a few months. He didn't care about hurting my family, causing them insufferable pain, ruining my career, or hurting the children and working families I could've helped as governor. He cared only about himself.

I am lucky to have a devoted daughter and son. In October 2012, Joseph asked the government's key witness, Nick Bailey, to meet for coffee. At the time, I wanted to get Bailey to go on CBS *60 Minutes* to amplify in person what he had told their reporter off camera in the segment that ran on my birthday, February 24, 2008.

"Is my dad really a criminal?" Joseph asked. "Did he solicit a bribe from Scrushy?"

"No. There was no agreement . . . Richard didn't get his appointment because he gave money . . . I know your dad. He can't be bought, he can't be bribed. It never happened that way."

"Then how did my dad get convicted?"

"Because of bullshit testimony from somebody like me. And he didn't have a fair judge or jury."

Joseph asked if Nick would consult with Doug Jones, formerly my lawyer, and later elected as Alabama's junior U.S. senator. I was so disappointed. Instead of representing my best interests, Doug Jones was looking out for Nick Bailey's. Doug said, "If Bailey recants, he could be prosecuted for perjury." Doug had put aside that it was Bailey's "bullshit testimony" that sent me to prison. Bailey agreed to talk to Doug, but Doug advised him not to go on *60 Minutes*.

Bailey would admit his perjury in private, but not in court or on camera. Joseph told me, "Dad, Nick is weak. He's not going to come forward with the truth."

My career was destroyed, my life's savings spent for lawyers, my family tortured, and I went to prison. By the way, as of this writing in May 2019, I've been under government supervision for nearly thirteen years. Bailey is living in Puerto Rico.

At least I knew for certain that the government's star witness had lied in exchange for favors from the prosecutors. We knew that the prosecutors and Jeff Sessions's retired FBI agents had pressured Bailey to lie and coached him on what to say to convict me of something they knew damn well had never happened. So much for their oath to seek truth and justice.

CHAPTER 74

MY JUDGE'S SEX, DRUGS, DOMESTIC VIOLENCE

Good news is rare in prison but some karmic news arrived in August of 2014. Mark Everett Fuller, my trial judge, was arrested in Atlanta. A woman pleading for help called 911. When police arrived at a suite in the Ritz-Carlton Hotel, they found broken glass, the smell of alcohol, blood on the floor, and a beaten woman. She was Fuller's second wife, Kelly, who told police, "He kept hitting me, beating me, kicking me as he dragged me around by my hair."

Her son, staying in a different room in the hotel, told police, "This wasn't the first time this has happened."

After the Fulton County prosecutor went easy on Fuller, Les and I worked on a draft complaint, requesting that Fuller be investigated. Congresswoman Terri Sewell agreed to push for Fuller's impeachment. The draft complaint was strengthened by Les, Joseph, and by female supporters: Barbara Turburton,

Diane Alvis, Pam Miles, Sharron Williams, and Anita Darden. The women took charge and filed it with the Eleventh Circuit Court of Appeals.

Following his arrest, Fuller's docket in the Middle District of Alabama was assigned to U.S. District Court Judge Clay Land of Georgia, who then became my judge. Les told me Judge Land was said to be fair-minded. We hoped his arrival might somehow help my appeal.

The authorities in Atlanta gave Fuller a break, because he lied and said it was just a domestic disagreement. He wasn't charged with felonious assault, he'd serve no jail time, spend no money on lawyers, and he would have no record. He was just required to complete an anger management class of sorts. Any other coward who viciously beat his wife would have been charged with a felony and been sent to prison. We have two systems of justice. Judge Fuller was allowed to resign, keep his pension, and return to his all-white country club to play golf and drink scotch with his pals. Justice? Not hardly.

More allegations came from Fuller's first wife, Lisa Boyd Fuller, who said he abused her, had an affair with his court clerk, and was addicted to prescription drugs and alcohol.

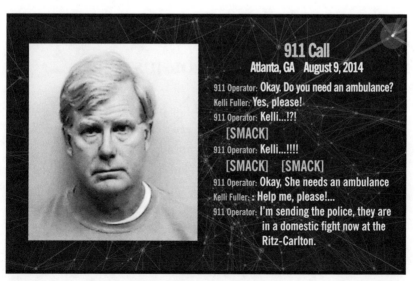

Mark Everett Fuller, arrested after at least eight violent assaults against his wife. (Courtesy Peppertree Films)

The U.S. Judicial Conference certified to the Speaker of the U.S. House of Representatives that it had "substantial evidence" for a "determination of impeachment" of Judge Fuller. "[A]long with a finding of perjury," the Judicial Conference determined that Fuller had "physically abused Kelly Fuller at least eight times" and that he "hit, kicked, and punched Kelly Fuller."

Fuller wasn't impeached. He had been a judge since President George W. Bush appointed him in 2002. His appointment had been a gift from U.S. Senator Jeff Sessions and Karl Rove for his years of Republican activism and disdain for me, not to any legal distinction. However, Mark Everett Fuller went from being "Siegelman's hanging judge" to "the wife-beating judge."

In the aftermath of Fuller's disgrace, newspapers reported his affair with a court employee. The affair was said to have lasted for several years and to have been common knowledge in the courthouse. The woman, who had two children, eventually divorced her husband. Lawyers pointed out that Fuller could have been blackmailed about the affair and should not have been serving as my judge. At least drunkenness and wife-beating had finally ended his power over the lives of others.

CHAPTER 75

GREG CRAIG'S QUEST FOR JUSTICE

My appeals continued. Greg Craig had successfully defended Bill Clinton when he faced impeachment and had been President Obama's first White House Counsel. To have him handling my appeal gave me hope. Greg was preparing for oral argument before the judge who had replaced Fuller. A hearing was set for December 14, 2014.

Greg said, "Don, all we have left is our plea for discovery, to prove that your prosecutor, who was conflicted because her husband was running your opponent's campaign, stayed involved though she was supposed to have had nothing to do with your prosecution. We have Tamarah Grimes saying Canary stayed involved and sent the email suggesting a 'gag' order."

The goal of the discovery process was to force the prosecution to hand over emails and other documents that would prove Leura Canary had stayed involved in my case. Hopefully, this would be enough for my new judge to order a new trial, a fair one, one in which I would testify.

Greg added, "We'll have a chance with this new judge. He has ordered your appearance in court. I've asked the judge and warden to allow us to pick you up and have you back at the camp within twenty-four hours."

Acting U.S. Attorney Louis Franklin objected. The warden of Oakdale denied our request. They had a better idea.

FORTY-NINE DAYS IN SOLITARY

I would be transported from Oakdale to Montgomery, Alabama, by U.S. marshals. I rode in buses, planes, and vehicles for several thousand miles in a journey that could have been made in six and a half hours. Instead, it took more than a month. This was senseless except as additional punishment for my seeking justice. It was the "diesel therapy" that Susan James had warned me about.

It was a long, painful, and cruel process during which I was chained, handcuffed, and shackled. My trip began by way of a bus from Oakdale to Oklahoma, 545 miles, then by plane to Jacksonville, Florida; then by bus to the prison in Atlanta, another 347 miles.

In Atlanta I was taken to a private prison, given a cold hot dog, and put into solitary confinement. After a few days, I was visited by Greg and my new appellate counsel, Clifford Sloan, a former assistant White House counsel to President Clinton. I liked Cliff immediately. I was exhausted, but their visit cheered me.

A few more days passed before two guards drove me from Atlanta to the federal courthouse in Montgomery, another 161 miles. I slept in the back of the van, handcuffed, chained, and shackled. During the drive to Montgomery, the marshals "forgot" my meal. At the federal courthouse in Montgomery, where I was tried in 2006, I was locked in a cell, then transferred by van to the Montgomery County Jail. There I was placed in a medical holding cell where the lights stayed on twenty-four hours a day. A young inmate recognized me and slid a book under his cell door. A guard kicked it back at him. Later the CO delivered the book, a Bible. I was immensely grateful for his kindness. During my ordeal, I would read the Bible several times a day between my pushups. I focused on the Old Testament and every word attributed to Jesus. I like history.

I was in solitary confinement again, to await the hearing on December 14th. I knew there was little chance I'd make it back to Oakdale before Christmas.

Not only were the lights in my cell on twenty-four hours a day, but I wasn't allowed outside for recreation, nor allowed to shave. At least I was given food. Bad food, but food.

By the time of the oral argument, I had dark circles around my eyes and a two-week growth of stubble. I shuffled into court, cuffed, and shackled, wearing a reddish-orange prison jumpsuit. Greg asked that my handcuffs be removed. Judge Land said it was fine if it was okay with Louis Franklin, the prosecutor. Greg's request angered Franklin. It was as if a mass murderer had demanded a gun. My cuffs stayed on. This was the Louis Franklin who was described in *Atticus v. The Architect* as someone who prosecuted with a chip on his shoulder. He was the figurehead leader of my prosecution, but he had lots of help. Leura Canary was supposed to be recused, but she was continuing to direct him, meet with him daily, and even write press statements for him.

Greg's argument for discovery made sense. The prosecutors made inane arguments about why a search for evidence of prosecutorial misconduct would unduly burden American justice. Judge Land professed to favor our argument.

After the hearing, I was returned to solitary in the Montgomery County jail. Two weeks later, Judge Land denied discovery, although he seemed to think we were entitled to it. He said we were in an impossible position. The evidence we needed to get a new trial was in the hands of the prosecutors, who were not legally required to let us see it. Because he believed the Eleventh Circuit Court of Appeals would deny discovery, he denied our motion.

Weeks later, I was still in solitary confinement in Montgomery, until Susan James asked the court why I remained there. The next day, I was driven to Atlanta in a thirty-two-passenger bus with three guards. I was the only passenger. Our government is so wasteful, I thought.

I was in solitary in Atlanta for several days, then driven by bus to the airport. I was chained, shackled, and handcuffed for the flight to Oklahoma City. Put back in solitary. Eventually, I was flown by a circuitous route to Lake Charles, Louisiana, and put on a bus to Oakdale prison camp.

The ordeal ended after forty-nine days and an estimated 4,500 miles. The entire time, I was either chained, handcuffed, or shackled, and was in transport or solitary confinement. Cruel but not unusual punishment, and very expensive. It should be illegal, but in fact it's common.

The endless travel, being shackled, purposefully disoriented, cut off from human contact, was an insidious form of torture. Sometimes, confused and exhausted, I tried to remember what my "crime" had been. It seemed to have something to do with having won elections against Republicans and trying to help all children get a better education.

The point of "diesel therapy" is that it both discourages inmates from appealing their cases and enables wardens and prosecutors to inflict extra punishment on troublemakers who persist with an appeal—people like me who fight for justice. What do they care how much all that travel and overtime pay for guards cost taxpayers? They obviously didn't care about my pain and suffering, nor did they mind wasting tens of thousands of dollars. It should have been a one-day trip that my lawyers offered to pay for. It's amazing how inhumane prosecutors and prison officials can be, as they dispense their twisted version of justice.

I reentered Oakdale bearded and haggard, greeted by laughs, jeers, and warm greetings from other inmates who had survived similar ordeals.

APPEALS COURT, ONE LAST CHANCE TO GET THE LAW RIGHT

Despite the setbacks, Greg Craig and my son remained determined to persuade the Eleventh Circuit to overrule Judge Land. We had to force the government to let us see the documents. The documents would expose the U.S. attorney and her husband's political motives and improper involvement in my case.

Clifford Sloan, Greg's partner at the prestigious law firm of Skadden, Arps, Slate, Meagher and Flom, had to be recognized even by these old conservative Republican judges. Cliff called on the Eleventh Circuit to make the government play fair, to turn over the documents, and "let the sun shine in."

I had a call from Greg and Cliff. "We thought we had a chance," they said, "but the Eleventh Circuit just wouldn't go there." My heart sank to the lowest point ever. I just knew the Eleventh Circuit would have to agree to what "Skadden" was saying. Instead, they denied our motion for discovery.

Greg added, "We want to petition the Supreme Court on the issue of acquitted conduct. Fuller tripled your sentencing guideline range based on acquitted conduct. We think we have a chance for *certiorari* to be granted. We believe it's worth a try." Now, I was so grateful for Greg's belief in my case, my heart lifted.

BACK TO THE SUPREME COURT

Although we had lost our fight for discovery, my spirits were lifted. If we could win on the issue of the unconstitutionality of adding years to a sentence based on acquitted conduct, it would, in part, exonerate me. More importantly, it would help countless other inmates who have been given additional years in prison on charges for which their jury had acquitted them. What a blessing to have lawyers who wouldn't give up fighting for justice.

With 113 former state attorneys general on board as amici, the Constitution Project filing an amicus brief, Skadden lawyers and my son representing me, we were returning to the Supreme Court on the question of acquitted conduct. We were asking whether my Sixth Amendment right to a fair trial was violated when Judge Fuller tripled the federal guidelines length of my sentence based on the RICO charges, for which the jury found me not guilty!

The Solicitor General, speaking for President Obama, argued that judges should have the right to impose prison time for such charges. How can our Supreme Court allow it? It's so blatantly wrong. But the Court denied our petition "without comment." I was bewildered.

JUSTICE GONE WILD

As a prisoner, far more than when I was a lawyer and attorney general, my eyes were opened to the reality of prosecutors who will do anything for a conviction. Suborned testimony, evidence withheld, felons "pressured and cajoled" to lie—all are commonplace. Vindictive or politicized judges, dishonesty that leads to pointless imprisonment, and people not reasonably punished but crushed—all work to destroy our democracy. When people lose faith in our system of laws, our democracy is threatened.

CHAPTER 76

MY PRISON ADMINISTRATIVE ASSISTANT

I wrote to law professors, members of Congress, journalists, and anyone else who might take an interest in my case. One day I was blessed by a letter from a woman in Seattle. Barbara Tarburton, who helped rescue Leroy, was sixty-plus years of age. She became a supporter after hearing me on Thom Hartmann's radio show in 2008. She told me there were many people who wanted to see justice in my case.

Barbara began doing research, getting my letters individualized and delivered for me. I sent letters via prison "email" that she would print, sign for me, and send. Sometimes Barbara personally delivered my letters to members of Congress or the media. She had retired from Northwest Airlines and could travel cheaply to Washington and to see me in Oakdale. "It's more impressive if I give them the letter personally," she said.

Soon we agreed that Barbara should have a title.

"I'll be your AA," she said. "Administrative Assistant."

"No," I say, "You're my PAA."

"What's that?" she asks.

"My Prison Administrative Assistant."

With me in Oakdale, Barbara and I laughed a lot, spoke regularly, wrote and emailed multiple times a day. She made it possible for me to communicate with more people faster.

Barbara did work that I couldn't have asked Dana or Joseph to do. They, along with Les and Chip, were already overloaded. Nothing was done or would be done about my 2002 election being stolen or the $20 million in dark money that was used by Karl Rove's friends to defeat me. So, we alerted members of Congress and all presidential candidates of the dangers the ruling in my case presented to candidates for any office and their donors. Can a political campaign contribution be prosecuted as a bribe? One was in my case. The campaign contribution was to a referendum not even to my campaign. There was no quid pro quo. I received no financial benefit. Yet the contribution, to establish funding for public education, sent me to prison. The decision in my case was a trap for the unwary.

CHAPTER 77

WARNING SENATORS MENENDEZ & SHELBY

Soon there were others being charged for similar but seemingly more egregious acts. Virginia's Governor Bob McDonnell and U.S. Senator Bob Menendez were two. Both, unlike me, had benefited personally by accepting personal gifts as well as personal campaign contributions. The question for them was how would their judge instruct the jury. Would they use the law as dictated by the U.S. Supreme Court in the 1991 McCormick case which required an explicit, asserted quid pro quo? Or would their judge use the standard invented by my judge allowing the jury to convict if they could imply a Quid Pro Quo. I wrote Menendez on May 31, 2015, giving him a heads up on the law, as I had Dick Shelby back in 2006.

Dear Senator,

I'm writing to lift your spirits.

You can take some solace knowing that if you go to prison, it may signify a tipping point for all Members of Congress. You can smile, thinking to yourself, "They'll all go to jail! And the President may be next." As the former Dean of Rutgers Law School, John Farmer, Jr., put it in his column in the *New Jersey Star-Ledger*, February 22, 2014: "What Governor Siegelman did was far less egregious than President Obama appointing contributors as ambassadors."

Senator, soon after I was convicted in 2006, I came to Washington to meet with your colleague, Alabama Senator Richard Shelby. Senator Shelby as you may know is notorious for raising bundles of campaign cash from donors seeking his vote or influence. I told Senator Shelby, "Think about it Dick . . . If they can send me to prison for what I did, they can execute you!"

I am however sending you some "good news" by way of my recent "Letter to The Editor" of the *WSJ*, 5/29/15, "You don't need a quid pro quo to wind up in prison."

The "good news" is that your "bribery" charges may not stick. The U.S. Supreme Court, in their last case defining "bribery" in a campaign contribution setting, said that campaign contributions evoke First Amendment protections. Therefore, to cross the line from politics to crime there must be an "explicit" quid pro quo, where the terms of the agreement are "asserted." (McCormick Case, 1991) From what is known of your case, an "explicit" quid pro quo doesn't appear to exist.

But then, here is some "bad news." Well, at least, bad news for me because I'm in prison for "bribery" based on a campaign contribution where there was no testimony of a quid pro quo, much less an "explicit" one that was "asserted."

To give your lawyers (and perhaps the Clintons') even more to chew on, there was no allegation of self-enrichment, no personal gain or personal benefit. The contribution wasn't even to my campaign.

The campaign contribution that sent me to prison was to the Alabama Education Foundation supporting a state referendum to benefit public education. The donor, a Fortune 500 CEO, had supported my opponent, and had never contributed to my campaign.

The "official" action? I re-appointed the CEO to a nonpaying board to which he had been appointed by three previous governors. I was the 4th governor to appoint him to the same board. I did nothing else to benefit the CEO, who got five years.

I had two "hung" juries that refused to convict . . . until the judge emphasized that they could convict by "inferring" or "implying" an agreement. My lawyers objected to the jury instructions because the Circuit Court of Appeals had previously adhered to the McCormick standard requiring an "explicit" agreement. The trial judge and the Circuit Court abandoned the McCormick standard and sent me straight to jail.

Just a word of warning: While my case is an anomaly in American Jurisprudence, it is nonetheless legal precedent and can be used against you or against any Member of Congress who votes in favor of a donor's interests.

Don E. Siegelman

Barbara had become my partner in my fight for criminal justice reform. Barbara, who moved from Seattle back to her family farm in Eagan, Minnesota, continued to work tirelessly on our projects. In 2015, I wrote a "treatise" entitled *A 2016 Presidential Primer on Criminal Justice Reform*. Barbara had it printed and got it into the hands of those we thought would care. I wrote letters to journalists, law professors, TV talking heads, and members of Congress. Two of my articles were published. One, on May 29, 2015, by the *Wall Street Journal*, "You Don't Have to Have a Quid Pro Quo to Wind Up in Prison," and another, on March 31, 2016, in the *Washington Post*, "How to Prevent Prosecutorial Misconduct."

In the *Primer*, I quote President Obama's Solicitor General, Elena Kagan, who declared to the Supreme Court in 2010: "U.S. citizens do not have a constitutional right not to be framed." That astonishing pronouncement came in the case of two black men who spent twenty-five years in prison for a crime they didn't commit.

CHAPTER 78

CONGRESS TALKS OF JUSTICE REFORM

Charles Koch, the conservative billionaire, not known for his compassion for inmates, had written in *Politico*, January 7, 2015, a rather bold "five-step approach to criminal justice reform" calling on Congress to make changes. I took this as a sign something could actually happen in Congress!

On February 5, 2015, less than a month later, Senator Orrin Hatch was published in the *Wall Street Journal* on the need for criminal justice reform. I immediately wrote Senator Hatch by way of Barbara Tarburton and sent copies to members of the House and Senate judiciary committees. Koch had given cover to timid Republicans and had emboldened Democrats, like Congressman Bobby Scott, to step forward. Even House Speaker John Boehner, on July 16, 2015, joined in. There was hope.

Dear Senator Hatch,

I applaud your commitment to criminal justice expressed in the *Wall Street Journal*: "Feds Criminalize Things That Aren't Crimes." Thank you for standing firm. Our justice system is broken. The Department of Justice and prosecutors will fight any change that makes convictions or guilty pleas something they actually have to work to prove.

Today, federal prosecutors get 99% of the indictments they seek, 97% plead guilty, about 60% before they get a lawyer. Of the 3% that go to trial, prison time is added for perjury or obstruction of justice if you testify on your own behalf and are found guilty. Plus prison time is frequently added for charges for which a jury found you not guilty, "acquitted conduct."

There are only two elements needed for a conviction: one is mens rea, criminal intent, the other an "unlawful act," a crime. The Department of Justice doesn't want to have to prove either element, that's why they gravitate to charges like "mail and wire fraud," "conspiracy" or "honest services fraud." They don't have to actually prove that a crime was committed. It's so nebulous, even legal scholars, like Justice Scalia, can't give a definition of honest services violations.

If that isn't enough, the government engages in "stings," using felons as paid informants to induce crimes promising a recommendation of "no time in prison" in exchange for the felon's testimony.

It's common for prosecutors to use felons to "frame" someone whom the prosecutor deems is a bad actor. Even President Obama's U.S. Solicitor General, now Justice Kagan, argued to the U. S. Supreme Court in 2010, that: "U.S. Citizens do not have a constitutional right not to be framed." (See *Los Angeles Times*, January 5, 2010, David Savage, legal correspondent)

How much more can the deck be stacked?

In the interest of full disclosure, I was sentenced to 88 months in prison in 2007 for something that 113 former state Attorneys General (including Utah's) said was not a crime. My trial judge and the 11th Circuit determined that a campaign contribution to a state ballot initiative referendum to benefit public education could be a "bribe," even without a self-enrichment scheme and even though I did not benefit by a single penny. Moreover, there was no testimony of a "quid pro quo," much less an express one. The court's instructions allowed a conviction if the jury could "imply" or "infer" an agreement, a dangerous oxymoron. (See attached: WSJ article, George Will's Washington Post column, and CBS 60 Minutes, 2/24/08)

Senator, please keep the momentum for criminal justice reform going. Your insistence on requiring criminal intent, before one can be convicted, will be the most significant step toward balancing the scales of justice since the Magna Carta.

Thank you for standing firm for justice. With every best wish for success, I am

Don E. Siegelman

On October 15, 2015, I called my friend Thom Hartmann's radio show, and talked about the need for criminal justice reform. The SAFE Justice Act was making its way through the House Judiciary Committee, and I was asking listeners to call their members of Congress.

"Something is wrong with our justice system when the president's own lawyer, the solicitor general, tells the U.S. Supreme Court that 'U.S. Citizens do not have a constitutional right not to be framed.'"

"Siegelman, get off the phone," a prison official ordered.

"I'm being told I have to hang up." Click. I was told to stand there and I did.

The unit manager and a guard arrived, outraged, saying I had disobeyed FBOP policy. "You knew better!" she exclaimed.

The guard brandished handcuffs. "Hands behind your back."

CHAPTER 79

FREEDOM OF SPEECH SUSPENDED

I was taken to a cell in the Special Housing Unit—solitary confinement. I knew what was coming. I just didn't know for how long.

Working through Barbara, Les, with Sharron Williams pushing Facebook messages, and my "webmaster," Anita Darden, I nonetheless on January 15, 2016, spoke out from solitary confinement, knowing the risks.

My Friends,

I was hand cuffed, chained and shackled. I'm being punished for speaking to the media.

They have tried to silence me, they do not want my story told. I continued to speak out even from solitary confinement: helping other inmates, encouraging Congress to take up criminal justice reform, and partnering with highly talented artists producing a documentary exposing the political motives of my prosecution. We have filed a complaint in federal court to expose political motivation and misconduct, and we are actively seeking a pardon.

I will never quit. I will not give in. I refuse to be silenced.

The documentary "Atticus v. the Architect" hits Karl Rove and exposes the raw political truth underlying my prosecution; it will stir questions about Karl Rove and the abuse of power. Now more than ever, I need you to help me fight for the truth, for our democracy, and for my freedom by giving what your heart compels.

Former Vice President of the United States, Al Gore said:

"Don Siegelman is not just fighting for his freedom-he is fighting for the integrity of our democracy. As Americans we have a responsibility to help preserve our democracy from those who would take advantage of it and abuse their power"

With deep personal appreciation, I am

Don E. Siegelman

Governor of Alabama, 1999–2003

I was excited. The documentary exposing links between Karl Rove and my prosecution was finally being readied. Not so exciting was the news my daughter was thinking of marrying.

Weeks went by. Solitary isn't always solitary when they're out of cells and have two inmates double up. That means sharing a small space with someone you'd just as soon not know. Or sometimes with someone who's okay. I had one entertaining cellmate. We did push-ups and played gin or poker. He showed me how to mark cards. My mind was often elsewhere. I was worried about Dana, my daughter. She was on and off with this guy. She had brought him to Oakdale saying she was in love and wanted my consent to marry him. I told her I was not the one to make that decision for her. If she thought he would make her happy for the rest of her life, then she had my consent. She added, "Daddy, I won't get married until you are out of prison."

Helpless in Prison

In prison, one seems helpless, and solitary makes it worse. The rules on solitary vary from prison to prison and guard to guard. You're supposed to have an hour of exercise every day, but that doesn't always happen. A CO can always find a corner of the bed untucked, your toothbrush out of place, or some lame excuse to deny you the hour of exercise. COs grow tired of having to go outside and watch prisoners exercise, so they find ways to cancel your one good hour a day.

There were no visitors in solitary except perhaps your lawyer. Mail was opened, read, then stapled shut and given to you. Paper and pencils were in short supply, so writing was difficult. The food was lousy and the extra food you could buy once a week was mostly candy bars, nothing nourishing.

So much is done in the real world while time stands still in prison. I thought about time differently. How my life was being taken. Wasted. With each passing hour, my time on earth was ticking away.

So many lives ruined. The Bureau of Prisons seems to place inmates as far as possible from their homes. I could have been put in a camp forty-five minutes from my home. Instead, Judge Fuller and my prosecutors made sure I was as far away from my family as possible. I was in prison nearly five hundred miles away, an eighteen-hour round trip. Inmates miss funerals, birthdays, anniversaries, graduations, Thanksgivings, and Christmases. In solitary, I missed my chance to object to my daughter's marriage. The distance and inconvenience destroyed relationships with spouses and children. I saw it every day. The longing to know sons and daughters, to be able to talk with them, to be part of children's lives added mental anguish to the ongoing punishment. A humane president could make one phone call to the FBOP and change this cruel policy.

Inmates could be placed as close as possible to their homes and families; instead all are shipped as far away as possible. A U.S. statute entitles inmates to fifty-four days off their sentences for each year that they have "good conduct," yet under Presidents Bush and Obama, inmates were not given full "Good Time" credit; a president could direct the FBOP to give inmates the full fifty-four days. More inmates could be directed to home confinement. The president could make an attitudinal shift telling U.S. attorneys that he repudiates the solicitor general's argument to the U.S. Supreme Court that "U.S. Citizens do not have a constitutional right not to be framed." A president could direct U.S. attorneys not to seek additional time for "Acquitted Conduct." Pretty basic. But presidents rarely worry about prisoners. Nevertheless, I wrote to President Obama telling him what he could do to improve the system, without a vote of Congress.

I wrote to the *Wall Street Journal* commending President Obama for his first grants of clemency to nonviolent offenders:

> What President Obama has done is to help spur a national dialogue on the need for criminal justice reform.
>
> One such reform is the SAFE Justice Act which adds "Good Time" credit to inmates who engage in work, programs to improve their lives, and maintain a clean record. The SAFE Justice Act could release many first time, nonviolent offenders earlier, freeing up prison space for offenders who do present a public safety risk. The SAFE Justice act will save taxpayers hundreds of millions of dollars each year.
>
> The good news for the country is that the President can accomplish much of the SAFE Justice act by executive order if Congress does not act.

After weeks in solitary confinement, I appeared before a disciplinary judge via Skype. I pointed out that published FBOP policy gave inmates the right to communicate with the media, that the FBOP approved the number I had called, and that I was not violating Bureau of Prisons policy.

"Nevertheless, I find that you disobeyed a staff member."

I knew they'd find a way to say I was at fault. No prisoner ever wins these legal arguments. Convicted again without breaking any rule. There was no use appealing. It would just extend my time in solitary and risk a punitive transfer to another prison.

PEPPERTREE FILMS PRESENTS

SPECIAL SCREENING

Atticus v. The Architect

The Political Assasination of Don Siegelman

Poster for the documentary film about my case. (Courtesy Cobb Theatres)

My crime was that I suggested changes in our criminal justice system and asked listeners to support a congressional proposal to reform criminal justice. It might embarrass higher-ups at the Bureau of Prisons. That's clearly something a prisoner should not do, even if he is a lawyer who, in theory, still possesses freedom of speech.

The isolation was painful but I knew it was just a game to them. I had spoken to a reporter. Before any inmate can make a call, the person and the phone number have to be approved. Thom Hartmann had been approved. A small pamphlet listing the responsibilities and rights of inmates specifically states that inmates may "communicate with the media." I knew they'd have to find some other excuse for sending me to "The Hole" and they did. All I did was speak the truth to a reporter.

At last, I was back at the prison camp.

A *Washington Post* INTERVIEW

Robert Barnes of the *Washington Post* wanted an interview. I wasn't about to give an interview and end up in solitary again. This time I went to my camp counselor for instructions. The reporter must make a request of the warden. Barnes could take notes but not record the interview and it must be over the phone. A prison official would listen in.

We had the interview on April 22, 2016. It was about a prison T-shirt I had bought from the Commissary and had auctioned online to raise money for the documentary about my case: *Atticus v. The Architect: The Political Assassination of Don Siegelman* by Steve Wimberly. The shirt netted $4,500!

Even though the interview had been approved, I was sent to solitary again. This time not for speaking to the media but for selling a T-shirt to raise money for the documentary exposing the corruption that brought me to prison.

BACK TO SOLITARY

My lawyers were notified by my son that I was in solitary. Greg Craig and Clifford Sloan wrote a blistering letter to the U.S. attorney general, citing my First Amendment rights and arguing that solitary had been unconstitutional punishment for what I said in the interview.

The Bureau of Prisons denied that I was there because of the *Post* interview but offered no other explanation. I was released after the *Post* wrote a follow-up story about my being in solitary. The rule of law didn't bother the people who put me in solitary, but the public exposure did.

ANOTHER DAY DOWN

"Another day down" is an expression by inmates that their sentence is decreasing, day by day.

Days to weeks to months to years. Inmates rejoice at the end of each day. I was over seventy years old; every day was precious. I was fifty-six when the false charges began. I often think about growing older in prison, the waste of lives and money.

Everyone knows when a month has passed or the seasons are about to change or his "out date" gets closer. It's hard because of the length of the sentences. It hurts me to think of all the young inmates being away from their families, homes, and children for so long. In so many cases, the punishment is needlessly cruel.

Every day in prison was one day closer to the end of my life.

Prisons are Human Warehouses

We know that prisons exist for warehousing, not rehabilitating. It's so sad to see men leave with nothing, no skills, and no way to earn a living.

Oakdale Federal Prison offered little in the way of education. Most inmates desperately needed help with social skills, life skills, language and job skills. There were no online courses and only one instructor for the 174 inmates in our dorm. The CO in charge tried to teach the basics to those who wanted to learn. All inmates were required to take "courses," mostly self-help manuals, to earn good-time credit which theoretically allowed inmates to leave earlier.

I told my new inmate buddy, Nick Colladdo, "I just saw Mr. Williams [an elderly black man]. We passed on my way to the Education trailer. He said, 'Governor, look what they gave me [displaying a stack of books]. They know I can't read.'"

Nick replied, "Bouteau and Guggi left yesterday. They've been in prison for a combined forty-five years and only worked as janitors while locked up. What chance do they have of making it?"

I added, "And Chappa left yesterday too. He'd been in for eleven years, and still couldn't read. It's pitiful."

It was all pitiful.

CHAPTER 80

TRUMP: SOUTHERN WHITE BOY'S CANDIDATE

With the 2016 presidential race taking shape, Nick Collado and I organized an in-house poll of inmates. Volunteers came forward for Hillary, Bernie, and Trump. No one wanted to work for Jeb, but many thought he and Hillary would emerge as the two nominees. The Oakdale prison poll put Bernie over Hillary among Democrats, with Trump a clear favorite for Republicans.

Trump's remarks about Mexicans shook me. Rapists, he said. I had worked closely with the Hispanic community as governor. They're good people. Will Trump ever stop his insults?

One inmate, Johnny, a quiet man about forty years old, a "Southern White Boy," and a fan of Fox News, said, "We finally have a candidate who represents us." He meant the white race. As the months passed, we could see Trump's support among white supremacists coalescing.

When I saw the rally with Jeff Sessions putting on his Trump campaign hat, I wrote a post for Free-Don.org reminding my friends of Jeff Sessions's racist past. Sessions, who was nominated for a federal judgeship by President Reagan, had been called out by Senator Teddy Kennedy for saying: "I used to think the Ku Klux Klan was a pretty good group of guys, until I learned they smoked pot." He was a strange little man, not known for his sense of humor. I had been in political and legal battles with Sessions dating back to when I was secretary of state. Even then he used race as a tool to win elections, to suppress the black vote in Alabama, and he had sent innocent African Americans to prison for his own political gain.

When Trump's reaction to the endorsement of David Duke, the "Grand Wizard" of the Louisiana KKK, wasn't an immediate rejection, and when he didn't back away from the Confederate flag in South Carolina, it was clear to me whose votes he was after. I had seen it all before with George Wallace. While the most ignorant and bigoted people in America supported him, there were many other rich, educated voters who thought Donald Trump should be president. Many conservative labor union members fell for Trump's BS about bringing back jobs that had been lost to international competition, or shifts in energy from coal to natural gas, just as they had fallen for Ronald Reagan.

When debate began over the Confederate flag in South Carolina in the summer of 2015, I wrote Governor Nikki Haley reminding her that when Governor Wallace raised the Confederate battle flag over the Alabama Capitol on April 25, 1963, it was five months later, September 15th, when the KKK laid dynamite outside the 16th Street Baptist Church killing four young girls.

Dear Governor Haley,

Like our nation, I grieve for those whose lives were taken. You have done the right thing by calling for the flag's removal. By doing so, you have lifted the national discourse and with it may come much needed healing.

While South Carolina has done remarkably well economically, think of what South Carolina will accomplish when THE flag comes down. The national business community will respond.

Alabama was much worse off than South Carolina. George Wallace was making his career off thumbing his nose at federal court orders and poking his finger in the eyes of Bobby and President Kennedy.

Because of George Wallace hoisting the Confederate battle flag with his defiant cry of "Segregation now, and Segregation forever," a green light was given to those prone to racial violence. Five months later, Sunday September 15th, 1963, a Ku Klux Klan dynamite bomb ripped through Birmingham's 16th Street Baptist Church killing four young girls.

Racially inspired murders, beatings of freedom riders, water cannons, clubs and ferocious police dogs used against children and "Bloody Sunday" in Selma, brought Alabama shame, and pushed Governor Wallace into the national spot light.

Wallace made it clear he would be the national voice for racial fear. He wanted votes. He was running for President of the United States. Donald Trump's unthinkable remarks about "Mexicans" in his announcement is just as dangerous and shameful as those of George Wallace, and made for the same reasons . . . votes. Americans must unequivocally reject this hate filled rhetoric.

Thank God, times have changed.

The Italian poet, Dante, teaches that "The hottest places in hell are reserved for those who in times of great moral crisis maintain their neutrality." You have acted in a time of moral crisis, and have cleared the way for debate by presidential candidates on the issues of race that still confounds our nation.

As Donald Trump bashed young immigrant children struggling, trudging hundreds of miles, risking their lives, separated from their parents, seeking a better life in America, I was troubled.

In prison, one might expect only self-pity, but seeing migrant children being turned away brought tears to my eyes. Our country's legacy, symbolized by the Statue of Liberty, is that of America saying: "Give me your tired, your poor, your huddled masses yearning to breathe free . . ." Yet America was now turning its back to those who would give up everything for a chance at a better life for their children. What I found most troubling was the silence of world leaders.

Trump & George Wallace, Two of a Kind

"Like peas and carrots," Forrest Gump might say.

Trump's support for those who attacked protestors at his campaign rallies only encouraged more confrontations. He kept finding new ways to pander to ignorance and racism. President Trump was using George Wallace's formula for getting conservative white voters at a new level.

I wrote about the 2016 Florida Presidential Primary comparing Trump to Alabama Governor George Wallace in his 1972 presidential campaign.

Here's how Hunter Thompson described the Wallace phenomenon in *Fear and Loathing on the Campaign Trail, 1972*:

> An opponent[of Wallace] denounces the winner of the Florida Primary as "a demagogue of the worst sort . . . a threat to the country's underlying values of humanism, decency, of progress."
>
> A [Wallace] fan sees it differently: "This guy is the real thing. I never cared about politics before, but [he] ain't the same as the others. He just comes right out and says it."
>
> A journalist: "There were no seats [at the Wallace rally] . . . everybody

was standing. The air was electric even before he started talking . . . He jerked this crowd around like he had them on wires. They were laughing, shouting, whacking each other on the back . . . .it was a flat-out fire and brimstone performance. The only one of the candidates this year who has broken every rule in the Traditional Politicians Handbook is George Wallace."

In 2016, from prison, I warned of Trump's similarities with Wallace.

George Wallace pulled off some amazing victories, first in Florida, then Michigan and Maryland. Wallace mounted a noisy rant but never became "presidential."

After his first big win in Florida, Wallace went to NASCAR at Daytona, spoke to nearly 100,000 flag waving (most likely confederate) fans with NASCAR driver Richard Petty, whose stamp of approval was worth as much as Bobby Knight's to Trump in Indiana.

Trump's ruthless attacks on the federal judge overseeing the law suit against "Trump U" is like Wallace's attacks on federal judge Frank M. Johnson who ruled against Alabama's legal positions in prisons, mental heath and civil rights. Wallace said he'd like to give the judge a "barbed wire enema."

Trump and Wallace excite the same base.

Times had changed, but not for the better. They had changed enough for DJT to get elected, largely using race, appealing to base nationalism, and with help from the Kremlin.

CHAPTER 81

MY END DATE APPROACHES

On January 27, 2017, the *Washington Post* reported that Justice Pryor was among the judges that the new president, Donald Trump, might consider to replace Justice Antonin Scalia on the Supreme Court. The *Post* noted that Pryor had defended Alabama's practice of handcuffing prison inmates to hitching posts in the hot sun if they refused to work on chain gangs. And that when the Supreme Court was considering sodomy laws Pryor filed an amicus brief arguing that "states should remain free to protect the moral standards of their communities through legislation that prohibits homosexual sodomy." He also called the court's *Roe v. Wade* decision, making abortion legal, "the worst abomination of constitutional law in our history."

Even knowing I might get sent back to solitary confinement, I had to speak out about Bill Pryor. I wrote a post for my "Free-Don" website:

Descent into the Bowels of Injustice

Evil and Pernicious Jurist To Replace Scalia, whose Pro Death Penalty & Pro-Life Stands Could Scare Pope Francis . . .

An involuntary scream came from my gut causing heads to turn as inmates also heard Bill Pryor's name drip from Trump's lips. Trump on Saturday night's Republican Presidential debate, named perhaps the most evil and pernicious jurist as Trump's choice to replace Supreme Court Justice Antonin Scalia. Bill Pryor is on the ultraconservative 11th Circuit Court of Appeals.

Bill Pryor has all the right credentials for a Right Wing nomination: an original member of the Federalist Society, an early supporter of the harshest mandatory minimums, Karl Rove's client, someone who started an investigation against me to damage my chances for reelection (and did). The presiding U.S. District Court Judge described the prosecution as "the most unfounded criminal case over which I have presided in my entire judicial career . . . totally without merit" [see letter to Eric Holder, May 9, 2009, by Judge U. W. Clemon]. The Department of Justice confirmed that Pryor's lead prosecutor "in charge of the Siegelman prosecution communicated directly with the campaign manager of Mr. Siegelman's gubernatorial opponent . . ." ["Project On Governmental Oversight," December 14, 2014]

Pryor is most frightening because of his closeness to Karl Rove and Jeffrey Beauregard Sessions.

Now, we now hear from Trump's own mouth that he has found the perfect possible replacement for Justice Scalia:

Bill Pryor, Sessions's creation, Karl Rove's client, a protector of corporate interests, a man who puts political prosecutions ahead of the truth and justice, an outlaw who orchestrated illegally certifying bogus elections results to ensure that Karl Rove's and Jack Abramoff's candidate for governor won in 2002, a Right Wing, "lock 'em up and throw away the key" blinded, fanatical anti-*Roe v. Wade* pro-life, a pro-death penalty Catholic. He is not an equal to fill Antonin Scalia's shoes.

The real danger is that Pryor is young and is just beginning his descent into the bowels of partisan injustice.

Jeff Sessions, who for his sins was tapped as Trump's new attorney general, had no doubt recommended his old partner in crime for Supreme Court consideration. However, the *Post* noted, "If his confirmation to the Eleventh Circuit is any indication, the judge is in for a lengthy battle if he is nominated by President Trump to the Supreme Court." As it turned out, Pryor was too dubious a candidate even for Trump.

LOSS OF FREEDOM—OPPRESSIVE IN ANY SEASON

The summers were hot and humid in the swamps of Louisiana. Green leaves, dried brown by Louisiana heat and drought, would fall. Later, Louisiana's mosquitoes would diminish as cooler fall air blew in from the north. Blue skies turned cloudy, a light drizzle drifted down. Seasons passed. A lone mockingbird sat on a telephone line, declaring a beautiful day. I had seen these same trees, and I swear I saw the same mockingbird, year after passing year.

My family and friends never stopped working to free me. Dana fought endlessly, day after day, year after year, through social media and media interviews, while my son dug into the law for nearly a decade with my lawyers. Joseph, Dana, and Les sacrificed their own need and personal goals to save me. Chip Hill and other dear friends fought everyday for my freedom.

Dana and others mustered nearly 100,000 contacts to the Obama White House. Les and Joseph worked with former New York Attorney General Bob Abrams and Lynne Ross, former director of the National Association of AGs, to coordinate more than one hundred former AGs trying to get the president's attention.

Les had always been there for me. How blessed to have had such a brother, such a friend, for my entire life.

Dana was fourteen and Joseph was eleven when this started. Both were in their thirties now. Dana pushed her own career aside to work to free me. Joseph became my lawyer. He altered his life to stay in Birmingham with his mother and to fight for my freedom. How could a father imagine that his children would become his protectors?

I counted my blessings, but when I thought about the toll this had taken on my children, my wife, my brother, my friends I could have, but didn't, curse those who did this and who stole free college education from Alabama's children.

I was grateful to the thousands of people who signed petitions asking the president to pardon me, for new friendships I would have never known and now will never forget. I continued to fight for the truth in my case but more importantly, to restore justice and to preserve our democracy.

My goal now was criminal justice reform. I saw my purpose as fighting for reform that would balance the scales of justice. Of course, I wanted President Obama to pardon me, but I was never given a break. While my cause had widespread support, we were fighting the Justice Department's determination to cover up their own wrongdoing. David Margolis, the chief puppeteer for prosecutors, was still in control. Bureaucracies don't admit error, much less dishonesty and lawlessness. They think they are immune from being held accountable.

As I awaited the end of my sentence, our hope again rose when journalist-legal analyst Jeffrey Toobin wrote in the January 14, 2015, *The New Yorker*:

> Since the midterm elections, President Barack Obama has been acting as if he feels liberated from parochial political concerns. After taking action on immigration, Cuba, and climate change, he should take on another risky, if less well-known, challenge by commuting the prison sentence of Don Siegelman, the former governor of Alabama.

President Obama did not pardon me. As an African American and a lawyer, he must have known how often our courts are guilty of injustice.

Yet he ignored my case, ignored the calls of members of Congress, governors, 113 former state attorneys general, countless legal scholars, and over 100,000 citizens. A great many civil rights leaders, including U.S. District Court Judge U. W. Clemon, Fred Gray (who had been Dr. King's and Rosa Parks's lawyer), Dr. Joseph Lowery, SCLC President Charles Steele, and the Reverend Fred Shuttlesworth all spoke on my behalf, but they apparently did not impress President Obama.

Had he relied on Eric Holder for advice? But the Department of Justice's priority was to protect itself. If they admit one man has been wrongly imprisoned, someone might claim there have been many more. There might even be calls for reform, and that, to some, would be unthinkable. With more than 1,500 exonerations, including more than 150 on death row, what more proof do people need to see that something is broken?

President Obama had a friendly relationship with Karl Rove in public settings. Or perhaps the problem was Eric Holder. As I pointed out, his law firm represented Rove and the National Republican Committee. When the Judiciary Committee subpoenaed Rove's emails and held Rove in contempt, Holder's firm defended the NRC. Rove was given a pass and was not required to testify under oath.

Holder had worked at the Justice Department before the Obama administration and been friendly with David Margolis, who had worked with Karl Rove and the Bush White House to fire and replace U.S. attorneys who refused to do "justice" Karl Rove's way. Or perhaps the problem was that Holder, like Obama, had never been part of the civil rights movement. Were they simply misled by DOJ's David Margolis? Did Karl Rove use his connections at DOJ? Were they so focused on their own careers that they turned a blind eye to justice?

President Obama left the White House on January 20, 2017. I stayed in prison until February 8, 2017.

CHAPTER 82

GOING HOME

The Federal Bureau of Prisons policy lets some inmates spend their final six months of confinement in a halfway house or, if there is a stable environment, at their own home. I was granted home confinement—essentially house arrest, which was to begin February 8, 2017. I notified my family and told them they wouldn't have to drive to Louisiana to retrieve me. I was told that if I had the money, I could fly to Birmingham. To save Lori and my kids the eighteen-hour round trip, driving from Birmingham to Oakdale and back, it just made sense for me to fly home. I did.

Just as in 2008, there were television crews at the prison gate. Neither I nor the prison authorities wanted me interviewed as I departed. After I was processed, the camp counselor drove me to the Alexandria airport. As we neared the prison gate, I ducked down as instructed, so the media wouldn't see me.

Barbara Tarburton, my faithful "Prison Administrative Assistant," didn't want me flying home alone. She was waiting at the airport to join me on the flight to Atlanta, then on to Birmingham, where friends and family greeted us as we made our way down the escalator to the street level. The media was there, too. Dana rushed up and put her hand to my mouth to remind me I had no approval for a press conference. She didn't want me sent back to prison. Neither did I. She was right. I was still a federal prisoner.

I said hellos, shook hands, exchanged embraces, and wiped away tears before climbing into Les's car. More friends were waiting downtown. Birmingham Mayor William Bell sent his security chief, Sergeant Harris, to escort us through the city. When we approached the city's main street, I saw the crowd gathered. With media cameras rolling, I smiled, fought back tears, waved, and touched some hands as we moved slowly past the crowd. It was wonderful seeing so many friends I had not seen in so many years.

As we proceeded to my home to greet Lori, Joseph, Dana, and Les wondered if our Chocolate Lab, Kona, would remember me. Kona was only six months old in 2012 when I went back to prison. I had been gone

Above: Waving to supporters who greeted me in downtown Birmingham on my homecoming in 2017. Below: celebrating my freedom at home with my brother, Les, and my dog, Kona.

for four years and five months. As I opened the door, I hugged and kissed Lori as Kona greeted me with all the enthusiasm I could have hoped for.

Doing time in prison, if you have the right attitude and understand why you are there, doesn't have to be a struggle. I knew who had put me away and why. Plus I had the thoughts, prayers, and hard work of so many people around the country. I even had the support of the national media and many in Congress. All this kept my spirits buoyed, even during the darkest moments.

There is nothing nice about prison. No one in solitary, in a cell, or in a camp wants to be there, but the real struggle and sacrifice was inflicted upon children and spouses. I saw families torn apart during my years in captivity. It was a blessing finally to be reunited with mine. I was still under house arrest but at least was away from the confines and correctional officers of Oakdale.

I met my probation officer at my home to go over the rules of my home confinement. I was fitted for an ankle monitor and could travel only 150 feet in any direction from the electronic transmitter in my kitchen. My PO soon agreed that I could go downtown to work in either my brother's office or my son's law office. That enhanced my sense of freedom even though I had to notify my PO which office I'd be in each day.

I spent most of the next six months working on this book, sometimes after having morning coffee with my brother. Later my PO agreed to let me walk from the office to a café across the street or to a restaurant in an adjacent building to my son's office. There Les, Joseph, and I would talk about what we could do to further the Freedom of Information Act lawsuit Joseph was working on. The idea was to show the judge how the government had acted in bad faith and was withholding documents which could result in a new trial. Joseph and his legal team eventually won the FOIA case, the only successful such case brought against the Obama administration. Yet, so much had been redacted by the prosecutors, the truth was still hidden.

Despite restrictions and frustrations, it was good to be home. Joseph had chosen to live in Birmingham to stay close to Lori and to work on my case. Dana, who had been such a warrior for me, had been wounded by a four-month marriage and came home to rebuild and recover. I was blessed to have my wife and both my children at home with me for the first time since Dana graduated from high school.

Lori continued to suffer from her terrible injuries in the 1984 car crash. She still returned to the doctor and dentist for the eye she lost and for periodic work on her teeth. Throughout this ordeal, her attitude always remained positive. Lori persevered by devoting herself to the arts, knitting scarves for children with cancer, and spending time with her elderly mother, who was also her best friend.

Now that I was home, I faced financial challenges. Despite my twenty years in public service I didn't have a retirement or even health insurance. Since the legal attack on me began in 2003 virtually all my savings had gone to lawyers. All I would have was Social Security and Medicare.

My most urgent goal was to write this book to tell the truth about the charges against me after so many years of lies and to suggest changes in our justice system. I had started work on the book in prison. By the time I left, my draft was over 650 pages. So, now out of prison, I set out to tell my story with more focus and brevity.

Writing was not my only concern. My health and physical conditioning had always been important to me. However, the workout schedule I'd followed in prison was impossible to maintain during home confinement. I went back to my dear friend and karate instructor, Seiko Shihan Oyama. I had been taking lessons since Les and I joined in October 1974. Earned my black belt in 1980, after thirty fights. Seiko Shihan and other old black belts welcomed me back.

When I broke my tibia and fibula in a karate tournament in 2009, I started taking boxing as a way to get in better condition for the 2010 karate tournament. When I got home, Martin Juarez, my boxing instructor, called and asked if I'd help him with a new endeavor, a boxing program for people with Parkinson's disease—the PD Fight Club. With my parole officer's approval, I began volunteering at least six hours each week.

Even as I was writing, enjoying my family, and volunteering with Parkinson's patients, I gave a great deal of thought to how America could create a system of justice that is more sensible, more fair, and more effective than the flawed and often cruel one I came to know all too well.

Left: Joseph, who had seen enough injustice, ran in 2018 for the office of state attorney general. He ran a flawless race but in red Alabama, he lost. (Beau Gustafson Photographer) Below: with Les right after we had proudly voted for Joseph, November 2018. (Photograph by Thomas Diasio)

CHAPTER 83

IN SEARCH OF JUSTICE

My mother, God bless her, used to say, "God works in mysterious ways." In prison, for a crime that never happened, I thought, "Yes, Mom, God sure does."

If there is a purpose in everything, or if we are to find a purpose in whatever situation we encounter, I felt like God sent me a clear message: "OK, Governor. Now you've seen what's wrong with our criminal justice system, go fix it!"

I should have a PhD in criminology for all I learned in trial, on appeal, and while in prison. It was an intensive, firsthand view of the failings of our system of justice, seen from the inside both from my own persecution and in the tales of countless others I met in prison. Now I'm compelled to speak out on injustice and the changes that are so urgently needed.

So what can be changed and how?

First, the adequate education of our children is the best way to reduce crime. That's why I wanted an Education Lottery to pay for early learning, Pre-K for every child, and free college education. Every child should have the hope and dream of being able to better themselves. With early education and free higher education there would be less crime, more jobs, healthier families, and less dependence on taxpayers.

When an inmate enters prison, that's when rehabilitation, by way of education, should start. Most inmates need skills: life skills, societal skills, language, reading and job skills. The president of the United States should appoint a director of the Bureau of Prisons who has a grasp on how to reduce recidivism. Human warehousing is not the answer. People who enter prison illiterate and unemployable should have a chance to leave literate and able to work. Each prison should have a human resources officer to match up inmates with jobs in their home communities before they are released.

It just makes sense to offer drug treatment to first-time nonviolent drug offenders. We have made some changes, but intensive drug treatment with deferred sentencing would help save lives and money.

We see record numbers of prisoners, wrongful convictions, the use of excessive force, draconian sentences, overcrowded prisons, wasted money, and families destroyed. This creates an ever-increasing financial burden on taxpayers and helps no one.

Certainly there are criminals who deserve to be in prison for the protection of society. The problem is that the worst criminals seize the headlines, leading to public demands to "get tough on crime." That's why prisons are filled not only with those who should be there, but with many others who shouldn't. Far too many are kept longer than makes sense. Juan Garcia was in for nineteen years for charges of "½ ounce or more" of marijuana!

So, we must reverse the "lock 'em up and throw away the key" mentality and adopt a mandate to reduce recidivism. Recidivism is the major source of crime. U.S. attorneys are political appointees, who perhaps have their eye on publicity, their next promotion, or higher office. Elected district attorneys, state attorneys general, and state judges often advance their careers by being "tough on crime." It's easy to proclaim a "war" on drugs or crime, but much harder to win that war if you think police and prisons are the only way to fight it.

Judges add years to a defendant's sentence for "acquitted conduct" and "relevant conduct." Only 3 percent go to trial, and those who testify on their own behalf but are convicted are then subject to additional punishment. The justification is that if a jury then convicts, the defendant must have lied or tried to obstruct justice. This nonsensical and unconstitutional notion must be reversed by Congress or the U.S. Supreme Court.

Another obstacle to reform is that when prisons are full, everyone in the criminal justice system keeps their job. The system, therefore, seems to have an insatiable appetite for new inmates and strong incentives to win indictments and convictions, sometimes, by any means possible. Correctional officers and private for-profit prisons have become political forces, and it is in their interest to keep prisons full.

As I told Senator Hatch in 2015, grand juries give prosecutors almost every indictment they ask for, and almost all of those charged, even when innocent, agree to plead guilty, rather than risk a harsher sentence.

Political leaders, the media, and concerned citizens must keep watch on prosecutors who have virtually unchecked power to seek indictments. Black leaders increasingly see prison as "the new slavery." Poor black youths, Asians, or Hispanics are too often put away for long sentences based on easy arrests for minor infractions. In 2017, the rate of incarceration for blacks was six times higher than that of whites. Those overseeing the administration of justice need to keep a close watch on prosecutors, police, and investigators.

Prosecutors have the power to threaten a target with more time in prison or bribe a target (as they did Nick Bailey) with "no time in prison" if they will testify or even lie for the government. Many convictions are made on the testimony of paid informants who, like bounty hunters, do it for the pay or for a lighter sentence for themselves. Judge Alex Kozinski of the Ninth Circuit Court of Appeals declared that the withholding of exculpatory evidence by prosecutors is "epidemic." So it's not surprising that the government gets 99 percent of the indictments they seek.

No system of justice should tolerate such abuses.

More importantly, no system of justice should be based on President Obama's solicitor general's pronouncement to the U.S. Supreme Court: "U.S. Citizens do not have a constitutional right not to be framed."

Such a pronouncement is horrifying and repugnant in a true democracy.

Therefore, the single most important reform Congress could make to balance the scales of justice is grand jury reform.

1. Every interview of a witness or target should be recorded and those recordings should be turned over to the defense before trial. Recording all interviews would help keep prosecutors and investigators in line. This would ensure less bribes or cajoling, less pressure and threats, and fewer felons willing to lie for a shorter sentence.

2. Allow every target or witness to have a lawyer present to object to evidence or testimony, such objections to be decided in the same manner as they are now in depositions.

3. No prosecutor or investigator should be allowed to knowingly and willfully present false evidence or testimony or withhold exculpatory evidence to get an indictment. Repeal the immunity granted to prosecutors and investigators in the Federal Tort Claims Act.

Vice President Al Gore wrote to my supporters that as I was fighting for my freedom, I was also fighting for our democracy. That's what I now intend to do.

When the Department of Justice is used as a political weapon, when witnesses are coached and cajoled to lie, when political rivals are silenced, our democracy is abused. We have a national legal and moral crisis. Those who care about our institutions of justice must expose and stop this misconduct to restore justice.

The partisans who conspired to send me to prison put themselves above the law. They knew that justice could be corrupted. They gladly did so in their quest for political power.

What We Learned from the Nixon Era

"Impeach the Cox Sacker" was the public cry that emerged after President Nixon fired Archibald Cox, who had been appointed as special counsel to investigate what became known as "Watergate."

Election interference, laws broken with impunity, a president thumbing his nose at Congress, lies, deception, cover-ups, abuse of power. It all sounds familiar. There is a big difference in the intensity in the mood of the electorate with Trump as compared to 1974 with Nixon.

After his election in 1968, Nixon started a secret fund to finance his 1972 reelection using longtime friends John Mitchell and Bebe Robozo as bag men. Rebozo funneled hundreds of thousands of dollars into Alabama in an attempt to hinder George Wallace's 1970 election to another term as governor. Nixon wanted to have a lock on conservative Southern whites and George Wallace's segregationist Dixiecrats. The Republicans' "Southern Strategy" which emerged is now claimed by Donald Trump as his own.

Nixon's attempting to manipulate the election with cash, tapping DNC phones, using dirty tricks, and spying on Democratic opponents was not so different from the Russians' influence in 2016.

What is different is that many citizens had reached the end of tolerance as protests teetered from civil disobedience to resistance after the killing of students at Kent State by Ohio National Guardsmen and the students at Jackson State College in Mississippi by the police. Hundreds of thousands of people participated in anti-war protests throughout the United States and the world. Anti-war sentiment was heightened by Nixon's lies about his "secret plan" to end the Vietnam War, McNamara's air of indifference, Kissinger's arrogance, Don Segretti and Karl Rove's dirty tricks, and President Nixon's corrupt team that was determined to lie, steal, or do whatever was necessary to win and maintain power at any cost to our democracy. Those men and others would go down in infamy: Roger Ailes, G. Gordon Liddy, Bob Haldeman, John Ehrlichman, James McCord, Bebe Rebozo, and Attorney General John Mitchell.

One honest man, Attorney General Elliot Richardson, appointed Archibald Cox as special counsel to investigate White House corruption. Cox was promptly fired by Nixon. Hence the cries to "Impeach the Cox Sacker."

President Nixon resigned when confronted by Republicans with the fact he would be impeached if he didn't step down.

What We Learned From The George W. Bush Era:

Not wanting to operate outside the Department of Justice to conduct dirty tricks as Nixon had done, Rove and Bush made sure all new DOJ employees were ideologically in sync with far-right Republican values and were Rove clones. Before they could be confirmed, all new U.S. federal judges and U.S. attorneys were first screened by Rove. If U.S. attorneys didn't live up to Rove's political expectations, they were fired. Others who prosecuted Democrats were praised.

The Trump Impeachment

In 2019, we heard calls from President Trump demanding that U.S. Attorney General Bill Barr investigate those who investigated the link between Trump and Russia's interference in our elections. Barr launched a formal DOJ criminal investigation.

Meanwhile, Donald Trump and his personal lawyer, former New York Mayor Rudy Giuliani, engaged in what might have been quid pro quo political extortion/bribery to extract from the president of Ukraine a public investigation of Joe Biden, who was at the time perceived as Trump's strongest 2020 Democratic opponent. Donald Trump's apparent abuse of power, the use of the DOJ as a political weapon, receiving what arguably was a dark-money bribe from a foreign national to fire the U.S. ambassador to Ukraine, threatening to withhold U.S. military aid to Ukraine unless it investigated Trump's opponent—all could have been impeachable crimes. This conduct clearly violated the U.S. Supreme Court's 1991 *McCormick* ruling.

What we learned from the Don Siegelman case:

You don't need a quid pro quo to wind up in prison. There was no Quid Pro Quo, much less an express one. I was raising money for a ballot initiative to send children to college for free. There was no allegation I benefited by a single penny. I was sentenced to prison.

What we learned from the Trump Impeachment:

Even with an express Quid Pro Quo, where the terms of the agreement were asserted, if you are a Republican president you can avoid jail time and impeachment.

The legal definition of "bribery" is exchanging official action for something of personal value. That standard hadn't changed for 100 years, before the Impeachment trial of President Trump.

For the rule of law to work, allegations of Quid Pro Quo corruption has to apply equally to everyone: either our President's alleged actions constitute bribery or they don't. But if they don't, I never should've been prosecuted.

So, as proof that DOJ can be used as a political weapon, I would call Donald J. Trump as my witness.

It was Trump who fired FBI Director James Comey to stop the investigation of Russian collusion with the Trump campaign. It was Trump who then fired FBI Director Andrew McCabe. It was Trump who fired acting U.S. Attorney General Sally Yates and hired his "Southern White Boy" buddy Jeff Sessions, then replaced him with Bill Barr who doesn't go to work each day without doing something to protect President Trump from some Congressional probe.

But, if you need further evidence that the DOJ can be used for political ends, I would call Karl Rove to the stand. There was sworn testimony that Karl Rove got the DOJ to pursue me.

It was Karl Rove's client, the state AG, who started the investigation. It was Karl Rove's Alabama partner's wife, Leura Canary, who as President Bush's U.S. attorney, kicked my federal investigation into high gear while her husband was being paid to defeat me. It was Jeff Sessions's retired FBI agents who spent nearly four years building the bogus case against me, pressuring witnesses to lie, all at a time when Sessions was considering a run against me. It was Karl Rove's "bag man" Jack Abramoff, who illegally laundered $20 million of dark Indian casino money into Alabama, using Rove's friends, Ralph Reed and Grover Norquist, to defeat me. I could go on, but you've already read about it.

The use of our criminal justice system as a political weapon must stop. It threatens our democracy. Prosecutorial decisions by the Department of Justice must not be viewed as political or the public will quickly lose respect for those administering justice.

I still believe our democracy will survive. Our right to vote is our most precious right. Each of us can make a difference. We can change things and make things better. As voters, as jurors, as politically active citizens, we can fight for an honest and fair system of justice. Voting is the fuel that drives our engine of democracy. Voting gives us power. Our right to vote gives us a voice. We must use it.

My purpose now is to work for the changes needed to balance the scales of justice, to reset our moral compass, to preserve our democracy and protect those who otherwise might suffer unfairly.

If the assassination of my political career, my five years in prison, nearly twenty years of fighting for truth and freedom, and the terrible price imposed upon my family are to have meaning, it must arise from my speaking out about the harm a flawed system of justice and the abuse of power does to our democracy.

We can do better. We must do better. We must elect a president who'll fix what's broken. I pray that my story will help.

| EPILOGUE

In 2001, being mentioned as a dark-horse candidate for president edged me closer to announcing a run for president as soon as I won my reelection in 2002. I intended to enter the Democratic primaries as a Southerner, a New South progressive, a successful governor who had garnered support from Republicans and Democrats, from business and labor, from liberals and the NRA. I had put education, jobs, and working families at the top of my agenda. Having been secretary of state, attorney general, lieutenant governor, and governor, I had the potential for widespread national support. However, at the time, Governor Gray Davis of California was in the lead. Then a turn of events in California, linked to Karl Rove and his operatives Ralph Reed and Grover Norquist, took Governor Davis out of contention for president.

I didn't know if I could secure the top spot, as Southerners Jimmy Carter and Bill Clinton had, but I felt confident I'd be well in the running as a VP choice. Then, the Karl Rove operatives struck and took me out. I was fifty-six years old. Now, I'm seventy-three.

So today I'm not a candidate. Today, I'm writing as a Democrat who believes that for candidates to capture the attention of a majority of Americans, we must focus on the issues which trouble working families.

The 2020 election shouldn't be about Donald Trump.

Working families don't go to sleep at night worrying about Donald Trump. They worry about their children, their parents, and paying their bills. They want a better life for their children, and they know it starts with education. They want their parents to live out the remainder of their lives without stressing over how they can afford prescription drugs, food, and a place to live.

We live in the richest country in the world. No one should go hungry. Our democracy should work for working families as well as the rich.

Working families are concerned about their children and their children's future. That's why I believe education should be the single most talked about issue by all candidates for president.

I believe every child, regardless of where they're born or to whom, regardless of their parents' economic status, should have the hope and dream of reaching their God-given potential. It all starts with education. Every child should have the right to a head start with free, early childhood pre-K education. Here, every child can learn to read and to use a computer, and every child can be prepared to succeed all the way through school. Every child, whether citizen or immigrant, should have the hope and dream of being able to get free higher education, whether it's job training or college. Giving children the security of being able to go to college, regardless of their family's financial or legal status, will help keep them in school and out of trouble and make them productive U.S. citizens. This is in America's best interest.

So we need a president who'll offer universal early learning and free higher education and who'll push for after-school jobs or job training for every student who wants it.

We need a president who'll retire student loans. It's time to lift this weight off students' shoulders so they can move on with their lives and help jump-start our economy.

In addition to educational opportunities, we need a president who'll expand economic opportunities. It starts with a fair tax system. Working families are penalized by our current tax structure. Something is wrong when three families have wealth equal to half of the U.S. population. Something is wrong when the top 1 percent have more combined wealth than 92 percent at the bottom! Something is wrong when large profitable corporations pay nothing in taxes, while working families are sucked dry. It's time for billionaires, millionaires, and large corporations to pay their fair share of taxes just like the rest of us do.

Raising revenue to pay for progress starts with a president who'll work to create a fair tax system. It is simply what's right and what's fair.

We need a president who'll work for more and better-paying jobs and recruit new manufacturers and new technologies.

We need a president who will raise the minimum wage to a living wage. Working families are struggling to feed their children and to prepare for their children's futures. As it now stands, it falls on the government to create policies that fill the gap. Increased wages will lower debt, increase spending, and boost our economy.

We need a president who'll work to save our planet from climate change.

We need a president who commits to rebuilding our infrastructure, our roads and bridges, protecting our coastal waters, rivers, lakes and streams, providing clean water, building waste water treatment plants, and creating new uses for renewable energy. By investing in twenty-first-century infrastructure, we can put more people to work, create after-school jobs to keep kids out of trouble, and teach them the value of earning money for themselves at an early age.

We need a president who knows healthcare must be a right for all citizens not just those who can scrape up enough to pay the premiums, co-pays, and deductibles.

We need a president who is civil, couth, and a role model for our children. Someone we respect and look up to.

We need a president who respects the rights of women.

We need a president who understands history, who understands the importance of Freedom of Speech to our democracy, and who respects the role of the media in preserving it.

We need a president who'll fight for justice—economic justice, social justice, racial justice, environmental justice—and for criminal justice reform. While I'm a dreamer, these are not pipe dreams. I'm a practical politician, a father, and someone who has seen the inside of the federal prison.

That's why I want a president who understands that our justice system is broken. It's broken when we have two million people locked up. Many who are nonviolent, first-time offenders. It's broken when we spent nearly $100 billion a year to warehouse them. It's broken when people enter prison without job skills and leave the same way.

I want a president who will work to solve the problem of recidivism, who recognizes that crime is too often related to drug addiction, and who knows that state prisons and local jails are filled with inmates with mental disorders. We need a president who'll confront mental illness, opioid and other drug addictions, one who recognizes the cost effectiveness of treatment programs.

Criminal Justice reform should be in the national presidential debate by Republicans as well as Democrats.

I want a president who understands that our system of justice is capable of political abuse, who wants to right wrongs and fix our justice system.

We must restore justice, preserve our democracy, protect the integrity of our elections, and balance the scales of justice to end mass incarceration. If my political opponents can put me in prison, a governor with the resources I had to fight them, think of what a politicized prosecutor can do to you and your family.

I believe America can be everything we want it to be, everything we can imagine it can and it should be, but it depends on us.

We must find candidates in whom we believe and trust, help them get elected, and work with them to accomplish their goals. After the election, we must make sure they stay true to their commitment. We must hold them accountable for the promises made in their campaign.

We need a president who is not trigger happy. The U.S. has been in too many "political" wars—Vietnam, Afghanistan, and Iraq—costing hundreds of thousands of soldier and civilian sacrifices and trillions of dollars. No one is a winner in these wars except those who make and sell weapons. Presidents who are ignorant or arrogant, who fail to heed the lessons of history, or who put their own political popularity over the lives of our soldiers or innocent civilians should never be elected. If elected, such a president should be impeached.

A Republican president who wanted to hold the military industrial complex accountable was Dwight Eisenhower. "Ike" put it this way: "Politics like war is too important to be left to the professionals." Ike meant the voices of citizens should be heard on these matters and not dismissed or denigrated.

If we want to preserve our democracy, then all of us must be soldiers doing our duty as citizens by voting. We must do our part to make sure our democracy functions in the best interest of our country, our future, and working families.

Oliver Wendell Holmes said our right to vote is our most precious right. That's because all of our freedoms are impacted by the people we elect to public office. Mayors can fix potholes and U.S. senators can curtail the president's war powers. Everything from fixing potholes to peace depends on who we elect to public office.

I'm writing this book to kickstart a conversation, to engender talk about the issues important to everyone, especially working families. I hope to wake some people up and to get voters motivated.

I'm living proof elections can be stolen, and not just by Russians. In addition to securing borders, we need to secure our elections. We need to vote on paper ballots that can be hand-counted when there is a question of accuracy.

The bottom line is that as voters we must be undaunted, we must be proactive and provocative. The struggle to restore justice and preserve our democracy depends on us. We must never ever give up. We must be willing to get into the arena and fight for the soul of our democracy, to fight for the truth and justice.

One of my favorite presidents, Teddy Roosevelt, was a renegade Republican, a founder of the Progressive "Bull Moose" Party. Teddy famously said:

> The credit belongs to those who are in the arena, whose faces are marred by dust and sweat and blood, who know the great enthusiasms, who spend themselves in a worthy cause knowing, if they should fail while daring greatly, at least their place will not be with those cold and timid souls who know neither victory nor defeat.

So I thank every voter, commend you, and encourage you to stay in the arena. Keep fighting for those ideals you hold dear, keep working for candidates in whom you believe and trust, and hold their feet to the fire once elected. Thank you.

▍ NOTES

All documents cited can be accessed on the author's website: www.donsiegelman.org.

1 "New District Attorney Named" (Dothan, AL: WTVY News 4, Dec. 23, 2002); *see also* Kim Lewis, "Circuit Judge McAliley applies for position as district attorney" (Enterprise, AL: *Southeast Sun*, Dec. 11, 2002).

2 Michael Kramer, "For Pete's Sake" (New York: *Time*, Mar. 27, 1995).

3 Adam Zagorin, "Selective Justice in Alabama?" (New York: *Time*, Oct. 4, 2007)

4 Jack Abramoff, *Capitol Punishment: The Hard Truth About Washington Corruption from America's Most Notorious Lobbyist* (Centreville, VA: WND Books, 2011), 185–87).

5 *The Kiplinger Letter*, March 28, 2001.

6 Manuel Roig-Franzia, "Post-Election Alabama Is Seeing Double" (*Washington Post*, Nov. 8, 2002). Beiler, David, "Case Studies: Southern Trilogy, How Republicans Captured Governorships in Georgia, South Carolina and Alabama" (Arlington, VA: *Campaigns & Elections* magazine, June 2003).

7 Dahleen Glanton, "Governor of Alabama concedes to Republican (*Chicago Tribune*, Nov. 19, 2002).

8 James H. Gundlach, "A Statistical Analysis of Possible Electronic Ballot Box Stuffing: The Case of Baldwin County Alabama Governor's Race in 2002" (Auburn University, April 11, 2003).

9 Adam Zagorin.

10 United States' Motion to Reduce Sentence under Rule 35 for Substantial Assistance (Doc. 89, ¶ 4), *United States of America v. Clayton Lamar Young, Jr.*, M.D. Al. (2:03-cr-135-MEF).

11 Memorandum from Peter Martin Fernandez, Federal Inmate 21215-051, to Vince Kilborn, attorney for Governor Siegelman (Sep. 17, 2007), p. 1.

12 Letter from U.S. District Judge U.W. Clemon to The Honorable Eric Holder, United States Attorney General (May 13, 2009), p. 2.

13 Testimony of Senator Doug Jones, Oct. 23, 2007, Subcommittees on Crime, Terrorism and Homeland Security and on Commercial and Admin. Law, Hearing, p. 12.

14 Affidavit of Nick Bailey, Government Witness, at ¶ 8.

15 Doug Jones, pp. 8-11.

16 Brett Blackledge, "Prosecutor: No political push in Siegelman case" (*Birmingham News*, Oct. 31, 2007), p. 1A.

17 Brett Blackledge and Mary Orndorff, "Prosecutor says Montgomery led Siegelman case," (*Birmingham News*, Oct. 28, 2007), p. 1A.

18 Blackledge and Orndorff; Bob Johnson, "Prosecutor offers different take on Siegelman" (Associated Press in the *Decatur* (Alabama) *Daily News*, Nov. 4, 2007).

19 Blackledge and Orndorff.

20 Doug Jones, p. 13 (emphasis added).

21 Will Evans, "Money Trails to the Federal Bench: State-by-state report on campaign contributions from federal judges appointed during the Bush Administration" (Oakland, California: Center for Investigative Reporting, Oct. 31, 2006), p. 17.

22 For background on Fuller's animus toward me, see *supra*, note 1, WTVY and Kim Lewis; and "Letter from Gary McAliley, Circuit Judge, to Don Siegelman, Governor" (Dec. 10, 2002).

23 Scott Horton, "The Pork Barrel World of Judge Mark Fuller" (New York: *Harper's*, Aug. 6, 2007).

24 Motion for Downward Departure (Doc. 49, p. 3, and Doc. 46, p. 2), *United States v. Nicholas D. Bailey*, M.D. Al. (2:03-cr-00133-MEF).

25 Plea Agreement of Nicholas D. Bailey (Doc. 6), *United States v. Nicholas D. Bailey*, M.D. Al. (2:03-cr-00133-MEF).

26 Affidavit of Nick Bailey, Government Witness, at ¶ 4.

27 "Letter from Tamarah Grimes, Former Paralegal for the Middle District of Alabama U.S. Attorney, to the Honorable Eric Holder, Attorney General of the United States" (June 1, 2009), p. 3 (emphasis added).

28 Transcript of Amy Methvin Interview, p. 2 (emphasis added). Methvin is the wife of Thomas J. Methvin, president of the Alabama State Bar in 2009–2010. She was interviewed on videotape in August 2006 for a documentary relating to this case.

29 Affidavit of Nick Bailey, at ¶ 9 (emphasis added).

30 Affidavit of Nick Bailey, at ¶ 5 (emphasis added).

31 United States' Sentencing Memorandum; *see also* United States' Motion for Upward Departure.

32 Scott Horton.

33 Rove and Bill Canary were/are good friends, and Rove admitted having spoken with him during this time. See Unofficial Transcript of Interview by U.S. House Judiciary Committee Members of Karl Rove at p. 96 (July 30, 2009).

LEGAL NOTES

Scott Horton, Columbia Law professor writing for *Trial Lawyer* in 2008, dubbed me "Political Prisoner #1," saying:

> The biggest political target of all for the Bush White House and the Karl Rove prosecution machine was in Alabama. Don Siegelman (former Secretary of State, Attorney General, Lt. Governor and Governor) was the most successful Democratic politician in post-Wallace Alabama. His case marks an amazing odyssey . . . but the constant that links the many strands of his case is Karl Rove.

DOJ's longtime Associate Deputy Attorney General, the late David Margolis: "the way DOJ managed this case, if brought to light, *would do real harm to the reputation of the department.*"[1]

DOJ had succeeded in keeping the political nature of my prosecution under wraps until my son found a willing Congressional whistleblower. The story was broken on December 11, 2014, when the Project on Government Oversight ("POGO"), an independent nonpartisan non-profit organization, published an article discussing a June 3, 2010 letter from DOJ to the Chairman of the U.S. House Judiciary Committee.[2] The letter, by DOJ's Office of Professional Responsibility ("OPR"), exposed I had been targeted by partisans. The letter revealed that DOJ's lead prosecutor heading up my investigation was in communication with the campaign manager of my opponent about his efforts and those of "likeminded conservative prosecutors" to find criminal charges against me. The plain language, "*conservative prosecutors,*" indicates clear political motivation. There couldn't be a legitimate reason for the AUSA with "supervisory authority over public corruption cases" to be telling the campaign manager of my opponent of his and other "conservative prosecutors" commitment to find charges against me.[3]

Yet DOJ reported to the U.S. House Judiciary Committee "political motivation" played no role in my investigation or prosecution.

---

1   Scott Horton, "The Case for a Presidential Pardon for Don Siegelman" (*Washington Spectator*: A Project of the Public Concern Foundation, Mar. 8, 2016), emphasis added.
2   Adam Zagorin, "Justice Department Downplays Evidence of Politics in Probe of Governor" (Project on Government Oversight, Dec. 11, 2014). .
3   Letter from Ronald Weich, U.S. Assistant Attorney General, to John Conyers, then-chairman of the U.S. House of Representatives Committee on the Judiciary (June 3, 2010), p. 4.

DOJ Was Steadfast in Their Pursuit of Creating a Crime

The same year I was prosecuted, 2006, several U.S. Attorneys were fired evidently "for partisan reasons."[4] DOJ later acknowledged that the firings "severely damaged the credibility of the Department and raised doubts about the integrity of Department prosecutive decisions."[5] Karl Rove, President George W. Bush's Deputy Chief of Staff who advised the firings,[6] indicated having influenced DOJ's decision to prosecute Siegelman.[7]

Upon recognizing "[the] prosecution was completely without legal merit,"[8] Chief Judge U. W. Clemon dismissed the case with prejudice on October 5, 2004, the first day of testimony.[9]

Shortly after my attorney, then Doug Jones, now U.S. Senator Doug Jones, received a call from an Assistant U.S. Attorney: "We had a meeting in Washington and we were told to go back and look at everything again from top to bottom."[10] Another Justice Department attorney confirmed: "'Washington' had ordered them to start over with the investigation."[11] "Start over" because only a few months earlier, DOJ had insufficient evidence to proceed with charges. "In early July 2004," My attorneys met with prosecutors and "left convinced that the investigation would close without any charges being brought."[12]

The government concluded the evidence didn't support charges against me was based on earlier determinations by DOJ's career prosecutors. "Charles Niven, a 26-year career prosecutor, [who] served as acting U.S. attorney supervising an investigation of the Siegelman administration from the summer of 2002 until 2003" said he "did not see evidence to link Siegelman to the investigation."[13] Mr.

---

4   "An Investigation into the Removal of Nine U.S. Attorneys in 2006" (Washington: U.S. Department of Justice Office of the Inspector General and Office of Professional Responsibility, September 2008), p. 1. [hereinafter "Report on Removal of U.S. Attorneys"]

5   Id., p. 358.

6   Email from David Leitch, Deputy White House Counsel, to Kyle Sampson, Chief of Staff to Attorney General Alberto Gonzales (Jan. 6, 2005; Exhibit 1).

7   Karl Rove on *This Week With George Stephanopoulos*, (New York: ABC News, Mar. 25, 2008); David Corn, "On the Siegelman Scandal, Rove Offers a Very Suspicious Non-Denial Denial" (San Francisco: *Mother Jones*, May 26, 2008)

8   Letter from Judge U. W. Clemon to U.S. Attorney General Eric Holder (May 13, 2009; Exhibit 2).

9   The government's witness "conclusively established that there was absolutely no basis for a conspiracy charge," after which Judge Clemon dismissed the conspiracy count in the indictment. *See* Id. The government itself then moved to dismiss the remainder of the indictment.

10   Testimony of Senator Doug Jones, Oct. 23, 2007, Subcommittees on Crime, Terrorism and Homeland Security and on Commercial and Admin. Law, Hearing, p. 12 (Exhibit 3).

11   Affidavit of Nick Bailey, Government Witness, at ¶ 8 (Exhibit 4).

12   Doug Jones, pp. 8–11, emphasis added.

13   Brett Blackledge, "Prosecutor: No political push in Siegelman case" (*Birmingham News*,

Nivens explained in 2003, "There wasn't sufficient evidence to seek an indictment against Governor Siegelman."[14] "John W. Scott, a senior Justice Department trial lawyer helping with the case," expressed the same.[15] Mr. Scott "opposed efforts to continue the investigation of former Gov. Don Siegelman and argued to end the case in 2004" because he "felt there was not enough evidence to go forward . . . ."[16] Acting U.S. Attorney Louis Franklin indicated that Mr. Scott was so disturbed by the persistence toward charges despite a lack of evidence that "when [Mr. Scott] left Montgomery he didn't come back."[17]

My attorney, Doug Jones, described the rejuvenation of charges against me as a directive from "Washington":

> What we saw beginning in early 2005 was much more than simply a top to bottom review . . . . it appeared that agents were not investigating any allegations of a crime, but were now fishing around for anything they could find against an individual. New subpoenas were being issued for documents and witnesses. Anyone that was a major financial backer of Don Siegelman or who had done business with the state during his administration began receiving visits by investigators and subpoenas by prosecutors. Every bank record, every financial record, every investment record of the Governor, his wife, his campaign and his brother were being subpoenaed.[18]

Several months later, I was indicted.[19]

ALLEGATIONS AGAINST TWO REPUBLICAN OFFICIALS, JEFF SESSIONS AND BILL PRYOR, ARE IGNORED

The case started with an investigation of businessman, Lanny Young, who accepted a plea deal in exchange for his "cooperation." Young provided allegations against me and two Republicans: then Attorney General Bill Pryor, and then U.S. Senator Jeff Sessions.[20] DOJ pursued only Young's allegations against me.

Initially, DOJ gave two reasons why they "did not pursue" Young's allegations against the Republicans, first, "concerns about Mr. Young's credibility."[21] Yet despite "concerns about [his] credibility," the government used Young's allegations

---

    Oct. 31, 2007), p. 1A (Exhibit 5).

14   Id.

15   Brett Blackledge and Mary Orndorff, "Prosecutor says Montgomery led Siegelman case," (*Birmingham News*, Oct. 28, 2007), p. 1A (Exhibit 6).

16   Id.; Bob Johnson, "Prosecutor offers different take on Siegelman" (Associated Press in the *Decatur* (Alabama) *Daily News*, Nov. 4, 2007).

17   Brett Blackledge and Mary Orndorff.

18   Doug Jones, p. 13, emphasis added.

19   *United States v. Don Eugene Siegelman, et al.*, M.D. Al. (2:05-cr-00119-MEF).

20   Adam Zagorin, "Selective Justice in Alabama?" (New York: *Time*, Oct. 4, 2007).

21   Letter from Ronald Weich to John Conyers (Exhibit 7).

as basis for RICO charges against me.

Young served only 11 months because prosecutors told the judge they "cannot overstate the importance" of Young to their efforts [to convict me].[22] A cellmate of Young sent an unsolicited statement:

> According to him [Lanny Young], he said whatever they (the "FEDS") told him to say. He laughs about it, and revels in the fact that he "made millions and got away with it" by becoming a "federal informant" and setting people up.
>
> No man should be allowed to trade his punishment for the crimes he committed for lies against the innocent.[23]

Another reason given for not pursuing Young's allegations of illegal contributions "to the campaigns of the prominent Republicans" was a "lack of resources."[24] A "lack of resources" didn't stop them from coming after me, the Democrat, in what was described as The Big Case:

> "The Big Case" was the most important case in the office and obtaining a conviction of former Governor Siegelman and Richard Scrushy was more important to the U.S. Attorney [Leura Canary] than anything else.[25]

Ms. Canary ensured resources for The Big Case. On January 25, 2005, Ms. Canary requested $91,000 "to fund the most important investigation pending in this office" adding that it "was absolutely necessary."[26]

---

22 United States' Motion to Reduce Sentence under Rule 35 for Substantial Assistance (Doc. 89, ¶ 4), *United States v. Clayton Lamar Young, Jr.,* M.D. Al. (2:03-cr-135-MEF).

23 Memorandum from Peter Martin Fernandez, Federal Inmate 21215-051, to Vince Kilborn, attorney for Governor Siegelman (Sep. 17, 2007), p. 1 (Exhibit 8).

24 Letter from Ronald Weich to John Conyers, p. 4 (Exhibit 7).

25 Report of Substantial Misconduct and Request for Investigation by the U.S. Department of Justice Office of Inspector General (Jul. 26, 2007), p. [hereinafter "Grimes Report"] (Exhibit 9).

26 Email from Leura Canary to Lisa Bevels (Jan. 25, 2005) (Exhibit 10). Ms. Canary wanted the money to pay a "contract employee" who she considered "critical to the success" of the prosecution. Email from Leura Canary to Sherri C. Hamilton (Sep. 15, 2005) (Exhibit 11). Unable to promptly get the funds, Ms. Canary left vacant an opening in the office in order to give that money to the Siegelman case. *See* Id. ("we won't fill the GS 12 open slot so that we will have some excess payroll money to help fund this"). On October 26, 2005, Ms. Canary received word that she would get the "critical" funds. Email from Leura Canary to Lisa Bevels (Oct. 26, 2005) (Exhibit 12). *That same day* her office announced its indictment of Governor Siegelman. *See* "Former Alabama Governor Don Siegelman, Others Indicted in Racketeering, Bribery and Extortion Conspiracy," *Department of Justice Press Release* (Oct. 26, 2005) *available at* www.justice.gov/archive/opa/pr/2005/October/05_crm_568.html.

U.S. ATTORNEY LEURA CANARY'S CONFLICT OF INTEREST

Leura Canary's husband, William "Bill" Canary, is a renowned Republican operative both in and outside Alabama: "'You drop him into some state where something needs fixing,' says former G.O.P. chairman Rich Bond, 'and it gets fixed.'"[27] *Time* called Mr. Canary a "legend in Republican circles."[28]

While U.S. Attorney Canary was investigating me (for nearly seven months), my attorney learned that the U.S. Attorney's husband was working for one of my gubernatorial opponents. He alerted DOJ of the conflict.[29] Despite Canary investigating me, a Democrat, during an election year while her husband was being paid by a Republican candidate for governor, DOJ's David Margolis wrote my attorney that "no actual conflict of interest exists."[30]

As the DOJ investigation was kicked into high gear, Leura Canary's conflict got worse. In my 2002 gubernatorial race, the U.S. Attorney's husband, Bill Canary, initially worked for Republican candidate Lieutenant Governor Steve Windom who was running for governor. When Windom lost the Republican Primary to Bob Riley, Canary then joined Riley's campaign as a consultant.[31] Following the politically damaging investigation, I narrowly "lost" the 2002 election, after 6,000 of my votes simply "disappeared,"[32] to Riley, who ran on a platform of "bring[ing] integrity back to Montgomery."[33]

---

27 Michael Kramer, "For Pete's Sake" (Time, Mar. 27, 1995).

28 Id.

29 Letter from Siegelman attorney David C. Johnson to U.S. Deputy Attorney General Larry D. Thompson and Kenneth L. Wainstein, Director of the Executive Office of U.S. Attorneys (Mar. 25, 2002, Exhibit 13).

30 Letter from U.S. Associate Deputy Attorney General David Margolis to Siegelman attorney David C. Johnson (May 15, 2002, Exhibit 14), p. 3.

31 *See* Beiler, David, *Case Studies: Southern Trilogy, How Republicans Captured Governorships In Georgia, South Carolina and Alabama*, Campaigns & Elections (June 2003) ("William [Canary] was a political consultant in the recurring employ of both [Bill] Pryor and Lt. Gov. Steve Windom…Canary later joined the Riley campaign") [hereinafter "Campaign Case Study"] (Exhibit 15).

32 The Associated Press announced Governor Siegelman had won reelection, but, after Democratic poll workers had gone home, a subsequent tally of votes shifted roughly 6,000 votes from Mr. Siegelman to Mr. Riley, which was enough to give Riley the election. See Steve McConnell, The changing of the guards: Bay Minette, election night, Baldwin County Now (July 20, 2007). Another client of Mr. Canary, then-Attorney General Bill Pryor certified the later tabulation and said that anyone "who opened the ballots would be committing a 'criminal act.'" Dahleen Glanton, Governor of Alabama concedes to Republican, Chicago Tribune (Nov. 19, 2002). Following the election, Auburn University professor James Gundlach did a statistical analysis on the results and concluded that they had likely been manipulated. See James H. Gundlach, A Statistical Analysis of Possible Electronic Ballot Box Stuffing: The Case of Baldwin County Alabama Governor's Race in 2002, Auburn University (Apr. 11, 2003).

33 *See* Remarks by President George W. Bush at a Luncheon for Gubernatorial Candidate Bob Riley in Birmingham (July 15, 2002). Phillip Rawls, "Siegelman, Riley square off in

Business Alabama described Bill Canary and Governor Riley's post-election rapport:

> Partisan politics will be high on Canary's agenda. Canary prides himself on being a well-connected Republican strategist. He has no patience with Democrats at any level. He is wired into Riley's policy-making, and as it stands now, he likely will be a cheerleader for Riley to seek a second term.[34]

CREATING THE EVIDENCE FOR A CRIME

Nick Bailey, my former aide, was the "linchpin" of the prosecutors' case.[35] Facing possible decades in prison, Bailey accepted a plea deal in exchange for a promise of a light sentence recommendation.[36] It was first said Bailey only met with prosecutors and investigators "two or three dozen" times "during the investigation"; the meetings "typically lasted two to three hours, and some of them extended from one day to the next."[37] A paralegal for the prosecution team, Tamarah Grimes, described one of the meetings:

> I particularly recall one meeting in which cooperating witness Nick Bailey was persuaded to recall something that he claimed he did not actually recollect. . . . Mr. Bailey repeatedly said he did not know and he was not sure. The prosecutors coaxed and pressured Mr. Bailey to "remember" their version of alleged events. Mr. Bailey appeared apprehensive and hesitant to disappoint the prosecutors.[38]

When this whistleblower voiced concern to the office's ethics officer, she was told "The Big Case was the most important case in the office and that U.S. Attorney Leura Canary would grant prosecutors virtually unlimited latitude to obtain a conviction."[39] The whistleblower was fired.

Amy Methvin, Bailey's friend, is the wife of Thomas J. Methvin, president of the Alabama State Bar in 2009–10. She was interviewed on videotape for a

---

first debate" (Associated Press in *Gadsden* (Ala.) *Times*, Aug. 6, 2002), emphasis added.

34 Bessie Ford, "Business Broods '06" (Birmingham, AL: *Business Alabama*, April 2004), p. 7 (Exhibit 16); Bessie Ford, "Getting Out While the Getting's Good" (*Business Alabama*, Aug. 2004), p. 14 (Exhibit 17).

35 Motion for Downward Departure (Doc. 49, p. 3, and Doc. 46, p. 2), *United States v. Nicholas D. Bailey*, M.D. Al. (2:03-cr-00133-MEF).

36 Plea Agreement of Nicholas D. Bailey (Doc. 6), *United States v. Nicholas D. Bailey*, M.D. Al. (2:03-cr-00133-MEF)

37 Bailey Affidavit (Exhibit 4, ¶ 4). *see also* Trial Transcript at 1090, Siegelman.

38 "Letter from Tamarah Grimes, Former Paralegal for the Middle District of Alabama U.S. Attorney, to the Honorable Eric Holder, Attorney General of the United States" (June 1, 2009), p. 3 (emphasis added).

39 Id. at 1; *see also* Grimes Report (Exhibit 9, p. 6).

documentary relating to this case in August 2006 and described a conversation with Bailey shortly before he testified:

> And then he said, "you know, I really feel bad about what's getting ready to happen, I really do." He said, "the Governor does not deserve this, he's a good man. I've never seen him take anything personally. And he gave and he gave and he was the best Governor we ever had."[40]

Mrs. Methvin asked, "Nick, what are you going to do if the lawyers ask you that under oath?" According to Mrs. Methvin, Nick's demeanor abruptly changed:

> And he went into this long speech without looking me in the eye. And I just – my mouth dropped open because it was absolutely—it was just the opposite of what he had just said. So I let him finish. And I said, Nick, you sound like a robot, like you have this thing memorized. And this is what he said to me, he said, "you would have it memorized, too, if you've heard the answers as many times as I've heard the answers."[41]

THE DEPARTMENT OF JUSTICE ENGAGED IN UNETHICAL CONDUCT

WITHHOLDING OF EXCULPATORY MATERIAL

Mr. Bailey had many meetings with prosecutors and investigators over the course of "well over four years."[42] Numerous notes were taken during the meetings:

> Bailey said, government representatives took notes at every meetings.
> When Assistant U.S. Attorney Julia Weller was present, she typed constantly on her laptop. My opinion is that Ms. Weller took verbatim notes. . . . After Assistant U.S. Attorney Steven Feaga was assigned to the case, he was generally accompanied to the interviews by J.B. Perrine, another AUSA, who took notes. Other government representatives generally took notes, on laptops or written by hand, at all of these meetings. When only agents were present (and such meetings would almost always include Keith Baker and Bill Long), one or both of them took notes . . . .[43]

Yet despite notes being taken DOJ made only a few[44] reports. Bailey said that

---

40 Transcript of interview of Amy Methvin, Exhibits 19 and 39, p. 2.

41 Id.

42 Letter from Kevin Di Gregory, Manatt Phelps & Phillips LLP, to Lanny Breuer, Assistant Attorney General for the Criminal Division (June 15, 2009, Exhibit 20), p. 11, n. 5—"a troubling aspect of this investigation is its extraordinary length."

43 Bailey Affidavit.

44 Di Gregory Letter, p. 12—"there is a deafening dearth of reports of interviews" (emphasis added); see also Trial Transcript at 1214–15, Siegelman.

the reports turned over to us "summarize *only a fraction* of the meetings that I had with government representatives."[45] He estimated that "there were *at least* 24 occasions when [he] met with government representatives . . . to discuss issues related to my case" for which no notes or materials were "provided to the defense team."[46]

EX PARTE JUDICIAL COMMUNICATION

Some of DOJ's officials met privately with the trial judge[47] to discuss an issue that was the subject of a new trial motion then before the judge.[48] DOJ disclosed this *ex parte* contact on "the eve of [our] briefing deadline to the Eleventh Circuit—too late for [my lawyers] to question the trial court about this *ex parte* communication or obtain any relief therefor."[49]

EX PARTE COMMUNICATION WITH JUROR(S)

A member of the prosecution team spoke to a juror shortly before the juror was to testify at a hearing concerning possible jury misconduct. Tamarah Grimes, the DOJ paralegal, heard Acting U.S. Attorney Franklin discuss the matter:

> Mr. Franklin state[d] that his legal assistant (Debbie Shaw) had spoken with a juror, whom he described as, "just a kid . . . she is afraid she is going to get in trouble." This was immediately prior to a hearing on potential juror misconduct at which this juror testified.[50]

At the time of this *ex parte* communication, there was a pending motion for a new trial based on jurors' improper exposure to extraneous information and evidence "that certain jurors began lobbying others for a conviction long before the trial was over."[51]

The prosecutors had casual communication with the jury as well.[52] "The jurors kept sending out messages through the marshals" to find out if a member of the prosecution team "was married"; one juror in particular, prosecutors learned, was

---

45 Bailey Affidavit, ¶ 9 (emphasis added).
46 Id., ¶ 5 (emphasis added).
47 Note 65, *infra*.
48 Letter from Siegelman attorney Vince Kilborn to U.S. Attorney General Eric Holder, (April 3, 2009, Exhibit 21), pp. 3–4; Letter from Patty M. Stemler, Chief of Appellate Section of Department of Justice Criminal Division, to Counsel for Don Siegelman and Richard Scrushy (July 8, 2008, Exhibit 22); *see also* Second Motion for Recusal (Doc. 1009), Siegelman.
49 Kilborn Letter to Holder.
50 Grimes Letter, p. 4; *see also* Grimes Report (Exhibit 9, p. 7).
51 Kilborn Letter (Exhibit 21), p. 4; Motion for New Trial (Doc. 467), Siegelman; Motion to Supplement the Record (Doc. 471), Siegelman.
52 There was a third potentially improper conversation between prosecutors and a juror. Richard M. Scrushy's Motion for New Trial (Doc. 953, ¶ 47), Siegelman.

"very interested."[53] "The prosecution team jokingly nicknamed the juror 'Flipper'" after learning she "entertained the other jurors by doing backflips in the jury room."[54] These communications occurred while the jury was deliberating. One might ask how the prosecutors knew what was going on in the jury room.

DOJ Converts a Campaign Contribution into a Bribe

As Governor, I wanted to establish an Alabama Education Lottery to raise funds to send students to college tuition-free, similar to Georgia's HOPE Scholarship Lottery. Voters would decide whether to establish a lottery in a referendum on October 12, 1999. The Alabama Democratic Party launched a campaign to promote the initiative—to combat the roughly $20 million laundered from Mississippi Choctaw Indian casinos into the state aimed to "stop Siegelman" and to defeat the lottery. In his 2001 book, Jack Abramoff wrote, "Located on the eastern border of Mississippi, our Choctaw client relied almost entirely on a customer base from Birmingham, Alabama, where Democrat Don Siegelman became the 51st governor in 1998. Siegelman vowed to enact legislation permitting a state lottery, which would have been the first breech [sic] in the Alabama anti-gambling wall. . . . It cost the tribe approximately $20 million to wage these battles, but the returns were worth it to them, Chief Martin called us the 'best slot machine' they had, and he was not exaggerating."[55] The Democratic Party incurred a debt supporting the initiative. The referendum failed. The debt remained.

On March 9, 2000, I agreed to become a guarantor on a loan to repay the Democratic Party's debt. Any contribution solicited by me to pay off the loan after that date could be construed as benefiting me. I asked and Mr. Scrushy made a sizeable contribution to the lottery campaign to pay down the Democratic Party's debt. However, to even contemplate this as a "bribe" the requisite *quid pro quo* arrangement between Mr. Scrushy and me would have to have occurred on or before July 19, 1999, the date of the first of Scrushy's two contributions to the lottery campaign.

In July of 1999, I wasn't a guarantor on the loan because, at that time, the loan did not exist. Therefore, it would've been (literally) impossible for me to contemplate getting any financial benefit from a contribution to the lottery campaign. Under no circumstances would I have been able to derive any personal financial benefit from Scrushy's contribution. Despite the unequivocal fact that there was no possible way for me to have benefited financially from Mr. Scrushy's contribution, prosecutors argued to the jury and later to appellate courts that "[Siegelman] benefited financially from the $500,000 because he was unconditionally liable as

---

53   Email from Assistant U.S. Attorney Patricia Snyder to Tamarah Grimes (June 15, 2006, Exhibit 23).

54   Grimes Letter, p. 4.

55   Jack Abramoff, *Capitol Punishment: The Hard Truth About Washington Corruption from America's Most Notorious Lobbyist* (Centreville, VA: WND Books, 2011), 185–87.

a guarantor for the campaign debt that was paid down with that money."[56]

Almost immediately upon being sent to deliberate, the jury returned with a question: "Is a contribution given to the [Alabama Education Foundation or Alabama Education Lottery Foundation] considered to be a thing of value to Governor Siegelman . . . or does it have to benefit Siegelman personally?"[57] Siegelman. In response, the trial judge (*see* note 65, *infra*) told the jurors that I could have benefited because I personally guaranteed the Democratic Party's debt and Scrushy's contribution to the ballot initiative could be considered a thing of value to me because I supported the Education Lottery Referendum.[58] He reminded the jury that the lottery was part of my platform when I ran for governor.

COURTS AND OFFICIALS HAVE NOTED OPR's HABITUAL BAD FAITH.

The Office of Professional Responsibility, like FOIA, was a product of the Watergate scandals. Amid concern about the ethical conduct of lawyers implicated in the scandal and the Department's integrity as a trustee of the American people's interest in justice, OPR was established by the Attorney General in 1975,

> to ensure that Department of Justice attorneys and law enforcement personnel perform their duties in accordance with the highest professional standards expected of the nation's principal law enforcement agency.[59]

But by 2007, OPR's "arguable ineffectiveness" had become so pronounced that OPR's *own leader of 22 years* called for abolishing it.[60]

Chief Judge for the U.S. District Court District of Massachusetts Mark Wolf, "who took pride in assisting" with the establishment of OPR, wrote the Attorney General in 2008 that he "sadly doubt[s] that it is now capable of serving its intended purpose" and that there are "serious questions about whether judges should continue to rely" on OPR.[61] U.S. District Court Judge Kurt Engelhardt of New Orleans wrote he had "no confidence" in OPR.[62]

Washington, D.C., District Court Judge Emmet Sullivan, who presided over the high profile case of late-Senator Ted Stevens which was ultimately dismissed

---

56   Brief for the United States as Appellee, *U.S. v. Siegelman* (11th Cir. 12-14373) (Sep. 30, 2013) at 6.

57   Trial Transcript at 7652,

58   Id. at 7686.

59   "About the Office" (Washington: OPR Policies & Procedures).

60   Ari Shapiro, "Ex-Chief Calls for Scrapping Justice Department Watchdog" (Washington: National Public Radio *All Things Considered*, June 1, 2007, 4 p.m. ET).

61   Letter from Judge Mark Wolf to Attorney General Eric Holder (April 23, 2009, Exhibit 24).

62   Order (Doc. 1070, p. 33), *U.S. v. Bowen, et al.*, E.D. La. (2:10-cr-204-KDE) (emphasis added).

for severe prosecutorial misconduct, appointed a special prosecutor to investigate because he considered the allegations "too serious and too numerous" to entrust OPR with investigating.[63] The special prosecutor discovered "systemic concealment of exculpatory evidence" and other "serious misconduct" which Judge Sullivan noted "almost certainly would never have been revealed" had OPR been left to investigate.[64]

At a Senate hearing on the misconduct, Senator Dick Durbin (D-IL) agreed that but for "an extremely conscientious judge" who "took the rare step of appointing an independent investigator" the misconduct would not have come to light.[65] In my own case, as detailed earlier, Judge Mark Fuller should have recused himself but did not.[66] Senator Sheldon Whitehouse (D-CT) explained that the revelations learned by DOJ about the U.S. Attorney firings may never have come to light since Attorney General Alberto Gonzales had attempted to refer the matter to OPR.

DOJ EXHIBITED BAD FAITH BY MISREPRESENTING TO CONYERS THAT THE SIEGELMAN CASE HAD NOT BEEN BROUGHT FOR POLITICAL REASONS.

DOJ's AUSA leading my investigation communicated directly with the campaign manager of my opponent about his efforts to find criminal charges against me. This AUSA emailed Bob Riley's campaign manager during the course of the investigation apprising him that "like minded conservative prosecutors" were trying to bring an indictment against me. Not only does the plain language, "*conservative* prosecutors," indicate clear political motivation, but what legitimate reason could possibly exist for this AUSA to communicate his (and others') commitment

---

63 Transcript of Hearing (Doc. 374, p. 46), *U.S. v. Theodore F. Stevens*, D.C. (1:08-cr-00231-EGS).

64 Order (Doc. 22, p. 4), In Re Special Proceedings, D.C. (1:09-mc-00198-EGS) (emphasis added).

65 *Hearing on the Special Counsel's Report on the Prosecution of Senator Ted Stevens: Hearings Before the United States Senate Comm. on the Judiciary*, 112th Cong. (2012) (Mar. 28, 2012), at 1:06, *available at* www.c-span.org/video/?305160-1/prosecution-former-senator-ted-stevens.

66 Judge Mark Fuller should have recused since, as governor, I initiated an investigation into Fuller's misconduct before he joined the federal bench. Fuller called it "politically motivated." *New District Attorney Named*, WTVY News 4 (Dec. 23, 2002); *see also* Kim Lewis, *Circuit Judge McAliley applies for position as district attorney*, The Southeast Sun (Dec. 11, 2002), (citing Letter from Gary McAliley, Circuit Judge, to Don Siegelman, Governor (Dec. 10, 2002)). Judge Fuller, as "a member of the Alabama Republican Executive Committee," had been tasked with defeating Governor Siegelman, the most prominent Democrat in the state at that time. Will Evans, *Money Trails to the Federal Bench: State-by-state report on campaign contributions from federal judges appointed during the Bush Administration*, Center for Investigative Reporting (Oct. 31, 2006) at 17; *see also 60 Minutes* ("This was a Republican state and [Siegelman] was the one Democrat they could never get rid of"), *infra* note 100. For a third reason for his recusal *see* Scott Horton, *The Pork Barrel World of Judge Mark Fuller*, Harper's Magazine (Aug. 6, 2007).

to finding charges against me to the campaign manager of my opponent? There can be no question that this AUSA with *"supervisory authority* over public corruption cases" was pursuing an indictment for political reasons. Moreover, the AUSA was not working alone on this partisan goal but rather with "a *small group* of like minded conservative prosecutors," if not with the campaign manager of my opponent as well. Nonetheless, DOJ reported to the Chairman of the U.S. House Judiciary Committee that "political motivation" played no role in the decision to investigate and prosecute me.[67]

The bad faith, or worse, evident in such a clearly false statement to a Committee of Congress with direct oversight authority is inexcusable, if not criminal.

DOJ EXHIBITED BAD FAITH BY NOT ADMITTING THE POLITICAL CONFLICT OF INTEREST FOR LEURA CANARY.

Thomas Gallion, a prominent Montgomery attorney and Republican who had been actively involved with the G.O.P. in Alabama, gave an affidavit in support of our motion to prove government "bad faith," saying in part:

> Sometime in late 2001 or early 2002, I received a telephone call from my long-time friend Winton Blount, III, son of former Republican Post Master General Winton M. "Red" Blount. Winton informed me that a group of Republicans in Alabama had set up a plan, which he called "Operation 2010." Their goal was to gain control of all branches of Alabama government, the executive, legislative and judicial, by 2010. He explained that, as part of this plan, a newly appointed Republican U.S. Attorney in the Middle District of Alabama, Leura Canary, would work with the group to prosecute statewide elected Democrats and their supporters. Winton further told me that Republican Congressman Bob Riley was running for governor against Governor Don Siegelman, and that they planned to indict Siegelman in the middle of the up-coming election.[68]

My attorney temporarily threw a wrench in the Republican plot on March 25, 2002 when he requested Ms. Canary's recusal after learning that her husband was working for one of my gubernatorial opponents.[69] However, Ms. Canary would be able to resume this effort[70] since DOJ, through David Margolis, Deputy AG

---

67 *See* Weich Letter (Ex. 7, p. 3 emphasis added).
68 Affidavit of Thomas T. Gallion III.
69 *See generally* Johnson Letter.
70 Canary publicly stated that she would recuse herself, but there is no evidence that she did. All available evidence indicates otherwise. *See, e.g.,* Grimes Letter (Ex. 18, p. 3) ("Mrs. Canary maintained direct communication with the prosecution team, directed some action in the case, and monitored the case through members of the prosecution team"); *see also* Scott Horton, *The Remarkable 'Recusal' of Leura Canary*, Harper's Magazine (Sep. 14, 2007) (emphasis added).

"conclude[d] that no actual conflict of interest exist[ed]."[71] Either Ms. Canary, in bad faith, misrepresented the true nature of her conflict to her superiors, or worse, DOJ's officials in D.C. knew about Ms. Canary's political conflict of interest and, DOJ, in bad faith, allowed her to remain involved in the case nonetheless. Did they also know of her political motivation described by Mr. Gallion?

In 2006, a Birmingham attorney, John Aaron, sought through a FOIA request to determine how Ms. Canary's conflict either was not learned or had become concealed, DOJ then engaged in bad faith reporting there were "no responsive documents" when "in fact there were more than 500 responsive documents." This was apparently done at the direction of "political appointees at the Justice Department." According to the DOJ, the only reason why "the false statements issued in response" to the FOIA request got corrected was because career personnel, against "a lot of political pressure . . . insisted that the false statements be corrected." A "senior Justice Department FOIA official" commented, "It was pulling teeth to get them to tell the truth." The Department of Justice's bad faith in that earlier FOIA case further undermined its trustworthiness in our FOIA action.[72]

DOJ MISREPRESENTED TO CONGRESS THAT I WASN'T SELECTIVELY PROSECUTED.

In a letter to Congressman John Conyers, then-Chairman of the United States House of Representatives Committee on the Judiciary, the Department of Justice stated, "The allegation that Mr. Siegelman was the subject of selective prosecution . . . was not supported by the evidence." Although Lanny Young's allegations against me, a Democrat, were pursued while Young's allegations against prominent Republicans Jeff Sessions and Bill Pryor were not, DOJ claimed to have reasons for not investigating the Republicans. DOJ explained that "the investigators and prosecutors in Alabama did not pursue" the allegations against then-Attorney General Bill Pryor or then-U.S. Senator Jeff Sessions "in part because of concerns about Mr. Young's credibility, and in part because of lack of resources." DOJ added as well that its Public Integrity Division ("PIN") later determined that the allegations against Pryor and Sessions "lacked merit and were probably time-barred at the time Mr. Young raised them."[73]

---

71 Margolis Letter.

72 Canary publicly stated that she would recuse herself, but there is no evidence that she did. All available evidence indicates otherwise. *See, e.g.,* Grimes Letter (Ex. 18, p. 3) ("Mrs. Canary maintained direct communication with the prosecution team, directed some action in the case, and monitored the case through members of the prosecution team"); *see also* Scott Horton, *The Remarkable 'Recusal' of Leura Canary,* Harper's Magazine (Sep. 14, 2007) (emphasis added), http://harpers.org/blog/2007/09/the-remarkable-recusal-of-leura-canary [hereinafter "Horton"].

73 Weich Letter (Ex. 7, p. 4).

DOJ justified its decision not to investigate the Republicans with four reasons: (1) Young's questionable credibility, (2) a lack of resources, (3) lack of merit to the allegations, and (4) potentially time-barred. These four reasons, however, did not stop DOJ's investigation and prosecution of me.

YOUNG'S CREDIBILITY CHANGED DEPENDING ON WHOM HIS ALLEGATION WAS AGAINST.

DOJ first cited "concerns about Mr. Young's credibility" for why it did not follow up on his allegations against Republicans Sessions and Pryor. However, DOJ's doubts about Young's credibility extended only to the Republicans; Young's allegations against me, the Democrat, translated into multiple counts[74] of indictment.[75] Moreover, while Young's credibility foreclosed investigation into potential misconduct by Republicans Sessions and Pryor, prosecutors did not hesitate to solicit testimony from Young against me.[76] Whatever "concerns about Mr. Young's credibility" DOJ may have had, those concerns somehow evaporated when Young gave allegations against a Democrat.

LEURA CANARY FOUND RESOURCES TO INVESTIGATE A DEMOCRAT BUT WOULD NOT PROVIDE RESOURCES FOR INVESTIGATING SESSIONS OR PRYOR, REPUBLICANS.

The other reason DOJ gave for not investigating the Republicans Sessions and Pryor was a "lack of resources."[77] The Republican U.S. Attorney Leura Canary, whether or not she recused herself from the Siegelman case,[78] retained control of her office's purse and staff. According to Canary's own emails, she devoted as much of her office's funding and personnel as possible to investigating and prosecuting me, the Democrat.[79] According to DOJ, Canary's exhaustion of her office's resources on me, the Democrat, prohibited any investigation of the Republicans, Jeff Sessions and Bill Pryor, who was Mr. Canary's (and Karl Rove's) client.[80]

---

74 Young's allegations formed the prosecution's most serious alleged offense, violations of Racketeer Influenced and Corrupt Organizations Act (RICO), of which the jury found me not guilty. *See* note 87, *infra*.

75 *See* Superceding Indictment (Doc. 61).

76 *See* Trial Transcript at 2588-3460, Id.

77 Weich Letter (Ex. 7, p. 4).

78 *See* Grimes letter, also see note 71, *supra*)

79 *See* Email from Patricia Snyder to Stephen Doyle (Apr. 6, 2005) (moving paralegal Grimes to work on the case) (Exhibit 26); *and* Grimes Report (Ex. 9, pp. 5-6).

80 *See* Campaign Case Study (Ex. 15, p. 32). After the election in 2000, I asked the attorney general who his political consultant was. "Karl Rove," Pryor proudly announced with a grin. I asked, "How do you reach him?" He pulled out his cell phone, flipped it open, scrolled, and showed me two phone numbers for Karl. "I usually just call him at the White House."

ALLEGATIONS AGAINST ME, THE DEMOCRAT, LACKING MERIT WERE PROSECUTED.

In addition to "concerns about Mr. Young's credibility" and a "lack of resources," the Department of Justice provided two others for not following up on the allegations against Pryor and Sessions.[81] First, DOJ claimed the Young allegations against the Republicans "lacked merit."[82] However, lack of merit was no obstacle to prosecuting me.[83] As discussed, DOJ's first case against me in 2004 was "totally without legal merit" such that the judge was ready to award me "attorneys' fees under the Hyde Amendment."[84] DOJ later admitted that its case "was weak," so weak in fact that they had to check whether its indictment violated "the Department's Principles of Federal Prosecution, which set forth the standards that govern charging decisions by federal prosecutors."[85]

The case against me in 2006 was no different, according to DOJ's senior-most career officials working on the case. Charles Nivens, "a 26-year career prosecutor," and John Scott, "a senior Justice Department trial lawyer" both determined that there were *no meritorious charges* that could be brought against me.[86] Moreover, Nivens and Scott reached that conclusion after *the DOJ had been investigating me for three to four years.*

DOJ USED TIME-BARRED ALLEGATIONS AGAINST ME.

The final reason DOJ gave for not investigating allegations against Republicans Sessions and Pryor was because they "were probably time-barred . . ."[87] However, DOJ actively pursued time-barred allegations against me, the Democrat. Circumventing the statute of limitations, prosecutors cloaked time-barred charges involving the campaign contribution by Scrushy to the lottery referendum as a violation of the Racketeer Influenced and Corrupt Organizations Act[88] (RICO). The contribution

---

81 Weich Letter (Ex. 7, p. 4).

82 Id.

83 I don't suggest that meritless charges should be brought against Republicans, but one can't ignore the fact that, given the DOJ's suggestion that it would never have brought a meritless charge, they did against me.

84 Judge U.W. Clemon's letter to President Barack Obama (Sep. 27, 2012) at 1 (Exhibit 27).

85 *See* Weich Letter (Ex. 7, pp. 3-4).

86 *See* Blackledge (Ex. 5); Blackledge & Orndorff (Ex. 6); Johnson, *supra* note 15.

87 Weich Letter (Ex. 7, p. 4).

88 Notre Dame Law Professor Robert Blakey, who authored the RICO statute, called the prosecution's RICO charges "trash" and "a joke." Adam Nossiter, *Ex-Governor Says Conviction Was Political,* The New York Times (June 27, 2007), www.nytimes.com/2007/06/27/us/27alabama.html. Pace University Law Professor Bennett Gershman, one of the nation's foremost experts on prosecutorial misconduct, opined that "it strongly appears the motive of the federal prosecutors in including the RICO counts in the indictment was for the inflammatory purpose of contaminating the jury by portraying Siegelman as part

was made in July of 1999. I was indicted in 2006, clearly time-barred by a five-year statute of limitations.

According to the Justice Department: (1) Lanny Young's allegations against me were credible, but his allegations against Republicans were not; (2) Because Leura Canary devoted the entirety of her office's resources to investigating me, the Democrat, none were available to investigate the Republicans, one of whom was her husband's client; (3) Allegations lacking merit against me became indictments, but allegations lacking merit against Republicans were disregarded; and (4) Allegations against me which were time-barred were prosecuted, allegations which *may have been* time-barred against Republicans Jeff Sessions and Bill Pryor were ignored.

All of the four reasons given by the Justice Department for not investigating the Republicans strengthen the argument that I was selectively prosecuted. However, DOJ told the Chairman of the U.S. House Judiciary Committee "[t]he allegation that Mr. Siegelman was the subject of selective prosecution . . . was not supported by the evidence."[89] The fact that DOJ would report to Congress that I was not selectively prosecuted—when every piece of evidence available indicated otherwise—represents bad faith, a crime or a shirking of its Constitutional obligations.

DOJ MISREPRESENTED WHO MADE DECISIONS IN MY CASE.

DOJ made repeated representations that all major decisions in my case were made either by local officials or the Public Integrity Section of the Criminal Division ("PIN").[90] There is no caveat in these representations. Yet we know—because DOJ's then-Acting Chief of the PIN Andrew Lourie admitted as much—**at least one critical prosecutorial decision came directly from the highest-ranking political appointees within the DOJ.**[91] After disclosing the source of the decision, Lourie stated that "he could not discuss the decision-making process any further and that he really should not have shared what he did . . . that he would be in trouble if it were known that he had shared the little information he provided . . . ."[92]

DOJ should not get to choose when it wants to tell the truth just because it can (usually) control whether anyone else learns it. If Lourie had not slipped up

---

of a corrupt conspiracy and thereby improving their chances of getting a conviction on something." Bennett Gershman, *Cruel Justice: The Case of Don Siegelman*, The Huffington Post (June 3, 2014). *See* Second Superseding Indictment (Doc. 61), Siegelman

89 Weich Letter (Ex. 7, p. 4).

90 *See, e.g.,* Weich Letter (Ex. 7, p. 4); *see also* note 93, *infra*.

91 According to Lourie, the decision of what plea, if any, by Scrushy would be allowed was made by the same individuals responsible for the U.S. Attorney firings. *See* Affidavit of Art Leach, Assistant U.S. Attorney (1983-2002) and former counsel for Richard Scrushy, at ¶¶ 16-20 [hereinafter "Leach Affidavit"] (Exhibit 28); *Allegations of Selective Prosecution in Our Federal Criminal Justice System*, Report by Majority Staff H. Comm. on the Judiciary, 110th Cong. (2007), (Apr. 17, 2008) at 14, Report on Removal of U.S. Attorneys at 357, *supra* note 4.

92 Leach Affidavit (Ex. 28, ¶ 20).

and accidentally disclosed the source of the decision, we would never have known that high-ranking political appointees maintained control over my case. Knowing DOJ misrepresented who the decision-makers were, we do not and cannot know who made what decisions.

Were there other decisions made in the Office of the Attorney General that were then passed down through the ranks from the high-ranking political appointee? What about if the lower ranks did something of which higher up political appointees did not approve; did the Office of the Attorney General reserve the right to veto or prod them in another direction or fire them? For example, when the AUSA reported that "the investigation in Montgomery would soon be coming to a close without any charges being brought," did the highest ranking political appointee object and tell them to "go back and look at everything again from top to bottom" sending the clear message that they wanted Democrat Governor Don Siegelman prosecuted?[93]

Just because DOJ holds the reins to the truth should not grant it impunity to misrepresent information at will to Congress (which it repeatedly did) or a court[94] (which it did) or to the public[95] (which it did regularly). By making these repeated misrepresentations, the Justice Department exhibited its bad faith.

DOJ Had Multiple Opportunities to Drop Its Vendetta Against Me.

In its pursuit of an indictment and conviction of me as Alabama's Governor, a Democrat, DOJ would not allow the truth to derail its determined outcome. The lack of interest in the truth exhibited by Department of Justice officials throughout my prosecution encapsulates the bad faith targeting of me. U.S. Senator Doug Jones, former U.S. Attorney and my former attorney, tried to enlighten prosecutors that their theory against me was entirely incompatible with objective evidence.[96] Doug Jones did this believing prosecutors would see the weakness of the case and end

---

93   See Doug Jones Congressional Testimony (Ex. 3, pp. 11-12).

94   *See, e.g.,* Government's Motion in Limine (Doc. 348, p. 10), Siegelman ("the Middle District of Alabama's U.S. Attorney's Office, the Public Integrity Division of the United States Department of Justice in Washington, D.C., and the Alabama Attorney General's Office have jointly made *all* of the substantive decisions").

95   *See, e.g.,* Statement of Louis V. Franklin, Sr., Acting U.S. Attorney in the Siegelman/ Scrushy Prosecution (June 6, 2007) at 2 ("**Canary has had no involvement in the case, directly *or indirectly* . . . a firewall was established**") (emphasis added), *available at* http://blog.al.com/bn/2007/07/Franklin%20Statement.pdf; Id. ("***unfounded*** **accusations that her husband's Republican ties created a conflict of interest . . . no conflict, actual *or apparent*, existed**") (emphasis added); Id. ("I alone maintained the decision-making authority"); *see also* Statement from Acting United States Attorney Louis V. Franklin, Sr., United States Attorney's Office, Middle District of Alabama, *Siegelman, Scrushy Prosecutor Refutes Rumors,* WSFA 12 News (Oct. 5, 2007), www.wsfa.com/story/7176844/ siegelman-scrushy-prosecutor-refutes-rumors.

96   *See* Jones Congressional Testimony (Ex. 3, pp. 9-10).

their pursuit toward an indictment.[97] Doug Jones was wrong. Instead, prosecutors reengineered their theory and shaped the testimony of Bailey to accommodate the information Mr. Jones pointed out.

Scrushy's attorney Art Leach, who had been an Assistant U.S. Attorney for 19 years, similarly tried to point out to prosecutors that their theory was not consistent with the actual facts, but his explanation too fell on deaf ears.[98] Even Bailey apparently tried to inform prosecutors that the inferences a jury may draw from his testimony would be contrary to his own personal knowledge. "These tactics resulted in Mr. Bailey giving testimony at trial that had been shaped by the government so as to allow the jury to draw inferences that were actually contrary to Bailey's own beliefs."[99] Exhibited at multiple intervals, DOJ proceeded in bad faith toward an indictment and conviction of me, the Democrat, disregarding the truth.

DOJ's Bad Faith Was Again Exhibited by Mischaracterizing 60 Minutes' Exposé.

CBS's *60 Minutes* aired a segment on the Siegelman prosecution highlighting some of the political abnormalities of the case including Karl Rove's involvement. *60 Minutes* producers interviewed Bailey, and their segment touched on two troubling aspects about his preparation for trial: (1) the number of times he spoke to prosecutors and (2) how prosecutors shaped Bailey's testimony. DOJ acted in bad faith by attempting to discredit what *60 Minutes* revealed while knowing it to be true. The disputed comments are listed below and compared to comments made by George Beck, Bailey's attorney and former U.S. Attorney:

---

97   Id. at 10-11.

98   Leach recounted a meeting with PIN officials:

> On October 4, 2005, I had a discussion with Mr. Pilger [Richard Pilger of PIN] . . . During this conversation Mr. Pilger set out a factual scenario which essentially equated to Mr. Scrushy entering into a quid pro quo with the Governor for the CON seat. He went on to say that if Mr. Scrushy could not say exactly what he had set out then Mr. Scrushy would have a problem. I asked what would happen if Mr. Scrushy's statement did not completely correspond to the scenario that Mr. Pilger had outlined. Mr. Pilger responded that Mr. Scrushy would be indicted. This brought on a heated response from me to Mr. Pilger in which I asked whether he wanted the truth or his version of the events.

Leach Affidavit (Ex. 28, ¶ 10) (emphasis added). Leach expressed his dismay over the behavior by Defendant in this case:

> The efforts by prosecutors Pilger, Feaga and Franklin, along with Mr. Lourie of Public Integrity were all calculated to get Richard Scrushy to present facts at trial which were not true and would have, without question, resulted in the conviction of Governor Siegelman . . . .

Id. at ¶ 22.

99   *See* Methvin Interview (Ex. 19, p. 2); *see also* Richardson Affidavit (Ex. 30, ¶ 6)

60 MINUTES: Bailey "spoke to prosecutors more than 70 times."[100]

BECK: "There's some 70 times that" Bailey spoke to prosecutors/investigators.[101]

60 MINUTES: Prosecutors had Bailey "write his proposed testimony over and over."[102]

BECK: Bailey "met with them, went over and over the testimony."[103]

First, DOJ falsely accused *60 Minutes* of a statement it did not make. DOJ ascribed to *60 Minutes* the comment that "Bailey *met with* prosecutors to prepare for his testimony *in* the Middle District trial more than 70 times."[104] *60 Minutes* actually stated, "*Before* the Siegelman trial, [Bailey] *spoke to* prosecutors more than 70 times." These seemingly subtle changes make material differences to accuracy. *60 Minutes*' actual statement is true; the statement DOJ attributed to *60 Minutes* is false. The fact that DOJ distorted what *60 Minutes* reported in order to discredit the otherwise factual statement exhibits bad faith.

While not all of the "some 70 times" involved scripting Bailey's testimony against me, *60 Minutes* and U.S. Attorney Beck are consistent on the number of conversations between Bailey and government officials. They are also consistent regarding the extensive preparation of Bailey's testimony. In addition to Bailey's account to *60 Minutes*, other evidence supports that Bailey practiced his testimony by making written notes and that such had been directed by a prosecutor.[105]

DOJ, in its letter to then-Chairman Conyers, wrote that "the evidence did not support" *60 Minutes*' comments. DOJ's bad faith effort to dismiss *60 Minutes*' reporting seeks to deflect attention from the critical underlying issue. In reality, the specific number of conversations prosecutors and investigators had with Bailey does not matter. Nor does it matter whether Bailey made written notes of testimony prosecutors wanted memorized. What matters is, regardless of the number of meetings or methodologies used, prosecutors "coaxed and pressured" their witness to conform his testimony to their liking.[106] That fact was not lost on DOJ when it made its disingenuous statement to Mr. Conyers regarding *60 Minutes*. This bad faith attempt to detract from *60 Minutes*' reporting is yet more evidence of DOJ's bad faith effort to mislead Congress and conceal the political nature of my prosecution.

---

100 *60 Minutes: The Prosecution of Siegelman*, CBS News (Feb. 24, 2008), *transcript available at* www.cbsnews.com/news/did-ex-alabama-governor-get-a-raw-deal [hereinafter *60 Minutes*].

101 Di Gregory Letter (Ex. 20, p. 8) (citing Sentence Hearing Transcript at 41, Bailey).

102 *60 Minutes, supra* note 99.

103 Motion for Downward Departure (Doc. 49, p. 8), Bailey.

104 Weich Letter (Ex. 7, p. 5) (emphasis added).

105 *See, e.g.,* Affidavit of Harrison Hickman at ¶ 12 [hereinafter "Hickman Affidavit"] (Exhibit 29); *see also* Affidavit of David Richardson at ¶¶ 11-12 [hereinafter "Richardson Affidavit"] (Exhibit 30).

106 Grimes Letter (Ex. 18, p. 3).

DOJ's Refused to Come Clean about Its Own Misconduct.

Other than the *ex parte* communication between DOJ's officials and Judge Fuller, all misconduct I've discussed was exposed by independent media reports and a whistleblower's disclosures.[107] Is there any other misconduct yet still hidden? The fact that even (comparatively) minor infractions—such as jurors passing messages through the U.S. Marshals to communicate an amorous interest in a member of the prosecution team were not self-reported by DOJ—engenders suspicion as to what else the Justice Department may still be hiding.

One example would be the email communication between the DOJ prosecutor and the campaign manager of my opponent while that prosecutor led the investigation to find charges[108] against me. Until POGO, in 2014, exposed the June 3, 2010 letter to then-Chairman Conyers, DOJ had concealed the evidence that the AUSA in charge of my investigation plotted with "a small group of like minded conservative prosecutors" (and the campaign manager of my opponent) to bring an indictment against me.[109]

Unless and until the Department of Justice comes forward with all the information it has on my prosecution, no matter how unsavory or disheartening the content, frankly the full truth may not become known and justice never done. By not doing so, the Department of Justice can continue its pattern of bad faith in other cases against Democrats or Republicans.

DOJ's Request for Life in Prison Shows a Bad Faith Vendetta

It is undisputed that neither I nor my personal campaign received a penny from the alleged contribution by Scrushy to the Education Lottery campaign or to pay off its debt. It is also undisputed that *no financial benefit to me could have even been contemplated* at the time the alleged bribe would have occurred. Nonetheless, DOJ recommended that I be imprisoned *for life*.[110]

DOJ sought the draconian punishment by asking that I be punished for acquitted conduct, *i.e.*, conduct the jury found that I did not commit. The acquitted conduct used by prosecutors to drastically increase my sentence originated from allegations by Mr. Young, who, as we now know, the Department of Justice didn't even believe. In addition, unlike Bailey who was difficult to manipulate, Young

---

107 While DOJ disclosed the *ex parte* judicial communication, it did not do so until more than a year after it occurred and after I would have been able to inquire about it or seek any relief therefrom. *See* Stemler Letter (Ex. 22, pp. 2-3); Kilborn Letter (Ex. 21, pp. 3-4).

108 The AUSA had stated "he hoped" their investigation "would go to the highest levels of the Siegelman administration." Jones Congressional Testimony (Ex. 3, p. 8).

109 Weich Letter (Ex. 7, p. 3)

110 *See* United States' Sentencing Memorandum (Doc. 589), Siegelman; *see also* United States' Motion for Upward Departure (Doc. 591), Id.

apparently "said whatever they (the 'FEDS') told him to say."[111] The fact that the Department of Justice tried to send me to prison for life—for charges of which I was exonerated and DOJ knew to be baseless[112]—screams political motivation, a vendetta. If a life sentence wasn't enough, DOJ also wanted me to serve additional time for charges the Eleventh Circuit dismissed due to the "absolute lack of any evidence whatsoever."[113]

DOJ REWARDED THOSE WHO ADVANCED THE PROSECUTION AND FIRED THE WHISTLEBLOWER WHO EXPOSED THEIR MISCONDUCT.

In addition to ensuring funding and "grant[ing] prosecutors virtually unlimited latitude to obtain a conviction," Canary further incentivized the prosecution of The Big Case.[114] She threw parties "at the Marina" to celebrate milestones such as "when the superseding indictment was unsealed" and "when the convictions were handed down."[115] She also gave "cash awards" to Mr. Feaga, and specifically, "AUSA Feaga [ha]d be[en] given virtually unlimited latitude to get a conviction in this case."[116] "Management felt that the priority was to keep AUSA Feaga 'happy' by whatever means necessary."[117] Part of the management was AUSA Patricia Watson, Canary's first cousin-in-law, to whom Canary gave "a 40 hour time off award."[118] "FBI Agents also received perks and rewards for their work on the case."[119] Tamarah Grimes, however, the DOJ paralegal on my case who courageously blew the whistle on the prosecution was threatened with criminal prosecution after she submitted her report, then fired.[120] This was apparently at the hands of Ms. Canary, then approved by David Margolis.[121] ("Ms. Grimes has become the subject of a criminal investigation reportedly initiated by USA Canary who requested an investigation of Ms. Grimes");[122]

---

111 Fernandez Memo (Ex. 8, p. 1).

112 See also note 87, supra.

113 U.S. v. Siegelman, 561 F.3d 1215, 1232 (11th Cir. 2009); see Di Gregory Letter (Ex. 20, p. 12).

114 Grimes Letter (Ex. 18, p. 1).

115 Id. at 5.

116 Id.; Grimes Report (Ex. 9, p. 6).

117 Id.

118 Grimes Letter (Ex. 18, p. 8).

119 Id. at 5.

120 See Letter from Scott Bloch, United States Special Counsel, to The Honorable Michael Mukasey, United States Attorney General at 3 (Apr. 18, 2008) (Exhibit 31).

121 See Id.

122 See Id. and see also Letter from Tamarah Grimes, Paralegal for the ALMD, to Steven K. Mullins, Assistant U.S. Attorney for the Western District of Oklahoma (Aug. 1, 2008) at 2 (Exhibit 32); Whistleblower Witch Hunts: The Smokescreen Syndrome, Government Accountability Project (Nov. 2010) at 20, available at www.whistleblower.org/sites/default/files/WWHfinal-1.pdf.

Getting nowhere with the Office of Inspector General, who declined to investigate her disclosures, Ms. Grimes wrote directly to the U.S. Attorney General.[123] Ms. Grimes was fired eight days later. The bad faith exhibited through the treatment of Ms. Grimes—beginning almost immediately after she disclosed unethical and, in some cases, illegal conduct—can be described only as a disgrace of the United States Department of Justice—and another example of how our democracy is stolen.

DOJ's Misconduct Amounted to Illegality, Not Just Bad Faith.

In addition to repeated, blatant bad faith DOJ's officials also engaged in illegal conduct during my investigation and prosecution. DOJ's illegality should have eliminated any justification for DOJ to refuse to turn over documents underscoring its misconduct.

First, Leura Canary Violated Federal Law by Failing to Abide by Her Recusal.

Leura Canary's continued involvement in my case violated 18 U.S.C. § 208. Section 208 provides that no officer of the United States may participate "personally and substantially . . . through decision, approval, disapproval, recommendation, the rendering of advice, investigation, or otherwise" in any matter where the official or his/her "spouse . . . has a financial interest . . . ."[124] The statute imposes a prison sentence of up to five years and a fine of up to $50,000 for *each* violation.[125] DOJ has never denied that the USA's husband stood to benefit financially from my political assassination. DOJ also openly acknowledges that Ms. Canary approved decisions concerning the case and made recommendations and rendered advice to the prosecution team.[126]

While the extent of Canary's continued involvement has never been evaluated,[127] her personal and substantial participation in the case is palpable nevertheless. Just the limited information known strongly suggests I may not have been prosecuted *at all* but for Ms. Canary's integral involvement. Canary made multiple personal pleas for additional funding for her prize case, The Big Case, "the most important

---

123   *See generally* Grimes Letter (Ex. 18).

124   18 U.S.C. § 208(a).

125   *See* 18 U.S.C. § 216.

126   *See, e.g.,* Gov't Br. at 28 ("USA Canary approved staffing the case with paralegal Grimes in 2005, Doc. 953-38, and forwarded unsolicited advice to seek a gag order, and sent material from my campaign to her prosecution team. Doc. 953-36"), brief for the United States as Appellee, *U.S. v. Siegelman* (11th Cir. 12-14373) (Sep. 30, 2013) at 6 (emphasis added).

127   Siegelman asked for discovery on the issue, but his request was denied. *See* Order by Judge Clay D. Land (Doc. 1165, pp. 28-30), Siegelman ("Defendant has been prevented from making the record more robust. Thus, he faces an unenviable conundrum.").

investigation pending in this office."[128] These were not routine funding requests that Ms. Canary handled as part of her administrative responsibilities—rather, this funding was "critical," "*absolutely necessary*," "*there is* no other *funding available*."[129] The very day Ms. Canary received word that she would get these funds, her office announced its indictment of me.[130] Ms. Canary was not exaggerating—her office apparently could not prosecute me without this funding, which was obtained only through repeated personal pleas by Canary who had supposedly disqualified herself and was prohibited from any involvement in my prosecution.

CANARY'S TOP AIDE'S INVOLVEMENT VIOLATED FEDERAL LAW.

The Code of Federal Regulations states in pertinent part:

> No employee shall participate in a criminal investigation or prosecution if he has a personal or political relationship with any person or organization substantially involved in the conduct that is the subject of the investigation or prosecution. 28 CFR § 45.2 (a)(1).

According to Mrs. Weller, she investigated the alleged illegal contributions to Mr. Pryor's and Mr. Session's campaigns when her husband had been a high-ranking staffer for both the Pryor and Sessions campaigns.[131] Ms. Weller also helped broker the plea agreement for Mr. Young, whose allegations against Pryor and Sessions became buried as his allegations against me grew legs.[132]

Mrs. Weller should have "report[ed] the matter and all attendant facts and circumstances to h[er] supervisor at the level of section chief or the equivalent or higher," but according to DOJ she "fail[ed] to . . . alert her supervisors" of her and her husband's ties to Sessions and Pryor.[133] In addition to violating 28 CFR § 45.2, if Mrs. Weller's husband maintained a financial interest through his relationships with either Sessions or Pryor, she, like Ms. Canary, would have also violated 18 U.S.C. § 208.

---

128 *See* note 26, *supra*.

129 Id. (emphasis added).

130 Id.

131 Kenny Smith, *Davis Says Siegelman Prosecution Is Unjust*, AL.com (Oct. 24, 2007), http:// blog.al.com/spotnews/2007/10/davis_says_siegelman_prosecuti.html; Check out Friends of Sessions Senate Committee 1996 Annual Report, Office of the Secretary of State of Alabama (Exhibit 33); *and* Attorney General Bill Pryor Committee 1998 Annual Report, Office of the Secretary of State of Alabama (Exhibit 34); *see also* Profile of Christopher W. Weller, Capell & Howard (2005) (Exhibit 35).

132 *See* "Former Alabama State Official, Others Plead Guilty to Federal Corruption Charges," *Department of Justice Press Release* (June 23, 2003), *available at* https://www.justice.gov/ archive/opa/pr/2003/June/03_crm_380.htm.

133 28 CFR § 45.2 (b); Weich Letter (Ex. 7, p. 6).

DOJ Official's Illegality Was Widespread.

Section 1622 of Title 18 of the U.S. Code provides, "Whoever procures another to commit any perjury is guilty of subornation of perjury, and shall be fined under this title or imprisoned not more than five years, or both." 18 U.S.C. § 1622. During the investigation, then-Assistant U.S. Attorney Matt Hart, appears to have knowingly suborned false testimony during grand jury proceedings.[134]

DOJ violated federal law in "pressuring, cajoling" Bailey to lie.

Section 1512 of Title 18 of the U.S. Code provides, "Whoever knowingly uses intimidation, threatens . . . with intent to influence . . . the testimony of any person in an official proceeding . . . shall be fined . . . or imprisoned not more than 20 years, or both."[135] A close friend of Nick Bailey attested as follows:

> For example, Nick said the prosecutors told him that his brother, Shane Bailey, was in a "situation." The implied threat was implicit as the government apparently never said they would prosecute Shane if Nick did not say what they wanted him to say. Nick told me, however, that the import of what the prosecutors were saying about his brother was clear, and that it made a difference in his willingness to go along with what the prosecutors wanted him to say.[136]

This friend of Bailey went on to describe another instance when "one federal prosecutor threatened to cause purported information of a highly personal nature about Nick to be disclosed."[137]

Special Assistant U.S. Attorney Joseph Fitzpatrick at one point stated that prosecutors "shaved witness testimony to fit what they needed" during grand jury deliberations for the Siegelman case.[138] "The tone and manner of which he spoke concerning the deliberations" strongly indicated that "serious violations occurred" and that "unprofessional and or illegal activities were used by U.S. [a]ttorneys to get indictments against Gov. Don Siegelman . . . ."[139] Mr. Fitzpatrick expressed that the conduct "rose to the level of him making a decision to change careers," stating "what they did in the Siegelman case was wrong, and I cannot work with people like that."[140]

---

134 *See* Letter from Don Siegelman to J. Anthony McLain, General Counsel of the Alabama State Bar, and H. Marshall Jarrett, Chief Counsel of the Office of Professional Responsibility (Feb. 10, 2005) at ¶¶ 3, 5 (Exhibit 36).

135 18 U.S.C. § 1512.

136 Hickman Affidavit (Ex. 29, ¶ 10); *see also* Richardson Affidavit (Ex. 30, ¶ 18).

137 Id.

138 Affidavit of Kenneth Marshall at ¶ 1 (emphasis added) [hereinafter "Marshall Affidavit"] (Exhibit 37).

139 Id. at ¶¶ 1-2.

140 Affidavit of Paul Hamrick at 2 (emphasis added) (Exhibit 38).

Mr. Fitzpatrick, who "was emphatic that he couldn't discuss the Grand Jury deliberations," did not give any more information.[141] But one can safely assume that the witness whose testimony was "shaved . . . to fit what they needed" was Nick Bailey.[142] By using various threats to induce this "shaved" testimony, the prosecutor(s) clearly violated 18 U.S.C. § 1512.[143] The prosecutor(s) also violated 18 U.S.C. § 1622 if this constituted the procurement of false testimony. Finally, Mr. Fitzpatrick said "*they* shaved witness testimony" which indicates others participated and/or knew the prosecutor(s) had committed the federally prohibited act(s), in which case these other individuals violated 18 U.S.C. § 3, 18 U.S.C. § 4 or both.[144]

DOJ's DISCLOSURE OF GRAND JURY INFORMATION VIOLATED FEDERAL LAW.

Pursuant to Federal Rule of Criminal Procedure 6(e), attorneys for the government "must not disclose" grand jury information, yet one or more of Defendant's officials appears to have done so. Fed. R. Crim. P. 6 (e)(2)(B)(vi). My attorney described some of the recurring leaks in a letter to Defendant:

> On Sunday, February 10, the *Birmingham News* reported that state and federal prosecutors have subpoenaed Governor Siegelman's financial records as part of an ongoing joint investigation. The newspaper cited anonymous leaks as the source for its story. . . .
>
> More recently, on March 16 the *Montgomery Advertiser* reported, "Vaughan said Friday the newspaper [the *Mobile Register*] was led to the story by Claire Austin, a lobbyist with ties to Republicans, who wanted to get back at her former business partner, Lanny Young . . . Austin confirmed Friday that Young was a former business partner but denied providing information to the newspaper. 'But I can't really be talking to you about this because of other reasons,' Austin said. 'There are several more indictments pending.'" *Montgomery Advertiser,* Kleffman, 3/16/02. If this information is true, Ms. Austin appears to have broken the law, as has the person who gave her the information . . . .[145]

DOJ's OPR INVESTIGATION WAS A BAD FAITH COVER-UP.

DOJ exudes its bad faith in OPR's superficial investigation of prosecutorial misconduct in the case. As demonstrated, there was pervasive unethical and illegal conduct by DOJ's officials throughout my investigation and prosecution. OPR

---

141   Marshall Affidavit (Ex. 37, ¶ 1).
142   Id.
143   Id.
144   Id. (emphasis added).
145   Johnson Letter (Ex. 13, pp. 6-7) (emphasis in original) (alterations in original).

overlooked nearly all of it. What little improper conduct OPR did acknowledge, it dismissed as inconsequential. Despite even patent violations of federal law having occurred, some punishable by substantial jail time, OPR decided no DOJ attorney was guilty of anything more than "poor judgment."[146]

OPR conducted an essentially meaningless investigation, inquiring only where misconduct would not be found. As observed by Special Assistant U.S. Attorney Fitzpatrick who hinted that serious misconduct had occurred, "OPR is going in the wrong direction with their investigation," adding, "If they only knew . . . ."[147] OPR exhibited its manifest disinterest in actually reviewing the conduct of Defendant's prosecutors when OPR *did not even bother to interview the campaign manager of my Republican opponent* with whom DOJ's AUSA was in email contact.[148]

In its letter to HJC Chairman Conyers, DOJ made incredible assertions in the course of tiptoeing around potential misconduct. For example:

> OPR found no evidence that Mr. Rove spoke with any Justice Department official about Mr. Siegelman, and found no evidence that U.S. Attorney Martin or U.S. Attorney Canary were pressured by anyone to "take care of" Mr. Siegelman . . . .[149]

This statement of course avoids the possibility that Martin and Canary needed no such pressuring because they were eager participants, or that Mr. Rove did not need to speak with "any Justice Department official" because he could speak to his good friend, Bill Canary, husband of the U.S. attorney who was prosecuting me.[150] OPR also unremarkably "found no evidence that Mr. Rove spoke with any Justice Department official" yet *did not interview any of the DOJ officials with whom Mr. Rove would have most likely communicated.*[151]

When OPR cited misconduct, it minimized the impropriety. For example:

> OPR also concluded that U.S. Attorney Canary did not commit professional misconduct or exercise poor judgment in connection with her recusal from the *Siegelman* case, although OPR concluded that she should not have forwarded an unsolicited campaign letter she received via e-mail to the trial team with a comment about it possibly providing a basis for a gag order.[152]

---

146 *See generally* Weich Letter (Ex. 7).
147 Marshall Affidavit (Ex. 37, ¶ 1).
148 *See* Weich Letter (Ex. 7, p. 3) (emphasis added).
149 Id. at 4.
150 Unofficial Transcript of Interview by U.S. House Judiciary Committee Members of Karl Rove at 96 (July 30, 2009).
151 OPR did not indicate having interviewed any of Defendant's political appointees who retained decision-making authority in my case. *See* note 90, *supra*; *see also* Weich Letter (Ex. 7, p. 3); Report on Removal of U.S. Attorneys at 325, *supra* note 4.
152 Id. at 6.

This is the height of evasion. As discussed *supra*, her forwarding of a campaign email was the *least* of Ms. Canary's violations of her purported recusal and to chastise her for that relatively small infraction is to suggest that it was the only one. The disingenuousness of DOJ's comment lies in the facts it leaves out: that Ms. Canary actively sought funding for the case; that she repurposed employees to bolster the case's resources; that while she dedicated resources to prosecuting me, her office cited "lack of resources" as its rationale for not pursuing Republicans, who were implicated by *the same witness* whose assertions founded the case against me and whom her office would later paint as lacking credibility with regard to Republicans despite relying heavily on that witness to prosecute me, a Democrat. The omission of those details leaves room only for the conclusion that *at best*, OPR declined to pursue information that was available to it so as to avoid making troubling discoveries or, more likely, that they intentionally sought to keep knowledge of the severe misconduct under wraps.

It is clear DOJ has hidden the misconduct its officials committed, and made repeated false statements to Congress. This conduct is nothing less than stealing our democracy.

INDEX